# EMBRACING NON-TENURE TRACK FACULTY

The nature of the higher education faculty workforce is radically and fundamentally changing from primarily full-time tenured faculty to non-tenure track faculty. This new faculty majority faces common challenges, including short-term contracts, limited support on campus, and lack of a professional career track. *Embracing Non-Tenure Track Faculty* documents real changes occurring on campuses to support this faculty group, unveiling the challenges and opportunities that occur when implementing new policies and practices. Non-tenure faculty contributors across a diverse range of universities and colleges describe the change process on their campuses to improve the work environment and increase the quality of learning. Kezar supplements these case studies by distilling trends and patterns from a national study of campuses that have successfully implemented policies to improve conditions for non-tenure track faculty.

This invaluable research-based resource illustrates that there are multiple pathways to successfully implementing policy for non-tenure track faculty. *Embracing Non-Tenure Track Faculty* provides the tools to create a lasting culture change that will shape the work lives of all faculty and ultimately improve student learning. Outlining detailed strategies and approaches for providing equitable policies and practices for non-tenure track faculty on college campuses, this book is essential reading for both contingent faculty and higher education administrators.

**Adrianna Kezar** is Associate Professor of Higher Education at the University of Southern California, USA.

# EMBRACING NON-TENURE TRACK FACULTY

## Changing Campuses for the New Faculty Majority

*Edited by*

*Adrianna Kezar*

 Routledge
Taylor & Francis Group

NEW YORK AND LONDON

P-HE
Em 16
2012

First published 2012 by Routledge
711 Third Avenue, New York, NY 10017

Simultaneously published in the UK
by Routledge
2 Park Square, Milton Park, Abingdon, Oxon, OX14 4RN

*Routledge is an imprint of the Taylor & Francis Group, an informa business*

Library of Congress Cataloging-in-Publication Data
Embracing non-tenure track faculty : changing campuses for the new
faculty majority / edited by Adrianna Kezar.
    p. cm.
Includes bibliographical references and index.
1. College teachers, Part-time–United States. 2. College
teachers–Tenure–United States. 3. Universities and
colleges–United States–Faculty. 4. College teaching–United States.
I. Kezar, Adrianna J.
LB2331.72.E54 2012
378.1′2–dc23                                          2011036153

ISBN: 978-0-415-89113-4 (hbk)
ISBN: 978-0-415-89114-1 (pbk)
ISBN: 978-0-203-82843-4 (ebk)

Typeset in Bembo
by Cenveo Publisher Services

Printed and bound in the United States of America on sustainably sourced paper by IBT Global

Dedication: For all those fighting inequities wherever they exist and for the non-tenure track faculty leaders and their allies who fight to maintain the quality of education.

# CONTENTS

# PREFACE

*Adrianna Kezar*

Imagine: *Professor Smith patiently waits outside of the classroom while a proctor administers the student evaluation form to her Intro to History class. While 40 students fill out the form, Professor Smith thinks about how those evaluations may very well be the only factor that determines if she remains employed next semester or not. No one in the department interacts with her or really knows her, even though she has made efforts. She also uses the time to check her day planner, noting that she has 45 minutes to meet with six students at her makeshift office—the local coffee shop—before running to teach her next class at another college. Of course, meeting with these students is not considered "part of her load or paid for." She also thinks about that upcoming conference that she would love to go to: it is local and will cost no money, luckily, because she does not receive professional development funds. However, she dare not cancel or be late for a class or she risks being fired. Other faculty members pass her in the hallway, but no one shows any recognition. As she re-enters the room to teach the final class of the semester, she thinks to herself, "This was not how I imagined being a professor would be..."*

But Professor Smith's experience is not uncommon at all. In fact, she represents the majority of faculty teaching in higher education today. Two-thirds of the faculty members (across all institutional types) are now off the tenure-track (either full- or part-time) (JBL Associates, Inc., 2008; Schuster & Finkelstein, 2006). Three out of four new hires are off the tenure-track, so hiring trends suggest that this pattern will only continue to grow. A recent survey of college presidents conducted by *The Chronicle of Higher Education* identified that they prefer non-tenure track faculty and will advocate for hiring in this area (Stripling, 2011). Non-tenure track (often labeled contingent or adjunct) faculty may be full- or part-time, but regardless of their appointment type, they share the common work conditions: Short-term contracts—typically year-to-year (full-time) or semester-to-semester (part-time); lack of job security; lack of a professional career track; and, currently, limited or no policies and practices in place related to their employment (for example, no promotion policies).

In the last 20 years, the increase in contingent faculty happened due to the combination of unprecedented growth in student enrollment, administrative misjudgments of that growth, and decline in government funding and public support of higher education (Cross & Goldenberg, 2009; Schuster & Finkelstein, 2006). While the hiring of non-tenure track faculty began as a temporary solution to a set of problems, these positions have now become the new norm in hiring. Furthermore, in this same time period, support for tenure has declined among the general public, policymakers, and even higher education institutional leaders.

The shift in the faculty composition has received some, though limited, attention. A few early works tried to bring visibility to the largely ignored part- and full-time non-tenure track faculty, and these books also tried to convey the experience of being a contingent faculty member (Baldwin & Chronister, 2001; Gappa & Leslie, 1993; Schell & Stock, 2001). In the last five years, several other books and reports have documented the change in the nature of the professoriate, most prominently Schuster and Finkelstein's (2006) work *The American Faculty*. Thus there is now greater awareness of the sheer change in numbers. A few authors (Baldwin & Chronister, 2001; Gappa & Leslie, 1993) also document that changes are needed on college campuses because the growth of contingent faculty has led to a variety of problems:

1. a caste-based faculty system
2. short-term solutions for long-term problems
3. problems of educational quality because campus policies and practices do not support non-tenure track faculty.

In terms of a caste-based system, a three-class faculty system has emerged in American higher education. Tenure-track faculty have a relatively privileged position compared to both full-time non-tenure track faculty and part-time contingent faculty. The compensation, benefits, opportunities for professional development, workload, office space and clerical support are all less favorable for contingent faculty. However, full-time non-tenure track faculty conditions are closer to those of tenure-track faculty, and part-time faculty have the least favorable working conditions and appointment types (Baldwin & Chronister, 2001; Gappa & Leslie, 1993). Not only are their working conditions significantly different, but these faculty are also usually culturally divided with tenure-track faculty treating contingent faculty as second-class citizens. Faculty who are divided into different cultures typically do not communicate or interact regularly, which impacts the curriculum and educational experience of students (Kezar, forthcoming).

Another significant problem is that contingent faculty have been hired outside of any overall staffing plan and represent short-term solutions not embedded in any long-term institutional strategy. Cross and Goldenberg (2009) document how institutions moved to hiring non-tenure track faculty in a random and unplanned fashion that threatens educational quality and the institutional mission. Baldwin and Chronister (2001) note that many institutions with long-term needs are treating full-time non-tenure track faculty as short-term solutions—expendable and easily replaced. While institutions have the need for consistent teaching and often keep on part-time faculty for 15 years, they continue to provide these faculty with semester-to-semester contracts when clearly there is a longer-term need. Increasingly, higher education administrators have a short-term focus rather than emphasizing what is needed for the long term and what is effective for the institution.

In recent years a research has emerged demonstrating that institutions that rely heavily on part-time faculty may experience lower transfer rates, a decrease in the number of students graduating, less contact time between students and faculty, and subpar teaching practices (Jaeger & Eagan, 2009; Umbach, 2007). Recently, a few studies have begun to explore the effect of contingent faculty on institutions (i.e., motivation, productivity, or morale) and on educational outcomes such as graduation or transfer rates (Bland, Center, Finstad, Risbey, & Staples, 2006; Ehrenberg, 2005; Jacoby, 2006; Umbach, 2007). For example, part-time contingent faculty members have fewer contact hours (office hours) with students (Benjamin, 2003). Since there are no set policies for office hours for contingent faculty and it is often not part of their contract, this gap may be affecting students' access to faculty. Also, contingent faculty spend less time preparing for class (Benjamin, 2003; Umbach, 2007). Both contact hours and class preparation are generally not paid for by institutions, so contingent faculty would have to do this work on their own time. Also, given the lack of job security and high demands on many contingent (particularly part-time) faculty members (some working at multiple institutions), it is not surprising that they skimp on preparation. Contingent faculty tend to use less active learning, service learning, educational innovations, and culturally sensitive teaching approaches (Banachowski, 1996; Jacoby, 2006; Umbach, 2008). All of these pedagogical approaches require time, which is scarce for contingent faculty within current working conditions. It is important to note that the problem appears to be non-tenure track faculty working conditions, not the contingent faculty themselves (Baldwin & Chronister, 2001; Gappa & Leslie, 1993).

These smaller impacts appear to shape more macro outcomes. Schools with larger numbers of non-tenure track faculty have lower graduation rates and lower transfer rates from two-year to four-year colleges (Eagan & Jaeger, 2008; Ehrenberg & Zhang, 2005; Jacoby, 2006; Jaeger & Eagan, 2009; Umbach, 2007). For example, Ehrenberg and Zhang (2005) found that institutions with larger numbers of non-tenured track faculty had significantly lower graduation rates than institutions that employed fewer non-tenured track faculty. Eagan and Jaeger (2009) found that students in the community college sector with greater levels of exposure to part-time faculty had a significantly lower likelihood of transferring to four-year institutions. And Jacoby (2006) found that, as institutions employed greater percentages of part-time faculty, their graduation rates decreased. These findings are particularly problematic as research demonstrates that faculty and student interactions are one of the strongest predictors of student retention and success in college (Astin, 1993). None of these studies control for working conditions, so they cannot determine what accounts for outcomes. Researchers hypothesize that institutions can likely ameliorate these outcomes with thoughtful policies and practices.

In the end, all of the noted problems relating to the growth of contingent faculty suggest that the unplanned nature of this change, without any policies and practices in place, threatens the quality of higher education. There is an imperative for education leaders to take responsibility for institutions—to create a faculty that can best serve the needs of students while also balancing concerns about affordability, flexibility, and budget deficits. Research demonstrates that leaders have focused only on the issues of affordability or flexibility and have largely ignored issues of educational quality and planning of the faculty (Cross & Goldenberg, 2009). Even if we agree that increasing the use of contingent faculty members is justified because it introduces staffing flexibility and saves money, more attention needs to be paid to what conditions will contribute to the success of the contingent faculty.

Why is this issue of the faculty composition so important now? The United States is focused on having more students complete college, aiming for an additional 8 million students by 2020. These students include those who are historically under-represented (low socio-economic status, racial/ethnic minorities, and first-generation students). Contingent faculty members provide a large share of the classroom experience for students. On many campuses, contingent faculty members teach 75 percent of the general education requirements (Schuster & Finkelstein, 2006). However, for these under-represented groups, contingent faculty may provide an even larger share of instruction. Contingent faculty members teach most remedial (often where many historically under-represented college students end up) and introductory courses on college campuses (Hollenshead et al., 2007; Schuster & Finkelstein, 2006). For these students especially, classroom experiences with faculty might change the chances for success. Their odds for success are greatly lowered when faculty have no office hours, lack an understanding of departmental or institutional learning goals, and lack time for mentoring students or class preparation. Also, students may find that their favorite teacher is gone the next semester, or that a faculty member is not available to write a letter of recommendation for a scholarship necessary to stay in school.

While many campuses are now aware that they have a significant number of contingent faculty, they have not necessarily created intentional policies and practices for including them. In fact, much of the early research efforts by Gappa and Leslie (1993) for part-time, and Baldwin and Chronister (2001) for full-time faculty, documented the frustration and concern among contingent faculty members who lived in conditions of uncertainty because campuses had not developed any policies and practices related to their employment. As of 2012, the landscape has changed somewhat and campuses are working to implement policies. A national study by Hollenshead et al. (2007) of four-year institutions demonstrated that many are trying to create policies around hiring, orientation, salary, professional development, mentoring, and other key areas related to the employment of contingent faculty. We know little about these efforts beyond the broad survey data that document the fact that some institutions are beginning to address these issues. We do not know how they are accomplishing the work to institutionalize changes on campus; the sort of struggles and challenges they meet as they institutionalize changes; the nature of the types of policies and practices that they are implementing; or the policies they implement first and why. Until this book, the whole process of researching and understanding implementation of policies and practices has gone largely undocumented.

## Unique Contribution and Focus

While a few sources have developed recommendations for new policies and practices that should be put in place on campuses (specifically Baldwin & Chronister, 2001; and Gappa & Leslie, 1993), few resources have documented the changes occurring on real campuses and the challenges that occur while implementing such policies and practices. This book builds on the earlier recommended changes to policy, such as implementing multi-year contracts, developing orientation appropriate to contingent faculty, and providing professional development options, by looking at actual cases where campuses have implemented these recommendations. The advantage is that we can understand several important empirical facts that we are unable to ascertain through abstract recommendations. First, through a study of the implementation process of policies and practices, we can see the actual mechanisms that are required to create change related to contingent faculty inclusion on campuses. Second, this book documents challenges and opportunities facing those implementing the changes. Third, the campuses have differing missions and structures, so the policies and practices needed may also vary; thus, we can capture modifications that respond to particular campus contexts. Finally, readers can get a sense of the various pathways to implementing new policies and practices, and align their strategy with the approach that best fits their particular context.

The value in this book lies in making transparent what is otherwise the 'black box' of the implementation process; e.g., change processes, challenges and opportunities, context-based approaches to modify policies, and multiple pathways to implement policy for contingent faculty. In order to meet this goal, authors from various campuses that have implemented changes in policies and practices were invited to document the change process on their campus. They have reviewed the policies and practices they advocated and why they chose those particular policies or practices. The authors have also documented any changes they were unable to make and why, the challenges and opportunities they experienced along the way, and how their particular mission or institutional culture affected their approach to change.

Another strength of this book is that it is based on a national study of campuses implementing policies to include non-tenure track faculty on campus. Therefore, it draws on more generalizable data about trends and patterns that are important for understanding the change process. Several of the chapters are based on a national interview and document study conducted by Adrianna Kezar and Cecile Sam. They interviewed representatives at 30 different campuses that had worked to implement policies, and have distilled lessons from these various campuses. They also reviewed several hundred union contracts for exemplary language and policies for including contingent faculty. Through these various sources, the editor supplements the case-study chapters with more national, generalizable research.

In addition, the book is unique in highlighting contingent faculty leaders and their important work to create change on campuses. One of the findings from the national study is that contingent faculty are leading the efforts on many campuses to create policies and practices for their inclusion. While earlier scholars documented this trend of growth in non-tenure track faculty and encouraged administrators to put policies and practices into place to address this issue, on most campuses, administrators have not taken a lead. Yet I should note that several cases highlighted in this book show administrators as allies, collaborators, and even leaders in change. Neither have tenure-track faculty taken the lead in implementing new policies and practices on campus, despite the assumption that they would, as part of their role in shared governance. Instead, most of the changes have been the result of the work of contingent faculty leaders, and this book highlights their bold leadership to change campuses and systems that do not work for them, often in the face of great resistance. This accomplishment is all the more remarkable since contingent faculty are often in marginal positions on campuses, but they have been in the forefront of developing strategies and approaches for policy development and implementation. In order to acknowledge the important work of these leaders across the country, this book will showcase contingent/non-tenure track faculty leaders from different campuses and the progress they have made to implement change. We identify contingent faculty leaders both at campuses that have institutionalized change for non-tenure track faculty, as well as campuses that are still in the process of doing so, to demonstrate the progression of change. We have also identified contingent leaders at different types of institution (community colleges, technical colleges, research universities, private institutions, religious-based, comprehensive, and regional public four-year institutions) in order to demonstrate the context-based nature of the change process. While there will be many similarities in the policies contingent faculty leaders address and the approaches they take, there will also be some unique elements to the change process. We have chosen faculty on unionized and non-unionized campuses because faculty are not able to unionize in all states, and we want to provide various approaches to change. We have also identified cases that highlight different nuances and key points such as the role of a senate subcommittee, exemplary departments, or external influences such as the media or accreditation. The contingent faculty authors have often interviewed and spoken with people on their campus to develop a full picture of the change process so that it does not just represent their own perspective, but a broader picture of the campus.

## Background on Contingent Faculty and the Nationwide Change in Faculty

Before describing the organization of the book, it is important to provide some background on contingent faculty and the meaning of the term "contingent." It is important to note that contingent faculty members are an incredibly diverse and heterogeneous group of individuals that has changed in composition over time. Forty years ago, contingent faculty were mostly part-time and located within community colleges and hired for their expertise in professional and vocational fields to supplement the educational experience by bringing in particular expertise. Later, four-year institutions and research universities also saw the advantages of bringing in business leaders, and retired lawyers, superintendents, and principals to help provide practical experience and knowledge within professional fields. However, in the 1980s, as state budgets declined and enrollments increased, and institutions were looking for more flexibility in meeting the needs of emerging fields, institutional leaders began to experiment with hiring non-tenure track faculty within fields where they had not traditionally been hired, such as English or mathematics, where they might have growing needs for instruction. As Baldwin and Chronister (2001: 17) note: "time term appointment faculty is in part a response to the uncertainty generated by fluctuating government financial support for higher education." Also, with the move to a more massified higher education system, remedial education grew and non-tenure track faculty were hired to teach in these areas. Additionally, with the overproduction of graduates with doctoral degrees, many fields found that they could hire non-tenure track faculty and not have to offer tenured positions—jobs that tied institutions to certain monetary obligations—and they could hire more faculty on these short-term contracts. Even medical schools began to move to a contingent faculty model and away from tenure, thereby increasing the number of non-tenure track faculty.

In the 1990s, campuses experienced a continued decline in state funds, the expenses to maintain a college or university were increasing, and institutions had to meet those expenditures. Institutions raised tuition, but still needed to find a way also to limit costs (Baldwin & Chronister, 2001). Hiring full-time non-tenure track faculty was a way to meet those fiscal needs. Institutional leaders found that it was often more efficient to hire a full-time non-tenure track faculty member who could teach several courses, rather than various part-time faculty with multiple recruitments and hiring processes. For some institutions, the full-time contingent faculty member was a more efficient model. Yet it can be a more costly model, as part-time faculty pay and benefits are much lower than those of full-time non-tenure track faculty, on average.

Over the 30-year period when contingent faculty grew on college campuses, the American workplace also changed significantly; temporary and contingent personnel became more commonplace. Many of the leaders who served on college boards worked in the corporate world where fundamental changes had been happening in the workplace and they brought these ideas into higher education. Also, in the 1990s, because of these changes in the business sector, boards and the general public began to challenge and critique tenure and campus efficiency. In response to various external factors (declining government support, change in the American workforce, loss of public confidence in higher education, and criticisms of tenure) and internal factors (rising costs, faculty workload and productivity, and changing student demographics), higher education institutions began to hire different sorts of faculty to respond to these various changing conditions.

As a result of this unplanned and largely random introduction of a new workforce, there are a variety of different kinds of contingent faculty on campuses— some still follow the early model of returning or retired professionals, others are in disciplines or fields that overproduced doctoral graduates seeking tenured positions, others are non-tenure track faculty who chose this role because of other obligations such as family.

Gappa and Leslie (1993) offer a helpful typology of the diverse groups of part-time faculty: career-enders; specialists, experts, and professionals; aspiring academics; and freelancers. According to Gappa and Leslie (1993), career-enders include not only those individuals who are in the process of retiring, but those who are retired. Many of them come from established careers outside of academia and have decided to continue in academia for a combination of various reasons: the supplemental income, keeping "a hand in the field," or simply because they enjoy the experience. Specialists, experts, and professionals are those who are employed full-time elsewhere, and come from a varied range of careers. They are hired for their specialized knowledge or success in certain fields, be it the arts or business. Rather than relying on the faculty position for income, these faculty members often take the position simply because they enjoy teaching. Some of these specialists can also add prestige to the institution. For example, the University of Southern California's School of Cinematic Arts promotes its cadre of award-winning faculty involved in the entertainment industry, many of them part-time or full-time non-tenure track faculty. The category "aspiring academics" takes into consideration those faculty members who are looking for a full-time or tenure-track position, including graduate students as well as those who may be looking for a position at the same institution as their partners. Faculty who manage to create full-time schedules from part-time faculty positions—"freeway fliers"—are also included in this category (Gappa & Leslie, 1993). Finally, there are the freelancers, predominantly faculty members who supplement their part-time positions from other jobs not in academia, or who may be caretakers at home, using the position for supplemental income. Research by Levin, Kater, & Wagoner (2006) also demonstrates that different disciplinary areas (arts and humanities, social and behavioral sciences, physical and biological sciences, computing and technology, professional programs, trades and services, and low status professional fields) have a different impact on the experience, motivation, and understanding of part-time faculty. There are two distinct groups across these fields:

1.   those possessing rare and highly valued skills and personal networks (often from vocational-oriented fields);
2.   those possessing common skills and limited personal networks (more academic-oriented disciplines).

While we do not know how many faculty fit into these groupings nationally, it is likely that the tenure-track aspiring group has become increasingly large as the job market has shifted and there are so few tenure-track jobs.

While part-time faculty are primarily teachers, full-time non-tenure track faculty often have a broader set of responsibilities. Baldwin and Chronister (2001) established a typology to better understand full-time non-tenure track faculty based on the terms of employment responsibilities: teachers, researchers, administrators, and other academic professionals. Teachers are those who spend over two-thirds of their time in instruction, and the rest of their time split between administrative tasks and research. Researchers are those specifically hired to conduct research for over half their time, with the other half divided between instruction and administration. Administrators are those who spend about half their time on administrative work (often being on committees) and spend the rest of the time in research and other activities. The final group is comprised of other academic professionals—full-time non-tenure track faculty who spend half of their time with activities other than teaching, research, or administration—these could be lab technicians, programmers, or community-service members. They usually spend a quarter of their time teaching, depending on their qualifications (Baldwin & Chronister, 2001). But, Baldwin and Chronister (2001) found that 70 percent of the faculty in full-time non-tenured track positions are focused on instruction; only 10 percent were primarily researchers.

Another way to categorize faculty can be in terms of voluntary and involuntary non-tenure track employment (either full-time or part-time) (Maynard & Joseph, 2008; Tilly, 1998). Though tenure has been a traditional goal for those in the academy since it was first introduced (Benjamin, 2003; Burgan, 2006; Chait, 2005), there are faculty members who actively choose not to take a full-time position or tenure-track position (Bataille & Brown, 2006; Chait & Trower, 1997; Gappa, Austin, & Trice, 2007; Hollenshead et al., 2007). These faculty members would be considered voluntary non-tenure track employees. Conley and Leslie (2002) note that there are part-time faculty who simply enjoy teaching and are not dependent upon the position as a career, while others choose to be part-time because it best fits into their lives or is only a supplementary career. Levin et al. (2006) divided part-time non-tenure track faculty in community colleges between those who had careers in other professions, and those who relied on the part-time position for sole income. Hollenshead et al. (2007) found that faculty also chose to be non-tenured to seek a work–life balance or adapt to geographic constraints. Chait and Trower (1997: 16) found that faculty members chose non-tenured positions for other benefits such as a "10 percent salary supplement, summer stipend, and the one year's severance pay [if a long-term contract was not renewed]," while others wanted either to teach more or to have an overall lessened load. Gappa et al. (2007) found that at some institutions, depending on department and campus context, full-time non-tenure track faculty did not have as many challenges as part-time faculty or some of the disadvantages of the tenure-track. These individuals opted for and preferred the full-time non-tenure track.

There are also involuntary part-time and full-time non-tenure track employees. These faculty members are typically looking for tenured positions in their field and currently hold the appointment while waiting for a tenure-track opening (Conley & Leslie, 2002; Gappa & Leslie, 1993; Gappa et al., 2007). Gappa and Leslie's group of "aspiring academics" reflects this classification. In some cases these faculty prefer a full-time position, but are unable to achieve this because of changes in the labor market or being part of a dual-career couple. The biggest factor seems to be that the percentage of tenure-track/tenured positions has decreased in last 20 years. Hollenshead et al. (2007: 4) noted "by 2003, full- and part-time non-tenure track appointments accounted for three out of five (65%) faculty positions in all types of institutions."[1] Many academics, who initially entered the field wanting a tenured position, faced dwindling job possibilities at that time. Also, in terms of part-time faculty being involuntary non-tenure track, there are those part-time faculty who would prefer full-time faculty employment of any kind (Conley & Leslie, 2002). The perceptions and experiences of voluntary and involuntary non-tenure track faculty may vary greatly. The main point is that there is a great variety of individuals within these positions and there are complexities of developing policies and practices among such a diverse group of people.

Researchers have documented non-tenured track faculty location in certain institutional types (more in community colleges, four-year research universities, and doctoral-granting institutions and less in baccalaureate institutions), the academic fields in which they are concentrated (for example, they are rising more in the humanities and social sciences than in the sciences), and their racial and gender composition (women are over-represented and minorities under-represented) (Schuster & Finkelstein, 2006). For more information about racial composition, gender, institutional distribution and other information pertaining to non-tenure track faculty, please see Kezar and Sam (2010).

We think it is also important to highlight the diversity of terms to refer to these individuals. There are over 50 terms referring to non-tenure track faculty. Most terms for this group of faculty reflect a particular element of focus: lecturer—that they teach; part-time—amount of time they teach; but these terms do not comprehensively reflect their status. Given the vast number of names in the literature, we wanted some clear terminology to break this confusion: thus our umbrella term when we are referring to similarities these groups share is either "contingent" or "non-tenure track." When there are meaningful differences, they usually reflect the part-time and full-time contract status, so we will use these two terms when relevant to identify significant differences in these groups within the book to provide clarity for the audience.

## Audience

This book will have broad appeal for two major groups: contingent faculty on college campuses and administrators trying to implement policies and practices for contingent faculty. This book will be particularly attractive to contingent faculty because it is written from the perspective of contingent faculty leaders at different types of campus. One of the criticisms leveled at the current literature is that contingent faculty are wary of research by tenure-track faculty members; instead they are looking for resources that contingent faculty members write themselves. A second audience for the book is administrators on college campuses. While administrators have not been responsive toward past calls to change policies and practices, the ballooning of numbers of contingent faculty on campuses has made it impossible for administrators to ignore this issue. Therefore, more recent surveys have found that administrators are looking for resources to address this issue, and recognize it is a significant priority (Hollenshead et al., 2007). Department chairs are one of the most likely groups to benefit from this book, as change often happens at the departmental level.

There are two other specific audiences that will be interested in this book. The first group is comprised of graduate students across a variety of disciplines, who are looking to obtain jobs in academia. They will be interested in understanding more about their future prospects and the ways that they can contribute and change the academy in the present. Graduate students have been active in organizing unions and fighting for better working conditions, and in many ways they are considered another subset of the contingent faculty category. In fact, some research does include them as part of this workforce. This book will help to provide graduate students with strategies they can bring into their own departments, both as students and in their first positions as faculty. The second group is composed of scholars who study faculty. A subset of faculty in higher education study and write about faculty and will find this book of interest. Given that contingent faculty in the academy has become such an important issue, and there are not many books or research studies dedicated to this population, I hope this will be viewed as an important new resource.

## Organization of the Book

The book is divided into three parts. Part I sets the stage with two chapters that provide the background and context for the case-study chapters. In Chapter 1, *Needed Policies, Practices, and Values: Creating a Culture to Support and Professionalize Non-tenure Track Faculty*, Kezar reviews the main recommendations that have been made in the literature, helping readers to understand what policies have been identified that can best support non-tenure track faculty. She provides a framework for understanding why a systemic approach is needed to support faculty from the time they are hired, through their first courses, and when they need retooling in skills. The chapter also examines the need to look not only at policies, but practices and the culture of the institution so that policies implemented are accepted into the institutional fabric. Finally, Kezar reminds us that policies need to be attentive to differences in context (i.e., institutional type and culture), a theme highlighted throughout the rest of the book, through the case studies. In Chapter 2, *Strategies for Implementing and Institutionalizing New Policies and Practices: Understanding the Change Process*, Kezar and Sam review the results of a national study examining campuses that have implemented progressive policies and practices for contingent faculty and highlight a three-phase model for change—mobilization, implementation, and institutionalization—looking across strategies and actions taking place at each phase. The three-phase model provides a framework for thinking about the strategies described in the case-study chapters that follow.

In Part II, a series of case-study chapters are provided, highlighting the experience of eight different campuses: Madison Area Technical College—MATC; Vancouver Community College; California Polytechnic Institute, Pomona (Cal Poly Pomona); San Francisco State University; Villanova University; Virginia Polytechnic Institute and State University (Virginia Tech); Mountain College (a pseudonym); and the University of Southern California, noting their specific policies, practices, contexts and change processes. These institutions represent the diversity of higher education—two-year/four-year; public/private; religious/ secular; research-intensive and teaching-intensive; technical and liberal arts; unionized and non-unionized; and from states throughout the country. Their stories range from those that shifted the entire culture of the campus (Vancouver Community College and MATC) to those which have just started to implement policies (University of Southern California and Villanova). Some have a long history of addressing contingent faculty issues (San Francisco State University) and others have more recently worked on the issues (Virginia Tech). We start with the three campuses that have moved the farthest and institutionalized changes (Vancouver Community College, MATC, and Mountain College) to give readers a sense of the end goal and work backward, through implementation (Virginia Tech, California Polytechnic Institute at Pomona, and San Francisco State University), and all the way to the early mobilization phase (University of Southern California and Villanova). Chapter 7 provides a more personal voice about the struggles that non-tenure track faculty face—some even self-inflicted— not believing they are worthy of changes to support their work. In not achieving a tenured role and based on negative feedback from tenured colleagues, non-tenure track faculty begin to absorb a self-loathing that can prevent change. While the case study explains how the campus achieved changes, it begins by describing important internal and psychological challenges and barriers that often need to be faced: this marks the beginning of activism and change. As a result of this objective, the chapter has a slightly different format from the others.

In Part III, the book closes with two chapters that synthesize lessons that can be learned from across all of these different cases—one written by Maria Maisto, the president of the New Faculty Majority, an organization devoted to improving the working conditions for contingent faculty; and one written by the editor. The final chapter by the editor synthesizes similarities in opportunities and challenges across the cases and compares the cases to the broader frameworks described in Chapter 1 and Chapter 2. Finally, the editor will draw implications and conclusions from the case studies.

## Note

1   Referencing American Association of University Professors (2006), *Trends in faculty status, 1975–2003*, Washington, DC: American Association of University Professors. Available at: http://www.aaup.org/AAUP/issues/contingent/resources.htm.

## References

American Association of University Professors (2006). *Trends in faculty status, 1975-2003*. Washington, DC: American Association of University Professors.

Astin, A. W. (1993). *What matters in college: Four critical years revisited*. San Francisco: Jossey-Bass.

Baldwin, R. G., & Chronister, J. L. (2001). *Teaching without tenure*. Baltimore: Johns Hopkins University Press.

Banachowski, G. (1996). ERIC review—perspectives and perceptions: The use of part-time faculty in community colleges. *Community College Review, 24*(2), 49–62.

Bataille, G. M., & Brown, B. E. (2006). *Faculty career paths: Multiple routes to academic success and satisfaction*. Westport, CT: Praeger Publishers. Retrieved from http://www.loc.gov/catdir/toc/ecip0613/2006014287.html.

Benjamin, E. (Ed.) (2003). *Exploring the role of contingent instructional staff in undergraduate learning*. San Francisco: Jossey-Bass.

Bland, C., Center, B. A., Finstad, D. A., Risbey, K. R., & Staples, J. (2006). The impact of appointment type on the productivity and commitment of full-time faculty in research and doctoral institutions. *The Journal of Higher Education, 77*(1), 89–121.

Burgan, M. (2006). *What ever happened to the faculty?* Baltimore: Johns Hopkins University Press.

Chait, R. (2005). *Questions of tenure*. Cambridge, MA: Harvard University Press.

Chait, R., & Trower, C. (1997). *Where tenure does not reign: Colleges with contract systems* (Forum on Faculty Roles and Rewards No. 3). Washington, DC: American Association for Higher Education.

Conley, V. M., & Leslie, D. W. (2002). Part-time instructional faculty and staff: Who they are, what they do, and what they think. *Education Statistics Quarterly, 4*(2), 97–103.

Cross, J. G., & Goldenberg, E. N. (2009). *Off-track profs: Non-tenured teachers in higher education*. Cambridge, MA: MIT Press.

Eagan, M. K., & Jaeger, A. J. (2008). Closing the gate: Contingent faculty in gatekeeper courses. In J. M. Braxton (Ed.), *The role of the classroom in college student persistence. New directions for teaching and learning* (pp. 39–53). San Francisco: Jossey-Bass.

Eagan, M. K., & Jaeger, A. J. (2009). Part-time faculty at community colleges: Implications for student persistence and transfer. *Research in Higher Education, 50*(2), 168–188.

Ehrenberg, R. G. (2005). The changing nature of the faculty and faculty employment practices. Paper presented to the TIAA-CREF Institute Conference on "The New Balancing Act in Higher Education," New York, NY.

Ehrenberg, R. G., & Zhang, L. (2005). Do tenured and tenure-track faculty matter? *The Journal of Human Resources, 40*(3), 647–659.

Gappa, J. M., Austin, A. E., & Trice, A. (2007). *Rethinking faculty work: Higher education's strategic imperative*. San Francisco: Jossey-Bass.

Gappa, J. M., & Leslie, D. W. (1993). *The invisible faculty: Improving the status of part-timers in higher education*. San Francisco: Jossey-Bass.

Hollenshead, C., Waltman, J., August, L., Miller, J., Smith, G., & Bell, A. (2007). *Making the best of both worlds: Findings from a national institution-level survey on non-tenure track faculty*. Ann Arbor, MI: Center for the Education of Women.

Jacoby, D. (2006). Effects of part-time faculty employment on community college graduation rates. *The Journal of Higher Education, 77*(6), 1081–1102.

Jaeger, A. J., & Eagan, M. K. (2009). Effects of exposure to part-time faculty on associate's degree completion. *Community College Review, 36*(3), 167–194.

JBL Associates, Inc. (2008). *Reversing course: The troubled state of academic staffing and a path forward*. Washington, DC: American Federation of Teachers.

Kezar, A. (forthcoming). Examining non-tenure track faculty perceptions of how departmental policies and practices shape their performance. *Research in Higher Education*.

Kezar, A., & Sam, C. (2010). *Understanding the new majority: Contingent faculty in higher education*. ASHE Higher Education Report Series, *36*(4). San Francisco: Jossey-Bass.

Levin, J., Kater, S., & Wagoner, R. (2006). *Community college faculty: At work in the new economy*. New York, NY: Palgrave.

Maynard, D. C., & Joseph, T. A. (2008). Are all part-time faculty underemployed? The influence of faculty status preference on satisfaction and commitment. *Higher Education, 55*(2), 139–154.

Schell, E., & Stock, P. (2001). *Moving a mountain: Transforming the role of contingent faculty in composition studies and higher education*. Urbana, IL: National Council of Teachers in English.

Schuster, J. H., & Finkelstein, M. J. (2006). *The American faculty: The restructuring of academic work and careers*. Baltimore: Johns Hopkins University Press.

Stripling, J. (2011, May 20). Most presidents prefer no tenure for majority of faculty. *Chronicle of Higher Education, 57*(37), A12.

Tilly, C. (1998). Part-time work: A mobilizing issue. *New Politics, 6*(4), 113–119.

Umbach, P. D. (2007). How effective are they? Exploring the impact of contingent faculty on undergraduate education. *The Review of Higher Education, 30*(2), 91–123.

Umbach, P. D. (2008). The effects of part-time faculty appointments on instructional techniques and commitment to teaching. Paper presented at the 33rd Annual Conference of the Association for the Study of Higher Education, Jacksonville, FL.

# PART I

# Setting the Stage:
# Background and Context

# 1

# NEEDED POLICIES, PRACTICES, AND VALUES

## Creating a Culture to Support and Professionalize Non-tenure Track Faculty

*Adrianna Kezar*

*John heads the non-tenure track faculty subcommittee of the academic senate and has been tasked with developing recommendations for contingent faculty at his liberal arts college. The campus has some part-time faculty and a growing number of full-time non-tenure track faculty. From conversations with non-tenure track faculty colleagues in different disciplines, he has realized they all have very different concerns and needs. He is perplexed where to start. In fact, he feels fairly paralyzed as if there is no common ground from which to start tackling the issue. He consulted a few reports on non-tenure track faculty issues, but they seemed more focused on community colleges and he is not sure how well the recommendations will apply to his campus. He calls a few colleagues at peer institutions who offer a few ideas, but mostly they express that they are similarly confused. John really is not sure how to proceed.*

This is the situation in which many of you will come to this book, a sense of not being sure exactly where to start or with what issues. While it is certainly important to know how to create change (the focus of much of the book), it is also important to understand and have a vision for what changes are needed. An underlying goal of all the changes recommended in this chapter and book is that they facilitate the professionalization of faculty, which helps make them more productive and improves performance. Several books have summarized general policies and practices for both full-time (Baldwin & Chronister, 2001) and part-time faculty (Gappa & Leslie, 1993) that likely support non–tenure track faculty on campuses. In this chapter, I build upon these thoughtful recommendations by placing them within broader frameworks of faculty work/organizational culture, and showing how matching change interventions to problems identified in particular campus contexts is critical to making effective policy. Why are such frameworks important? Gappa, Austin, and Trice's (2007) framework of essential elements of faculty performance demonstrates how current polices for non-tenure track faculty position them to perform poorly and highlights ways we can improve faculty outcomes. Furthermore, this framework helps expose gaps in policy areas that institutions and departments need to fill in order fully to capitalize on non-tenure track faculty. The culture and context frameworks illuminate how the generic recommendations will not be as successful if they are not modified to fit the campus culture. The culture framework showcases the need for institutionalized changes throughout the entire organizational system—policies, practices, and values.

In order to accomplish these goals, I begin the chapter by summarizing some of the more generic policy changes that have been recommended. The list of generic policy recommendations is not fully inclusive, but represents the key areas that have been found across various studies as problematic and affecting the creation of a quality learning environment, including lack of mentoring and professional development. In addition to the important policy, practice, and value changes described in this chapter, each individual case-study chapter in this book will describe an important set of changes made in either policy or practice, helping to provide more detail to the points highlighted in this chapter.

Next, these generic policy recommendations are placed within three meaningful frameworks that can assist change agents to think about and approach change strategically. First, I review Gappa et al.'s (2007) framework for making faculty effective in their work, and I place the non-tenure track faculty recommendations for change within this framework. Second, I review a change-culture framework that highlights how campuses need to address policies, practices, and principles/values as each of these contribute to the culture. Institutions too often focus only on policy change and ignore the practices and values that have shaped the culture; institutions miss the opportunity for deep and lasting change. The focus of this book is to give the reader the tools to create a lasting culture change that will shape the work lives of all faculty. Third, building on the importance of culture, I will describe some of the ways that these general policy recommendations need to be considered in a context-based framework. In terms of context, institutional type, union status, centralized versus decentralized structure, power, and resources, among other significant issues impact the type of changes needed on various campuses.

## General Policy Principles Advocated for Supporting Non-tenure Track Faculty

Scholars advancing recommendations to support non-tenure track faculty have been extremely comprehensive in thinking about the entire experience of being a faculty member: hiring, orientation, a career track, professional development, evaluation and performance issues, and so on. In this section, we highlight these various important policies. It is important to reinforce that each recommendation plays out slightly differently based on institutional context, whether the policy is in place to address full-time or part-time non-tenure track faculty, and based on the motivation and interests of the non-tenure track faculty member (see "Background on Contingent Faculty and the Nationwide Change in Faculty" in the Preface for more information about typology and the differences in motivation and interests). Some of these differences and how they play out are highlighted in the sections below.

### Regularize Hiring

Various studies of both part-time and full-time non-tenure track faculty demonstrate that contingent faculty are generally hired within departments without any standard procedures or processes (Baldwin & Chronister, 2001; Cross & Goldenberg, 2009; Gappa & Leslie, 1993). In fact, administrators within four-year and research institutions have little understanding of the standards and procedures used for hiring non-tenure track faculty members. Too often, a department chair identifies a candidate through personal contacts and simply picks up the phone and calls someone to teach a course or fill a position. This overlooks affirmative action or any systemic hiring process. In some community colleges, more systematic hiring approaches have been instituted, often a result of collective bargaining (Gappa & Leslie, 1993). Also Hollenshead et al.'s (2007) study demonstrates that there is a tendency to put more effort into full-time than part-time non-tenure track faculty, because the perception is that full-time faculty members will be on campus for a much longer time period, which is a fallacy given their data about longevity. It is recommended that institutions and departments develop a more rigorous and standardized process of hiring for both part-time and full-time non-tenure track faculty that mirrors the current system of hiring for tenure-track faculty members. Furthermore, non-tenure track faculty need to be recruited and selected based on stated qualities and needs designated by the department or program, not on happenstance criteria such as being available or knowing someone in the department (Baldwin & Chronister, 2001). However, standardization of hiring is difficult within some institutions where academic disciplines (e.g., department chairs) have much authority over hiring, particularly at research universities or within certain disciplines such as physics.

### Create a Systematic Socialization Process and Mentoring

Many reports document that non-tenure track faculty are typically not offered orientation, or it is offered infrequently or at a time they cannot attend (Baldwin & Chronister, 2001; Gappa & Leslie, 1993; Hollenshead et. al., 2007). Also, no mentoring process is offered to help them adjust and learn the formal and informal rules. Systems should be created to socialize non-tenure track faculty members, or they should be included in current orientation and mentoring systems serving tenure-track faculty. A hallmark of professionals is that they socialize new members to the expectations and standards of the institution (Baldwin & Chronister, 2001; Gappa & Leslie, 1993; Sullivan, 2004). Orientation programs should be offered at times when non–tenure track faculty can attend, and for part-timers it may have to be offered online. In addition to formal orientation programs, non–tenure track faculty members need to be included in departmental and university discussions about norms related to grading policies, teaching philosophy, co-curricular activities, and other campus normative processes; and they need to be paid for such participation.

Another way to communicate institutional norms is through mentoring programs. Tenure-track and senior non–tenure track faculty members who are familiar with the roles and responsibilities of the work should be included as mentors for non–tenure track faculty members. Often it is the practice to have other non–tenure track faculty, who are more senior, mentor newer non–tenure track faculty. It is important to remove the barriers between non–tenure track and tenure-track faculty. Socialization needs to happen among the two groups whenever possible; mentoring is an ideal place for this interaction. However, for some part-time faculty, socialization may be less important, as they may be teaching but not be interested in becoming part of the academic community. Yet part-time non–tenure track faculty still need to know some basics to be successful teachers, such as the characteristics of students in their classes or grading policies, and this is where mentoring from other faculty can help. Attention to the motivation of individual faculty members is critical in developing policies and practices that are meaningful.

## Multi-year Renewable Contracts, Seniority Systems, Non-rehiring, and Revised Re-appointment Procedures

The current system of largely one-year contracts for full-time non–tenure track faculty, and semester-by-semester contracts for part-time faculty is not conducive to creating professionals who can meaningfully invest in the institution. Data show that non–tenure track faculty are committed to their discipline, students, and teaching; but often not to their institution, which they perceive is not committed to them because of one-year or semester-to-semester contracts (Shaker, 2008). Without a multi-year system, faculty must constantly be job hunting and may not have time for student contact and teaching preparation. Also, institutions are increasingly needing non–tenure track faculty to take on additional responsibilities, which means faculty need assurance that they will be at the institution to execute these responsibilities. Commitment is a reciprocal endeavor. Most reports recommend that institutions move to multi-year, renewable contracts, often starting with shorter contracts of two to three years and moving to five-year contracts after some probationary period of three to seven years (AFT, 2005; Baldwin & Chronister, 2001; Hollenshead et al., 2007;

Rhoades & Maitland, 2008). Also, it is recommended that institutions should eradicate policies that limit or cap the number of years in which faculty can teach off the tenure-track. This policy ends up eliminating positions for strong long-term non-tenure track faculty simply because the institution wants to maintain the perception of protecting tenure through this policy. Clearly this policy has not protected tenure on many campuses.

For part-timers, creating a seniority system where long-term part-timers receive priority appointments for teaching demonstrates the commitment of the institution to them. Once faculty have taught for a certain number of semesters, they might be eligible before other faculty with less experience for teaching assignments the next semester. Also, for all non-tenure track faculty, reports recommend that contract renewal and termination dates be explicitly listed and honored (Baldwin & Chronister, 2001). While there have not been explicit recommendations about how to approach multi-year and seniority systems, I recommend that they be considered in light of evaluation processes and not be granted merely for time served. Faculty who receive seniority or multi-year contracts should demonstrate that they are performing to the expectations of the department. Seniority without any system of evaluation is being severely attacked in the K–12 system and has been a concern among the general public. There will be more support for seniority systems and multi-year contracts tied to merit and performance. For any type of contract, due process is recommended, where faculty members are given some explanation for not being rehired, particularly those who have had long-term employment with the institution and effective performance, which can be established through reviews (Gappa & Leslie, 1993).

## Compensation and Benefits

Non-tenure track faculty pay is significantly less than tenure-track faculty pay (60 percent less in several studies looking at part-time non-tenure track faculty) and benefits are often not provided or are partial (Baldwin & Chronister, 2001; Gappa & Leslie, 1993). Almost all reports call for equitable compensation and benefits, but often do not provide details, since this depends on whether a faculty member is full-time or part-time and varies according to the financial situation of the institution (Baldwin & Chronister, 2001; Gappa & Leslie, 1993; Hollenshead et al., 2007; Rhoades & Maitland, 2008). But each report recommends—when feasible—that institutions should provide more equitable pay and benefits, particularly for the priority benefits such as healthcare or retirement. Many propose salary and benefits equal to that of entry-level tenure-track faculty members for full-time non-tenure track faculty members (AFT, 2005). For part-timers in particular, office hours, governance, and service needs to be included in discussion of salary. If part-timers are expected to have office hours (for student contact), or participate in governance, they should be compensated for this work. Also, scholars recommend consistency of pay or salary rates within different departments of an institution. It is not uncommon for non-tenure track faculty to be paid different amounts within the same department, and this practice creates feelings of inequity (Gappa & Leslie, 1993). While there are market differences between tenure-track faculty, at many institutions there are already attempts at market parity within disciplines—examining issues such as gender or race. Thus, two non-tenure track faculty members in engineering should have pay parity.

## Clear Role Definition

Various scholars promote the need to define the non-tenure track faculty role better, particularly for full-timers where expectations have been changing (Baldwin & Chronister, 2001; Hollenshead et al., 2007; Rhoades & Maitland, 2008). Hollenshead et al. (2007) found that institutions and departments increasingly expect full-time non-tenure track faculty to perform service and research roles like tenure-track faculty, in addition to teaching. Issues such as office hours, class preparation, communicating with students, administrative responsibilities, supervising clinical work or fieldwork, committee work, training, and mentoring graduate students all need to be made explicit in contracts or faculty handbooks. Roles and responsibilities should also be included and followed in promotion and evaluation processes. Non-tenure track faculty have experienced the disconnection of being assigned responsibilities, and then being given poor evaluations because the evaluations were not based on the role they had been assigned (Baldwin & Chronister, 2001).

## Promotion and Evaluation

Contingent faculty members are much more likely to feel like professionals if there is a system of sequential ranks and opportunities for salary increases, as they advance over their career (AFT, 2005; Baldwin & Chronister, 2001). Standards should be developed for progression through the salary scale. In order to advance professionally, some suggest that a system of evaluation needs to be put in place that is responsive to and aligned with the contingent role, which is often more focused on teaching (Gappa & Leslie, 1993). Some non-tenure track faculty who have other careers or who are retired may not be interested in a promotion system, but evaluation of all faculty is important.

Gappa and Leslie (1993) also recommend that evaluation processes be used as part of reappointment decisions. When I described concerns about seniority systems, I mentioned that evaluation might alleviate concerns; therefore evaluation can serve multiple purposes. However, unions differ and are leery about evaluations being part of the reappointment process (AFT, 2005). They argue that, too often, institutions rely on weak indicators, such as student evaluations alone. Therefore, there is less agreement about the desirability or use of evaluations.

Reports recommend that non-tenure track faculty members be involved in the development of the promotion and the evaluation systems (Baldwin & Chronister, 2001). In addition, if peer evaluation processes are utilized, care should be taken that both tenure-track and non-tenure track faculty are included as observers or evaluators.

## Professional Development

One of the most important aspects of being a professional in academe is the ability to learn and grow over the course of one's career; this aspect is significantly related to being a productive and effective faculty member (O'Meara, Terosky, & Neumann, 2008). Yet studies have identified how non-tenure track faculty are routinely denied access to professional development, and if it is open to non-tenure track faculty, it is offered at non-amenable times (Baldwin & Chronister, 2001; Gappa & Leslie, 1993). Researchers recommend that non-tenure track faculty be provided with opportunities and support for professional development (Baldwin & Chronister, 2001; Gappa & Leslie, 1993). This recommendation includes issues ranging from funds for conferences, and workshops on teaching, to professional growth opportunities for scholarship similar to sabbaticals. It is also important that centers for teaching and learning develop workshops and programs specifically designed for non-tenure track faculty members, so they have the opportunity to meet each other and network on topics of specific interest to this population, such as the scholarship of teaching. However, it is also important for campuses to offer professional development, where both tenure-track and non-tenure track faculty have the opportunity to learn together, such as programs on including collaborative learning or using technology in the classroom. Non-tenure track faculty should be included in awards and be recognized for excellence in teaching and service. Like orientation, these programs should be offered at times when non-tenure track faculty can attend them, and some may need to be offered online. Consortia across similar institutions may be an important direction for creating professional development in an affordable manner. Part-time faculty who teach at several institutions will find it difficult to take part in such activities without compensation.

## Governance

A long-held characteristic of professionals is their involvement in creating their conditions of work and impacting the larger work environment. As professionals, non-tenure track faculty should be full participants in the governance process, both in departments and at the broader school or university level (AFT, 2005; Baldwin & Chronister, 2001; Rhoades & Maitland, 2008). Studies identify that part-time non-tenure track faculty are typically excluded from governance and not even invited to departmental meetings (Baldwin & Chronister, 2001;

Gappa & Leslie, 1993). Full-time non-tenure track faculty are often excluded from governance, but more likely to be invited to departmental meetings (yet voting rights in departments are often not granted). Token representation and invitation to participate are not sufficient: Non-tenure track faculty members need to be given the right to an equal vote, to have a proportional number of members on committees and the faculty senate, and should be included in all matters—particularly curriculum, teaching, and learning (which they are often excluded from currently)—with the exception of tenure decisions. Also, involvement in governance should range from faculty senate, and campus-wide committees, to departmental decisions such as input on course selection and scheduling (Hollenshead et al., 2007). Also significant is that non-tenure track faculty should be paid or compensated for involvement in governance. While not all faculty will be interested in participation, the right to participate should be made available, and these rights should be clearly articulated in a handbook or faculty union contract and compensation should be provided.

## Academic Freedom

Academic freedom policies in general should include non-tenure track faculty. Academic freedom as it relates to shared governance was more of a concern for non-tenure track faculty than academic freedom in the classroom (AFT, 2010; Baldwin & Chronister, 2001; Conley & Leslie, 2002). As a result, particular protection should be in place so that non-tenure track faculty members feel they can participate in governance without jeopardizing their jobs. Scholars recommend that campuses create explicit statements that protect individuals when they critique the administration as part of their shared governance role (Rhoades & Maitland, 2008). The move toward multi-year contracts and an evaluation system could assist in this process as well.

## Appropriate Office Space, Clerical Support, and Equipment

Employers should provide the necessary supplies and support for employees to be able to fulfill their job responsibilities. Faculty need to be provided with an individual or shared office space that gives them a place to meet with students and other colleagues, to prepare for teaching, and to meet other job responsibilities ranging from managing graduate assistants to field placements (Baldwin & Chronister, 2001; Gappa & Leslie, 1993). They also need appropriate clerical support for their teaching, service, and research demands, and appropriate access to equipment such as a computer, photocopier, phone, fax, and other basic office equipment necessary in order to do their work. Too often, non-tenure track faculty, particularly part-time, are expected to have a home office with all these materials and buy their own supplies (paper, printer cartridges, and other needed equipment) and do their own clerical support. This expectation puts an undue burden on a group of faculty that is already paid less than their colleagues (Baldwin & Chronister, 2001; Gappa & Leslie, 1993).

These policy recommendations have emerged from national reports; they were the focus of institutions involved in the national study and are recommended for other campuses beginning this process. I now provide some important frameworks for thinking about these recommended policy changes. Rather than conceptualizing these as a bullet-point list of items for professionalizing non-tenure track faculty, I want to demonstrate how to think about these items strategically as a more holistic package of changes needed to create an inclusive culture that makes faculty productive and high-performing. Here I will explain the first framework, giving the reader a detailed look into the essential elements. Then I will show how the policy recommendations described above fit into the framework.

## A framework for Creating Effective Faculty Work

Gappa et al. (2007) developed a framework of the essential elements for effective faculty work, which includes employment equity, academic freedom and autonomy, flexibility, professional growth, collegiality, and at the core, respect. These research-based essential elements are drawn from literature on faculty satisfaction and meaningful work. Their framework suggests that if these essential elements are in place, the outcomes are increased faculty satisfaction and a sense of meaningfulness, increased commitment to the organization, enhanced recruitment and retention, a broader spectrum of individuals represented on the faculty, and more strategic utilization of intellectual capital. While they do not examine whether the essential elements of faculty work lead to increased student outcomes, research by Kezar (forthcoming) suggests that when faculty lack these essential aspects of work, it does negatively affect the student learning environment. As noted in the introduction to this chapter, any changes recommended for contingent faculty should be embedded within a larger framework of what makes faculty effective. Figure 1.1 depicts the framework.

Gappa et al. (2007) note that the central concept of the framework is *respect* —a foundational requirement for the other elements to be operationalized. They note that, "respect is a fundamental entitlement for every faculty member and is at the core of any reciprocal relationship between faculty members and their institutions" (Gappa et al., 2007: 139). The issue of respect is often overlooked when making changes related to non-tenure track faculty. The administration or tenure-track faculty may feel that if they have addressed policies such as pay or length of contract, they have addressed the issue of respect. However, on most of the campuses highlighted within this book, it is the second-class citizenship that is often most problematic on campuses and reflects this lack of respect that non-tenure track faculty feel others exhibit toward them. It is lack of respect that leads to a lack of progressive policies and practices, and

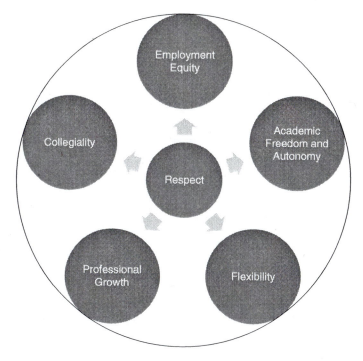

**FIGURE 1.1** Framework from Gappa, Austin, & Trice (2007)

*Source*: Gappa, J. M., Austin, A. E., & Trice, A. *Rethinking faculty work: Higher education's strategic imperative*. © Gappa, Austin, & Trice, 2007. Reprinted with permission of John Wiley & Sons, Inc.

outcomes such as retention problems, lack of commitment, tension and communication problems, and a poor work community. Decades of research on motivating people to work and work satisfaction demonstrates the importance of respect from co-workers as fundamental to enhanced work performance and growth that leads to higher performance and productivity (Gappa et al., 2007). Gappa and her co-authors recommend that departments and institutions conduct an audit of the institutional climate and culture to understand and address the issues around respect. This notion about the importance of data collection to tackle issues of climate will be addressed in the case studies.

Gappa et al. (2007) define *employment equity* as the right of every faculty member to be treated fairly with regard to his or her employment within the institution and its departments, and to have access to the tools necessary to do his or her job. Therefore, if the institution has a policy about evaluation or contract renewals, each department within the institution follows this policy. Gappa and her co-authors are clear that equitable treatment does not necessarily mean identical treatment. Instead they emphasize the importance of being treated fairly after differences among faculty members are taken into account (for example, market differences in pay between law and classics).

*Academic freedom and autonomy* is described as faculty members being free to express their views in research and scholarship, in the classroom when discussing the curriculum, and as citizens in society. Gappa et al. (2007) also suggest that autonomy is a fundamental aspect of faculty effectiveness and entails faculty being able to make decisions about how to perform their work assignments. Academic freedom is tied to autonomy, as faculty should be free to choose a curriculum and examples that fit into their perspective and not be constrained by politics or those in power—whether external or internal to the institution.

*Flexibility* is the ability of faculty members to construct their working conditions to maximize their contributions to the institution as well as for their work in teaching, research, and service. It also relates to providing career-path options such as multiple points of entry, exit, and re-entry into the faculty position, and the ability to shift between tenure-track and contract-renewable appointments. Flexibility includes the opportunity for leave for family reasons and caregiving, flexibility on load, on-campus childcare and work–family policies, career breaks, and half-time tenured appointments and job sharing. The notion of flexibility has become particularly important as leaders have tried to diversify the professoriate (i.e., by race and gender). A very narrow approach to a faculty career path has been demonstrated to decrease productivity and performance rather than enhance them.

The next element is *professional growth*—the opportunity to broaden knowledge, abilities, and skills to meet the demands of work and constantly to improve and find greater satisfaction in work. Clearly, it is important for faculty to be able to keep up on advances in their field that impact their teaching, whether they are tenure or non-tenure track.

The last element is collegiality—the ability to belong to a community of colleagues who value their contributions to the institution. *Collegiality* refers to a sense of belonging and sense of inclusion. All faculty should feel that they are part of the institution and this should be demonstrated through the policies and practices created—such as inclusion in governance, input on teaching, involvement in campus organizations and groups, an office space that puts you in contact with other faculty in your area, and invitations to meetings and events. Collegiality also denotes working for something larger than yourself as an individual—you are part of a collegium that entails students, other faculty, and staff who are all educators. Collegiality also relates to being part of and shaping that community and speaks to participation in consensus-type processes such as governance. Gappa et al. (2007) acknowledge that collegiality is the element of work that has been fraught with historic as well as recent challenges. Many of these characteristics are what have come to define professional work.

Under each essential element in this framework we can place the policy recommendations to support non-tenure track faculty reviewed earlier.

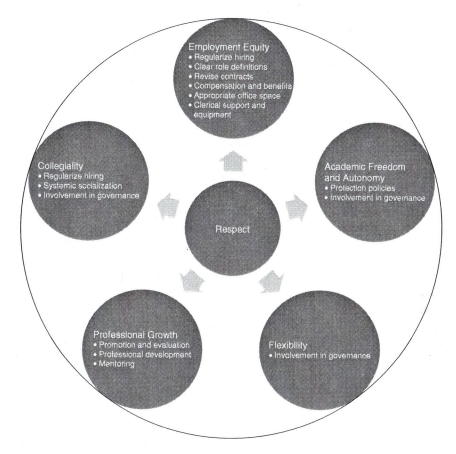

**FIGURE 1.2** Overlay of the framework with the policy recommendations for professionalizing non-tenure track faculty

See Figure 1.2 for an overlay of the framework with the policy recommendations for professionalizing non-tenure track faculty.

- EMPLOYMENT EQUITY—regularize hiring; clear role definitions; revise contracts, compensation and benefits; appropriate office space, clerical support, and equipment;
- ACADEMIC FREEDOM AND AUTONOMY—protection policies, involvement in governance;
- FLEXIBILITY—involvement in governance;
- PROFESSIONAL GROWTH—promotion and evaluation, professional development, mentoring;
- COLLEGIALITY—regularize hiring, systematic socialization, involvement in governance;
- RESPECT—all policy recommendations relate to this area.

It is important to note that recommended policies can be mapped onto the framework for effective faculty. The majority of current recommended policies focus on *employment equity*—an area where there has been great disparity for non-tenure track faculty. For example, by regularizing hiring, there is a greater chance that institutions will follow their equal opportunity employment policies, which are currently often disregarded in the hiring of non-tenure track faculty and can lead to inequitable hiring. Another critical issue is the lower compensation and lack of benefits for many non-tenure track faculty; the creation of greater equity in compensation and benefits is another way to create greater employment equity for non-tenure track faculty.

*Academic freedom* can be addressed through formal policies that guarantee academic freedom for non-tenure track faculty. The issues of *autonomy* as well as *flexibility* are primarily addressed through governance where decisions are made about curriculum and issues that impact the teaching and learning environment. Since non-tenure track faculty are often excluded from governance, they do not choose textbooks and are often given pre-created syllabi, thus hampering their autonomy and ability to capitalize on their strengths. As non-tenure track faculty are included in governance, they obtain agency to make decisions about the teaching and learning environment, which as a by-product creates autonomy for them. Through governance they also create flexibility by having input on a variety of decisions that impact their working conditions such as student admission, class sizes, the presence and amount of online learning, and various other decisions that affect their flexibility. However, it is important to note that few recommendations to date have been made related to non-tenure track faculty and issues of flexibility. The types of flexibility that tenure-track faculty obtain in terms of maternity or paternity leaves, career breaks, leaves without pay, family-friendly policies, or job sharing are not usually provided to contingent faculty. In fact, the opposite of flexibility is typically the norm for non-tenure track faculty who have very prescribed and heavy teaching loads and little involvement in research and service. Their careers are not envisioned with flexibility in mind and more recommendations in this area are needed. The flexibility envisioned is always to the benefit of the institution's flexibility in terms of when and if they teach; it is not a mutual process. Some institutions, highlighted in this book, are trying to obtain professional leaves for non-tenure track faculty, which demonstrates institutional efforts to provide greater flexibility.

*Professional growth* is ensured through contingent faculty being able to participate in institutional and departmental professional development, and being considered in the design of such curricula that might be oriented more toward teaching. In addition, having a promotion and evaluation system for non-tenure track faculty allows them to have ongoing growth and development as part of their career and to receive continual feedback.

Finally, *collegiality* can be fostered by hiring processes that include tenured and non-tenure track faculty in the selection process, so that individuals brought in are considered part of the overall professoriate, which adds to the collegiality among individuals. Not only hiring, but also the creation of a socialization process, foster collegiality by having new non-tenure track faculty meet with and be mentored by existing faculty and learn the norms of the department and discipline/field. Lastly, a hallmark of a professional and a key way to foster collegiality on campuses is through involvement in departmental and institutional governance. As non-tenure track faculty work with their tenure-track colleagues, it breaks down stereotypes and creates relationships that build collegiality.

It is also important to note that these essential features (and related policies) are reinforcing of each other and related. For example, inequitable employment policies may result in inequitable evaluations, or faculty who are collegial may be less likely to support policies that disadvantage contingent faculty. These various features should not be seen in isolation but can be linked, and if leveraged well, can build a strong foundation. But if some are not dealt with, the foundation can come apart and cause a domino effect to the other features.

Through this analysis, it is clear that existing recommendations for non-tenure track faculty fall short in certain areas and need further refinement. Current recommendations strongly address employment equity, and moderately address academic freedom and professional development, but flexibility and collegiality are woefully in need of more work. If we want faculty to be effective, we need to enhance recommendations related to flexibility and collegiality.

In this section, I highlight a few ways to enhance these areas that are under-developed that will also contribute to this framework of effectiveness. A way to foster *collegiality* is to cluster non-tenure track faculty in similar fields in offices. On many campuses, non-tenure track faculty are placed in offices with contingent faculty from other departments or units. In order to foster collegiality, non-tenure track faculty should be able to have some input into who is placed in their shared office space, so that more networks can be created and greater connection to the campus can be made. Another way to foster collegiality is to ensure that non-tenure track faculty are invited to all speaking events and social opportunities.

As noted earlier, there are very few policies in place to enhance non-tenure track faculty *flexibility*. Changing faculty contracts to include service work is important to providing the flexibility to be involved in governance and other service work. In turn, service work can help provide them with more flexibility in their role and enable them to move out of the constraints of extremely high teaching loads without any time for other types of work to contribute to the institution. Another flexibility issue is having policies that help non-tenure track faculty move to tenure-track positions if they so desire. A faculty member may, for example, initially prefer a non-tenure position in order to have a child, but later be positioned to move to tenure-track; these options are not often made available or encouraged.

By placing these changes within this broader framework, the importance of making a whole series of changes, rather than simply a few more obvious policy changes, such as improved pay or multi-year contracts, is made clear. While changes toward employment equity tend to be the focus, they fall short of creating the conditions necessary for the non-tenure track faculty to be effective members of the professoriate and to create the best learning environment for students.

## A Framework for Changing Culture: Policies, Practices, and Principles

Another framework to conceptualize these changes beyond a constellation of effective components for faculty work is to consider the way that campuses need to support faculty through various types of levers that include policies, practices, and principles, which amounts to a change in the culture. If change agents envision this process as a policy change rather than a culture change, they will likely make less progress than hoped. Research on change demonstrates that changing the culture of the institution is one of the most important ways to institutionalize changes, and it requires alteration of policies, practices, and principles/ values (Curry, 1992; Kezar, 2001; Schein, 1992). While these mechanisms work in concert, to focus only on policies in the hope that it will affect practices and principles is shown to be ineffective. Change occurs when leaders focus on alteration of all three areas (Kezar, 2001; Schein, 1992). Scholars such as Schein (1992) emphasize the importance of starting with underlying values and principles as these are embedded in policies and practices. By first addressing people's underlying assumptions, practices and policies are more likely to change easily. However, given the difficulty of changing underlying values and assumptions, some scholars have recommended changing policies and practices as a way to begin discussion of underlying values and to move toward alteration of principles that affect the culture (Kezar, 2001). While there is no definitive research on where to begin, it is clear that working on all three is important to change campus cultures, and perhaps working on all three simultaneously can best create change.

### Policies

Policies are formal institutional guidelines that are created to guide action, and include things such as employment contracts, hiring guidelines, compensation and benefits packages (many of which were described in detail above in the "General Policy Principles Advocated for Supporting Non-tenure Track Faculty" section). Policies are also related to inclusion in governance and voting rights, role definitions, academic freedom policies, and promotion and evaluation. Many of the disparate policies noted can be found in faculty handbooks or union contracts, so it is critical that the non-tenure track faculty leaders first start with becoming particularly familiar with these documents. Often there are rights for non-tenure track faculty members that are not put into practice, but which are stated in policy documents. Gappa and Leslie (1993) found that institutions do not inform non-tenure track faculty of their rights to benefits in the hope that many will not use them, which is what often happens. Also, at Villanova University, one of the institutions highlighted in this book, non-tenure track faculty have voting rights within departments on certain issues, but this was not known among non-tenure track faculty and not practiced by departments. Therefore, just becoming familiar with campus policy documents may shed light on policies that are not being followed. On a variety of campuses that I have visited or studied, non-tenure track faculty were surprised when they went to union contracts or faculty handbooks and found a series of rights that institutions were not following.

In addition to understanding the existing policies, it is also important that these policies be updated and revised as the composition of the faculty changes. The handbooks at many campuses do not refer to non-tenure track faculty and they may be excluded from mention within policies. By merely inserting the title of non-tenure track faculty into academic freedom policies, these policies can be extended to a new group. In addition to them being added on to current policies, new policies may need to be developed that are specific to non-tenure track faculty and their appointments. For example, reappointment processes and the way that evaluations will be used within reappointment may be an area that needs to be specifically designed relating to non-tenure track faculty. It is important to note that many individuals do struggle because even though they find out their rights, the only way to make the institution follow the policy is to voice a griev-ance or become involved in a lawsuit, which most faculty do not want to do. Yet, if individuals work more collectively and not individually (as will be described in the discussion of strategies in Chapter 2), they can get action without going to these extreme measures.

## Practices

In addition to examining campus policies, campus practices need to be reviewed for their effectiveness and inclusiveness related to non-tenure track faculty. Policies are often the first place where non-tenure track faculty leaders focus their work, and existing practices that marginalize contingent faculty are typically overlooked. Practices are the accepted behaviors, actions, and procedures that may not necessarily have a corresponding policy connected to them. Practices include hiring processes, orientation, mentoring, office space, equipment and clerical support, governance practices and traditions, promotion and evaluation processes, and professional development. While policies often shape overarching guidelines for certain practices such as hiring or governance, practices are the everyday execution of such processes and move beyond designation of who can be involved, to how they are involved, and the degree of respect and type of interaction that occur during hiring, governance, or mentoring processes. Non-tenure track faculty leaders need to look across various practices and ensure that these are offered to non-tenure track faculty and then examine the way that they are offered. Often professional development will be open to non-tenure track faculty, but it will be offered at times that they cannot attend and involve content that is of little interest to them. Therefore, opening up processes is not enough, they must be altered to meet the needs of contingent faculty. Another example might be mentoring that is provided by tenure-track faculty to non-tenure track faculty, but with the tenure-track faculty having little understanding of the non-tenure track role. In these instances, tenure-track faculty either need to be educated about the non-tenure track faculty role, or non-tenure track faculty need to play a more prominent role in mentoring their non-tenure track colleagues.

## *Principles*

Finally, in addition to examining policies and practices, principles or values also need to be examined carefully in order to alter the culture of the institution to support non-tenure track faculty. Gappa et al.'s (2007) framework suggests that respect is the foundation of effective faculty work. The notion of respect is probably the most important principle to address in relationship to the contingent faculty. Research demonstrates that tenure-track faculty and administrators often hold negative stereotypes of non-tenure track faculty (Kezar, Lester, & Anderson, 2006). For example, non tenure-track faculty are considered to have lesser qualifications, to be less competitive for faculty jobs, to be inferior teachers, to not understand the research process, and to lack the knowledge necessary to contribute toward governance. These stereotypes prevent tenure-track faculty and administrators from having respect for the non-tenure track faculty and seeing them as equal contributors within the institution. Unless these assumptions are unearthed and addressed, they will continue to prevent needed changes within the institution. While some faculty have explicit views about non-tenure track faculty, other faculty may be unaware of their implicit assumptions. These faculty may not state any negative views about non-tenure track faculty, but when you ask who the faculty are, they never mention non-tenure track or they talk about the "real faculty" who are tenure-track. These tacit views are important to unearth and sometimes are even more difficult to change. For more details about how stereotypes held affect non-tenure track faculty experience and the way to overcome them, please see Kezar et al. (2006).

In addition to the very basic notion of respect, institutions might examine their existing values and see how they support or do not support non-tenure track faculty. Mission statements may describe the importance of teaching, but institutional practices have moved away from teaching to focus on a research mission. Appealing to the teaching mission might provide support for the work that non-tenure track faculty are doing. Campuses also often have value statements that speak to particular principles that guide employees in working together, such as notions of community, mutuality, or ongoing learning and development. In looking at the way that non-tenure track faculty are treated, campuses may realize that contingent faculty are not being included as part of the community or provided with the opportunity for ongoing learning and development, and rethink current practices. Policies themselves often include value statements, and non-tenure track leaders should carefully evaluate these policies for the implied or explicit values. For example, in relationship to hiring, policy documents might speak to the importance of a fair and open process that follows principles of equal opportunity; however, these values are not followed in practice in the hiring of non-tenure track faculty. Pointing out how the happenstance hiring of non-tenure track faculty violates the campus's stated hiring policies and values helps to create change. Leaders can draw upon the stated values within various policies for changing existing practices better to reflect these more inclusive values. In general, the values reflected in mission or value statements and policies often reflect our highest ideals and can be a place to remind people how we should be striving to interact and work together.

A very important overarching concept around values and principles is that change agents need to convince internal and external groups and stakeholders about the need and reason to change non-tenure track faculty working conditions. Anyone who wants to change policies for non-tenure track faculty will have greater success if they demonstrate the greater value or principle this change is working toward, by explaining how these changes can benefit the institution, department, tenure-track faculty, and/or students. By making this link, change agents can help to ground policy changes for non-tenure track faculty in already existing values about increasing learning, and help non-supporters see how the non-tenure track faculty experience relates to the larger picture or mission. For example, including non-tenure track faculty in governance helps ease the increasing burden of faculty service left to the dwindling number of tenure-line faculty who are increasingly finding it difficult to grade papers and revise their syllabi. Providing multi-year contracts allows non-tenure track faculty more time to prepare for courses as well as giving them an incentive for course creation in areas with few tenure-track faculty, to meet the needs of students in burgeoning areas. In these examples, the change agent provides tenure-track faculty and their department with the need and reason to change contingent faculty work conditions and ties the changes to increased benefit to the department and tenure-track faculty.

## A Framework for Context-based Solutions

Institutions need to look at how their policies, practices, and values add up to support effective faculty work, looking across the various dimensions of respect, employment equity, academic freedom and autonomy, flexibility, professional growth, and collegiality. In addition to thinking about these two frameworks, as institutions approach making needed changes, they must also think carefully about a third framework: the type of institution in which they are located and the institutional culture and subcultures (Kezar & Eckel, 2002; Trowler, 2008). The case-study chapters illustrate the importance of understanding the institutional culture and structure when creating changes so that they respond to the problems of the institution. For example, as a Catholic Augustinian institution, Villanova University had greater equity when it came to compensation and benefits because of its focus on social justice, but it had unaddressed issues of respect and culture that particularly played out in exclusion of non-tenure track faculty from governance, professional development, and leaves. An examination of the institution (and subcultures by discipline) and its particular issues and problems related to non-tenure track faculty is important, rather than wholesale application of the various changes recommended in this chapter. In particular, certain areas might be more of a priority within particular institutional types and the problems which they face.

One of the best ways to identify context-based solutions is to conduct a survey (or run focus groups) of non-tenure track faculty to discover their concerns and needs. Rather than assuming contingent faculty needs based on the general recommendations offered within this chapter, it is important to identify the perceived or experienced problems within the institution. However, many non-tenure track faculty do not have a broader vision of what it would take to make them effective in their position, which is why the framework by Gappa et al. (2007) offered in this chapter can also be brought to focus groups, so that individuals can respond to other criteria and elements that may not have occurred to them as important for their working conditions. A combination of bottom–up identification of needs that respond to the context in addition to balancing these needs with a broader vision for making faculty effective is likely to create the best solutions for your campus.

In addition, it is important to evaluate the institutional characteristics and how these might alter particular recommendations for change. Gappa et al. (2007) suggest six important institutional characteristics that can shape the type of elements that are put in place to support faculty: mission, resources (fiscal, human, and physical), reward structure, leadership, governance and structure (e.g., centralized versus decentralized), culture and norms. For example, if you are at a resource-poor institution, focusing on compensation and benefits first is likely to be met with significant resistance, and looking to other issues such as involvement in governance and establishing a promotion and evaluation process is more likely a good use of time and energy. When examining the mission of the institution, if ongoing development and professional growth is an underlying principle but non-tenure track faculty are excluded from professional development, this may create a lever for change and be an important area of focus. Sometimes getting a change in place quickly builds momentum, so determining the "low-hanging fruit" can be a helpful strategy. If the reward structure is heavily focused on research and limited ways to evaluate teaching exist, then non tenure-track faculty will have to help develop models for altering the reward structure. On highly decentralized campuses with few policies that govern the overall institution, non-tenure track faculty leaders may need to focus more on institutional practices such as inclusion in governance, since the alteration of faculty handbooks will speak to very few issues, and changes will need to be made more departmentally and fit within the particular norms of that department. On campuses that have a strong ethic toward supporting diversity (an example of an institutional norm), leaders might promote the issue of contingent faculty as another issue of diversity (another marginalized group) and see the ways it can be paired with institutional changes made in the hiring or orientation of diverse faculty. In these many ways, institutional characteristics are taken into account in crafting the types of changes that can be made, prioritizing particular types of changes, and creating processes that work within the institutional culture and characteristics. Other examples may also be relevant as you think about your specific context.

In order to demonstrate the ways that campuses might address needed changes in very different ways, I provide the example of two very different institution types—a community college and a research university—to demonstrate that they identify quite different changes that are important within their context (examples adapted from Kezar & Sam, 2010).

### Private Research University

One private research university has been considering ways to improve policies and practices for contingent faculty. The contingent faculty comprises 50 percent of the total faculty, a large percentage being full-time. It is hard to know exactly how many part-time faculty are teaching, as the institution does not keep accurate records, but data suggest that many courses each term are also taught by part-time faculty. However, this institution needs to address the full-time contingent faculty in particular, as they have grown tremendously in recent years. Like most institutions, the university does not recognize the need to educate tenure-track faculty about the working conditions of non-tenure track faculty or address negative messages, so the non-tenure track faculty experience outright backlash from tenure-track faculty at proposals for change. The climate at this university is very negative toward those not on the tenure-track; a clear two-tier system is in place.

Because the institution has a very decentralized administration, enacting unilateral change at first is difficult. For example, the regularizing of hiring proves challenging. Deans and department chairs have very individual approaches to hiring. The provost calls for schools to devise standards and criteria for hiring non-tenure track faculty, both full-time and part-time. Schools have to submit plans and report annually on their progress to develop and meet their new hiring procedures, similar to affirmative action plans that the schools have developed in the past. Making the analogy to these already existing affirmative action plans helps the schools to understand how they might approach this process. Schools manage their own budgets, so contract terms are decided locally, but the provost recommends a new plan of multi-year contracts with a promotion schedule. The plan provides that while salaries vary by school, all full-time faculty should receive generally similar pay (this factor has not been a major issue at the schools as full-time contingent faculty pay is on par with tenure-track faculty pay). Because of the availability of part-time faculty who work in full-time jobs in other professions, they leave the part-time faculty pay at a lower range that fits the market situation of their area. Schools are encouraged to make part-time faculty who desire a full-time position, full-time so that the issue of pay is alleviated. Several schools put this into place right away, but others are reluctant. The provost provides money to the schools that made the changes to evaluate the progress over time, so there is data to report to the other schools to convince them of the value of such an approach. The provost organizes a campus-wide orientation, and contingent faculty are invited for the first time. The orientation includes a break-out session for contingent faculty, so they can also meet to discuss their specific needs. The turnout rate for full-time contingents is very high, but for part-time contingent faculty quite low. The administration recognizes that, due to part-time faculty schedules, a one-time orientation may not be as successful for this group, so a part-time orientation is also available online as a webinar to fit the schedules of part-time faculty.

The faculty senate takes the leadership for developing a subcommittee to look at professional development, governance, and mentoring of non-tenure track faculty. This proposition requires some strong-arming from the administration; luckily the provost finds a few allies among the faculty. The subcommittee consists of contingent faculty across campus, in order to take into account particular role variations in the arts, medicine, law, and business. The subcommittee makes a recommendation for a formal mentoring program, which the provost funds, and the Center for Teaching and Learning begins to offer new seminars aimed at contingent faculty, as recommended by the senate subcommittee. The subcommittee also develops a clear definition of the role for non-tenure track full-time faculty, which the provost distributes to the deans. The faculty senate votes to include contingent faculty in all levels of governance. The senate asks for schools to report annually about the progress made to include contingent faculty and to use the new non-tenure track role definition.

The subcommittee decides to conduct a survey of contingent faculty every other year to see how the mentoring, professional development, and governance activities are going, as well as to explore changes in their working conditions. The first survey suggests that certain areas have much more severe problems with climate—for example, the school of engineering and the composition program have hostile climates. They are not changing their governance policies even with the mandate of the provost. The faculty senate realizes it will need to focus its efforts on certain schools that are not making progress. Also, role definitions and suggested workload for full-time non-tenure track faculty are not being followed, and the workload for some greatly exceeds the recommendations of the faculty senate.

The decentralized nature of the university means that constant surveying and checking in all of the schools will be necessary. Also, faculty leaders will need to apply pressure to schools that are not responding to administrative dictates for change. Non-tenure track faculty in engineering and composition note that they feel captive to tenured faculty, who define the rules of the game. The context-based solutions vary because of the decentralized administrative structure, strong faculty power, the focus on full-time over part-time contingent faculty, less of a need to address salary and benefits and more of a need to address access to resources (professional development) and professional levers (promotion scale and mentoring), and the overt hostility toward non-tenure track faculty.

## Community College

The situation is quite different for a community college that has no full-time non-tenure track employees. Twenty-five percent of the faculty are all tenured or tenure-track, but 75 percent of the faculty are part-time, which has increased from 60 percent 10 years ago. The campus climate is quite favorable between tenure-track and part-time faculty. Part-time faculty are recognized as making a major contribution to the campus. In this scenario, the administration is preventing change. They feel that the part-time faculty are doing such a great job that they want to continue to utilize more of them. Without paying for benefits, the institution has more money for other costs including the brand new student center that was recently built. Administrative and service loads for tenured faculty have doubled in recent years. Some part-time faculty enjoy their positions, but over half would prefer a full-time position rather than piecing together classes between two or more colleges. Salary is quite low for part-timers, benefits are non-existent, and seniority does not exist. The campus is in a state that cannot unionize, so collective bargaining is not an option. The campus actually has quite a few resources for part-time faculty including a handbook, online and in-person orientation, access to governance and professional development related to teaching, and two professional development opportunities paid for each year.

The part-time faculty appeal to the tenured faculty for help, citing the dramatic decline in tenure-track positions and the increased workload for tenure-track faculty. The faculty senate decides to sit down with the administration with a proposal for changes to make the working conditions more favorable for part-time faculty. The faculty develop an agenda of items for the administration to consider:

1.  Request a staffing plan looking at the right composition of full-time to part-time faculty to run the campus adequately.
2.  Convert some part-time positions into full-time tenure lines and move back toward 60 percent full-time; they cite literature and research about the problems of the effect of excessive numbers of part-time faculty on institutional operation and student outcomes.
3.  Make part-timers eligible for benefits (pro rata) and increase their pay over time to become closer to full-time faculty, making the use of part-timers less attractive.
4.  Create a seniority system so long-time part-timers have priority for teaching and to reward their commitment.
5.  Include part-time faculty in the governance system more systematically and proportionally. The part-time faculty were added to the senate in recent years, but their voice is fairly inaudible and they are not paid for involvement. The part-timers have convinced the tenure-track faculty that it is in all their best interests for more part-timers to be on the senate.
6.  Create policies around teaching online courses, which are growing exponentially. While the part-timers are teaching most of these, full-timers are now being asked to teach them, and recognize the problems of large class enrollments, workload, and intellectual property that need to be sorted out. Also, computer support and perhaps even replacement computers should be considered for those teaching extensively online.
7.  Create more office space for part-time faculty. While they built one shared space for part-timers, it is inadequate given the increase in numbers.
8.  Pay for office hours, course development, and service is proposed. Part-timers are currently not paid for many activities that they perform outside of the classroom, making their pay even lower. The faculty believe that this needs to be paid for, as some part-time faculty cannot do this work without pay and it is unethical to ask people to do work when you are not paying them.

These issues are quite different from the research university's, which focused on full-time contingents and the hostile culture among the tenure-track faculty. At the community college, there is a united front among faculty, but the administration has moved toward an inexpensive business model and they have to work on key issues affecting the working conditions, which are mostly around pay/compensation and resources, like the office space and computer support.

The administration responds that given the high price tag for these issues, they need the list prioritized so they can address them over time. The faculty prioritize the list of items that require funding. They suggest that the administration looks for other funding areas to divert resources from in order to support some of these issues in the short term. Several faculty approach the local media about the concerns they have, and a story is run about the community college's dilemma and the rise in part-time faculty on campus. This event puts pressure on the administration to make some changes. In addition, the faculty are lucky that they have improved governance in recent years, and have strong leadership within the senate to negotiate with the administration. While the administration is taken aback at first, they later come back with some proposals for diverting expenses from one area to pay for the part-time salary increase. They begin on the road to change. However, change will take a while on this campus, as the funding structure cannot support many of the changes immediately. The context of interest in this case is—the largely part-time composition of the faculty, the diminished power of tenure-track faculty, the power of the administration, and the working conditions being largely framed around money rather than climate.

## Comparing Cases of Change

To summarize, at the private research university, attending to context meant that they needed to focus more on full-time non-tenure track issues; work within the decentralized structure (but benefit from and be able to capitalize on administrative support); address the negative climate; determine their change agenda related to orientation, governance, professional development, promotion, mentoring, and clarifying role definition. At the community college, context meant they were focused on part-time faculty; had a united faculty front, but unsupportive leadership as well as resource constraints; an agenda focused on job security, seniority, intellectual property, and more refined policy on governance. Different contexts demand different change agendas and change approaches.

## Caveat: Differences by Faculty Motivation/Interest

In addition to examining these recommended changes within these broader organizational frameworks, it is also important to acknowledge that recommendations will differ based on individual characteristics. In the Preface, I described how non-tenure track faculty are an extremely heterogeneous group when compared to tenure-track faculty—they have more diverse motivations for being a faculty member, approach the work differently, and may not see this position as their primary employment. Some campuses find that when they survey non-tenure track faculty, the interests and recommended changes are quite different and it is hard to come to consensus. Or they may find that only full-time non-tenure track faculty, who may be more engaged with the institution, respond, so they cannot develop a list of policy and practice changes that are inclusive. As noted in the recommendations above, some part-time faculty may only be interested in teaching, and socialization may be less important, as they are not interested in becoming part of the academic community.

It is important to survey your faculty to determine among the part-timers and full-time non-tenure track how many are: career-enders; specialists, experts, and professionals; aspiring academics; and freelancers. For the full-time non-tenure track, a survey can identify primary responsibilities as: teachers, researchers, administrators, and other academic professionals. It is important to examine if groups are clustered in any departments so that policies and practices might be focused on specific departments. Professional schools may find they need to do less in terms of the policies and programs as their part-time faculty are not interested in certain programs like mentoring and professional development. The case study of Virginia Tech (see Chapter 6) will demonstrate this issue of different types of non-tenure track faculty needing quite tailored policies. But, even as I advocate for understanding the motivation and interests of faculty, there is certainly no harm in creating global policies of inclusion and support that non-tenure track faculty can opt out of if they are not interested in participating.

## Conclusion

This chapter has tried to advance thinking about the types of changes needed to make contingent faculty successful on colleges and university campuses. I have presented the overarching policy recommendations that have been made for over two decades to advance the non-tenure track faculty and to improve their performance and include them on campus (Baldwin & Chronister, 2001; Gappa & Leslie, 1993; Kezar & Sam, 2010). Furthermore, I have advanced conceptualization about these recommendations by demonstrating how they fit into a framework of essential elements for faculty work. The chapter demonstrates how these policies/practices support respect, employment equity, academic freedom and autonomy, flexibility, professional growth, and collegiality. I also identify certain areas where policy recommendations have been lacking in support of essential elements such as flexibility, respect, and collegiality. In addition, I have examined how leaders tend to focus on policies and suggest the importance of also looking at practices and underlying values/principles that significantly affect the day-to-day experience of contingent faculty. I advocate for work on all three fronts: policies, practices, and underlying values and provide supporting data for this framework. Finally, the chapter addresses the importance of changes being made that fit the specific institutional context, both in terms of its structure and culture. This framework highlights the importance of conducting institutional surveys and research in order to understand changes that meet the problems of the context. Examples of context-based solutions and changes are also provided.

Once change agents have a vision for change—offered by this chapter—and have conducted necessary research on campus about the needs and problems, they will be well positioned to begin the change process. Leaders will be able to move forward and think about a change process needed to put these important recommendations into action. The rest of the book addresses this important question of how to actualize the changes that contingent faculty leaders envision. Chapter 2 will give key strategies for leaders going through the change process and the subsequent case studies will give detailed examples of change in particular institutions.

## References

American Federation of Teachers Higher Education. (2005). *Reversing the course: The troubled state of academic staffing and the path forward*. Washington, DC: American Federation of Teachers Higher Education.

American Federation of Teachers Higher Education. (2010). *American academic: A national survey of part-time/adjunct faculty*. Washington, DC: American Federation of Teachers Higher Education.

Baldwin, R. G., & Chronister, J. L. (2001). *Teaching without tenure*. Baltimore: Johns Hopkins University Press.

Conley, V. M., & Leslie, D. W. (2002). Part-time instructional faculty and staff: Who they are, what they do, and what they think. *Education Statistics Quarterly, 4*(2), 97–103.

Cross, J. G., & Goldenberg, E. N. (2009). *Off-track profs: Non-tenured teachers in higher education*. Cambridge, MA: MIT Press.

Curry, B. (1992). *Instituting enduring innovations: Achieving continuity of change in higher education*. ASHE-ERIC Higher Education Report No. 7. Washington, DC: George Washington University.

Gappa, J. M., Austin, A. E., & Trice, A. (2007). *Rethinking faculty work: Higher education's strategic imperative*. San Francisco: Jossey-Bass.

Gappa, J. M., & Leslie, D. W. (1993). *The invisible faculty: Improving the status of part-timers in higher education*. San Francisco: Jossey-Bass.

Hollenshead, C., Waltman, J., August, L., Miller, J., Smith, G., & Bell, A. (2007). *Making the best of both worlds: Findings from a national institution-level survey on non-tenure track faculty*. Ann Arbor, MI: Center for the Education of Women.

Kezar, A. (2001). *Understanding and facilitating organizational change in the 21st century: Recent research and conceptualizations*. ASHE-ERIC Higher Education Report Series, 28(4). Washington, DC: Jossey-Bass.

Kezar, A. (forthcoming). Examining non-tenure track faculty perceptions of how departmental policies and practices shape their performance. *The Journal of Higher Education*.

Kezar, A., & Eckel, P. (2002). The effect of institutional culture on change strategies in higher education: Universal principles or culturally responsive concepts? *The Journal of Higher Education, 73*(4), 435–460.

Kezar, A., Lester, J., & Anderson, G. (2006). Challenging stereotypes that interfere with effective governance. *Thought and Action, 22*(2), 121–134.

Kezar, A., & Sam, C. (2010). *Understanding the new majority: Contingent faculty in higher education*. ASHE Higher Education Report Series, 36(4). San Francisco: Jossey-Bass.

O'Meara, K., Terosky, A., & Neumann, A. (2008). In K. Ward, & L. Wolf-Wendel (Eds.), *Faculty careers and work lives: A professional growth perspective*. ASHE Higher Education Report Series, 34(3). San Francisco: Jossey-Bass.

Rhoades, G., & Maitland, C. (2008). Bargaining for full-time non-tenure track faculty: Best practices. In *The NEA 2008 almanac of higher education* (pp. 67–73). Washington, DC: National Education Association.

Schein, E. H. (1992). *Organizational culture and leadership*. New York, NY: Jossey-Bass.

Shaker, G. (2008). Off the track: The full-time non-tenure track faculty experience in English [Unpublished doctoral dissertation]. Indiana University, Indiana.

Sullivan, W. (2004). *Work and integrity: The crisis and promise of professionalism in America*. San Francisco: Jossey-Bass.

Trowler, P. (2008). *Cultures and change in higher education*. London: Palgrave Macmillan.

# 2

# STRATEGIES FOR IMPLEMENTING AND INSTITUTIONALIZING NEW POLICIES AND PRACTICES

## Understanding the Change Process

*Adrianna Kezar and Cecile Sam*

A future scenario: *Melissa, a mathematics professor at a community college, sometimes has to pinch herself because things seem so different from 15 years ago. She used to walk around campus feeling like a second-class citizen. She struggled with her bills and the unstable employment gave her ulcers; her car was a makeshift office, and it was certainly not a great place to meet students. Melissa remembers the constant frustration of finding out a few days before class that not only had her teaching schedule changed, but also discovering that the textbooks or learning goals had been changed. She would scramble to make changes, but lacked clerical support.*

*Times have changed. Non-tenure track faculty feel generally included in the campus culture, and can be found on campus listings of the faculty and in pictures on the walls of the departments. Compensation has improved, and department chairs go out of their way to give each faculty member as many courses as possible. While the benefits are not perfect, faculty can obtain them after teaching a certain number of courses and if they contribute toward a benefit pool. Between the greater guarantee of courses, the pay increases, and the benefits, Melissa is more secure, less stressed, and now able to focus on teaching. She appreciates the opportunity to participate in professional development on campus and recently went to a seminar on teaching large courses, which helped her to integrate clickers (personal response systems) into her class. Melissa notes the importance of being able to have input into curricular decisions that impact her classes and is happy with the recent textbook changes she helped to make. As she walks to her class, Melissa wonders, "How did these changes happen?"*

For many non-tenure track faculty, often due to limited access to decision-making mechanisms such as committees and the faculty senate, the change process can be a veritable "black box"—where various factors (advocates, state legislation, agendas, politics, revenue, etc.) go into the mix and the outcome results in new policies and practices. Even for those faculty and administrators involved in the change process, sometimes the difference between successful and failed attempts seems arbitrary. For leaders wanting to create changes at their institutions, understanding the change process can help them identify ways to strengthen their change attempts, as well as be wary of possible challenges along the way.

This chapter first explains why promising practices and policies for contingent faculty can be considered institutional innovations. Advocating for innovations requires a different set of strategies and encounters specific challenges compared to policies or practices that are amendments to the status quo. Next, we explain the change process by using institutionalization theory—a theory that looks at how institutions eventually adopt innovations. We ground this theory in the experiences of 45 faculty leaders at 30 campuses, all of whom are trying to enact positive changes for non-tenure track faculty on their campuses. These lessons from faculty leaders stem from a nationwide study we conducted of institutions with positive practices and policies for their contingent faculty members.[1] Here we will provide a brief note about the study from which this three-stage model emerged. This chapter is an adaptation of a nationwide study of over 400 faculty contracts and interviews with 45 faculty leaders at 30 institutions (Sam & Kezar, forthcoming). We used the contracts to determine positive policies or practices[2] for contingent faculty as well as identify possible contingent-friendly institutions. Our interviews focused on the following information:

1. exemplary practices and policies, particularly ones not listed in contracts (both unionized and not unionized);
2. narratives about the policies and practices put in place;
3. challenges they experienced and ways they overcame challenges;
4. issues that emerged that shaped their progress toward institutionalization.

The institutions spanned many different types: two-year colleges and four-year institutions, public and private institutions, liberal arts and research focus, and unionized and non-unionized campuses. Our approach was to examine a cross-section of campuses in the institutionalization process.

From these experiences we found tactics and strategies that other faculty can use to help further advocate their own institutional changes. The goal for this chapter is to make the change process at the institutional level as transparent as possible and to offer practical advice for leaders to advocate successfully for their own changes. Yet, we should note that change is not just desirable at the institutional level, but change should also be advocated for by larger groups (state policymakers, unions, and outside groups like the New Faculty Majority). But our focus in this book is institutional, with some attention to how broader forces intersect and engage institutional leaders. Change happens because of on- and off-campus leadership efforts, but we highlight on-campus leadership more in this model.

## Innovation and Promising Policies and Practices for Non-tenure Track Faculty

Despite the evidence that non-tenure track faculty positions are currently the majority of all faculty positions in academia in the United States (Schuster & Finkelstein, 2006); that these faculty members experience poor working conditions at their institutions (Baldwin & Chronister, 2001; Gappa & Leslie, 1993; Schell & Stock, 2001); and that the current faculty situation may have negative effects on student performance (Eagan & Jaeger, 2009; Jaeger & Eagan, 2009; Umbach, 2007), few institutions have made any changes to incorporate positive practices and policies for non-tenure track faculty. For example, Baldwin and Chronister's (2001) in-depth study of full-time contingent faculty found little systematic orientation, socialization, evaluation, salary or promotion schemes; active exclusion of faculty from governance, professional development, and curriculum development; concerns about academic freedom related to institutional affairs; and a general lack of administrative or technical support. For many institutions, the status quo is to continue with policies and practices as though the majority of faculty are on the tenure-line.

We conceptualize the creation of a favorable non-tenure track faculty environment as an innovation or set of innovative policies and practices; like other innovations, this change is met with resistance as it challenges the status quo. Establishing positive policies and practices for contingent faculty, such as multi-year contracts, orientation and professional development, and voting rights may mean that institutions would have to acknowledge two ideas. The first idea is that a change in the faculty composition has occurred, making the current policies and practices for faculty inapplicable to the majority of faculty. The second idea is that change needs to occur for institutional policies and practices to align with the new faculty majority, because ignoring the issue is unsustainable; long-term inaction would lead to negative impacts on the professoriate, the institution, and the students. These shifts in understanding can constitute a novel perspective for many people on campus, a perspective that would challenge past understandings and previous policies and practices.

## The Change Process and Institutionalization Theory

Creating sustained change can be challenging for advocates. We have all experienced new or changed policies or practices that either quickly fall into disuse or never even become implemented. In order to understand how innovations become an integral part of a campus or department, we use the framework of institutionalization theory to make sense of the process. Institutionalization is the global framework that lets us see the change process as it has occurred in numerous institutions with varying policies. Institutionalization refers to "the point at which an innovative practice having been implemented loses its special project status and becomes part of a sustained behavior of the institutional system" (Curry, 1992: 10–11). If long-term change is wanted, then institutionalizing the innovations is one way to create that change.

From conceptual beginning to institutionalization, an innovation (or change) goes through a series of phases, each one with the potential to lead to the next phase. It is a process that occurs over time and that entails the entire organizational system. Curry (1992: 5, citing Curry, 1991) offers a three-stage model of institutionalization to illustrate this process:

1. mobilization—"the system is prepared for change";
2. implementation—"the change is introduced";
3. institutionalization—"the system is stabilized in its changed state."

See Figure 2.1 for a visualization of the model. Since organizational evolution is a process over time, these three stages are more of a continuum rather than set delineated stages.

Mobilization is the first stage of the model. In this stage, the organization begins to prepare for change. This preparation ranges from initial awareness of a problem to laying the foundation for policy implementation. In this stage, people begin to gather around a common cause or reform. Change agents begin to question and challenge the status quo—those previous practices and policies that are enmeshed within the current institutional culture. This stage is associated with two aspects: galvanizing members and creating the initial structural change to the organization. Galvanizing members toward action can occur through raised awareness or disseminating information. Structural change is where "innovations are reflected in a concrete fashion throughout the organization" (Datnow, 2005: 124). Initial structural changes can range from setting up agendas and priorities at meetings to changing mission statements.

| MOBILIZATION | IMPLEMENTATION | INSTITUTIONALIZATION |
|---|---|---|
| • Galvanize members<br>• Create initial structural change | • Create infrastructure and support for reform<br>• Incentives and/or disincentives are introduced<br>• Maintain momentum | • Change value system of organization<br>• Members come to consensus<br>• Innovation is stable and part of the organization |

**FIGURE 2.1** Three-stage model

Implementation is the second stage, which focuses on creating infrastructure and support for the reform or change. During this stage, initiatives begin to materialize in the organization, and support for the structures is developed to maintain momentum (Curry, 1992; Kezar, 2007). These initiatives may take the form of reward/incentives or sanctioning for new behaviors. Also, other groups and people begin to cooperate and new members may join in for additional support. Barriers often emerge at this point and technical assistance and trouble-shooting occur (Curry, 1992; Fullan, 1989). At this stage, new policy and behaviors are becoming part of the standard operating procedures of the organization (Curry, 1992). Members are conducting new work, but have not fully accepted the procedure. Furthermore, they have not formulated an evaluation of the innovation, nor do they think about it as part of ongoing planning; it is still an innovation. Continued incentives, new people, and problem-solving are needed throughout implementation.

Institutionalization is the final stage of the process when the innovation moves from explicit policy to implicit standard operating procedures, altering the actual value system of the organization. Members come to a consensus, accept the value of innovation, and see the innovation as normative behavior for the institution. At this level, authors connect institutionalization with the changing of the organization's culture and core understanding (Curry, 1992; Kanter, 1990; Kezar, 2007). The innovation has maintained stability within the organization to be virtually indistinguishable from the rest of the institution. In a bit of irony, an innovation reaches the institutionalization stage, and is successful when it no longer is seen as an innovation; rather it is just a part of the organizational framework.

It is important to note that simply because an innovation or change makes it to one of the stages, it does not necessarily mean that it will easily move onto the next stage, or even move at all. Institutionalization theory suggests that changes are more likely to be maintained within an organization if they move into the fabric or culture of the institution—its basic assumptions, norms and values, and policies and practices (Schein, 1992). Changes that can gain a foothold in the existing culture of the institution may have a better chance of moving through all three phases. Culture incorporates both the policies and practices of an institution, but also moves to more abstract values, ideas, and principles such as whether contingent faculty are respected. Finding ways to link change to values and specific contexts can be beneficial for the change.

## Institutionalization Theory and Practical Applications

Institutionalization provides a useful framework because it allows for an understanding of how leaders establish permanent innovation at their institution. The framework is pivotal as research on innovation adoption demonstrates that leaders need to use different strategies when an initiative is new to an organization as opposed to when the initiative is already partially incorporated into the organization or institutionalized (Alexander, 2005; Curry, 1992; Kezar & Eckel, 2002). However, while institutionalization provides a global framework, we wanted to examine the specifics of how contingent faculty innovations move through the three phases toward institutionalization so that leaders have more specific and concrete advice.

The following section breaks down institutionalization into its three respective phases: mobilization, implementation, and institutionalization. In each of those stages we share important tactics that leaders can use to try and move change forward—we offer explanations as well as let the leaders describe in their own words the ways they went about change. Afterward, each section will highlight challenges specific to each stage that leaders may encounter.

## Mobilization

Three important tactics characterized the mobilization phase:

1.  developing awareness;
2.  creating a network;
3.  breaking invisibility.

The major outcomes of the mobilization phase are new practices that create a collective group, such as the development of communication tools, networks and regular meetings, and unionization. Campuses in the mobilization phase had few established policies for contingent faculty and had a climate that was antagonistic toward contingent faculty.

### Developing Awareness

Mobilization was very unlikely to occur unless awareness was developed and apathy, fragmentation, and isolation were overcome by contingent faculty. Almost all the people we interviewed mentioned how development of awareness was the first key factor to mobilizing, and it could occur in many different ways. For some institutions, the apathy toward poor work conditions was overcome by a significant galvanizing event such as a person being unfairly fired, a major grievance that was filed, or a non-tenure track faculty member being excluded or thrown off a governance body. While people could ignore these events, contingent faculty leaders worked to make these inequitable acts visible to the community. A second way that campuses created awareness was through data collection, demonstrating how poor the work conditions were compared to either other institutions or to those of tenure-track faculty members. These contingent leaders often looked for model institutions or more exemplary contract language with which to make comparisons to their particular campus. One contingent faculty leader described the way they used data:

> Contingent faculty weren't really aware of the disparity in salary between non-tenure track and tenure-track faculty. I think at some level they were, but to see it in black-and-white and to be told how underpaid they were by a percentage hit home more.

Another part of awareness was also becoming cognizant of differences in the experience of contingent faculty on the same campus. For example, a contingent faculty member in composition, the medical school, and social work may each experience different treatment on campus. This awareness was pivotal in moving toward implementation as they could see pockets to target (the composition department), models to follow (the medical school), or allies with whom to collaborate (the professional schools). An example of this developing awareness was the non-tenure track faculty committee at the University of North Carolina that brought together representatives from each unit. While the first year was extremely difficult, as they could not find common ground, the discussions helped them realize the complexity of the issue and engage better in brainstorming activities that led to more complex solutions. The solutions focused on an understanding of the multiple experiences and working conditions within the same university.

## Creating a Network

In our study we found that the second major practice during mobilization was creating networks. Once a community developed awareness, there was an opportunity to capitalize on this attention, and creating communication vehicles (i.e., newsletters, listservs) became a way to disseminate information as well as further unite individuals. The most prevalent mechanisms for communicating and connecting people were campus-based listservs, websites, and electronic or printed newsletters. Contingent leaders also encouraged people to join the national contingent faculty listserv (adj-l), which further created awareness about the problems and developed enthusiasm for mobilization. As one contingent faculty member explained: "Our campus listserv has been invaluable in letting people know about the bad experiences contingent faculty are facing and the reason working together is important. We've also gotten out lots of data through the listserv." Mobilizing, newsletters, flyers, and word-of-mouth had been used in previous years, but the onset and ease of technology now makes mass communication easier. Technology also connected contingent faculty to off-campus networks easily. For example, information about large nationwide events like Campus Equity Week can be disseminated in a matter of minutes.

---

### CALIFORNIA POLYTECHNIC INSTITUTE, POMONA

Cal Poly Pomona has created a council made up of non-tenure track faculty representatives from various departments. They meet monthly to discuss issues of importance to non-tenure track faculty. Through the council, they become aware of emerging problems that may need to be resolved. It also serves as a vehicle for mobilizing people when they need to address a particular problem—professional development being denied within certain departments. This also serves as a way to understand progress in the implementation of policies and practices created.

---

### *Breaking Invisibility*

The third major practice used to mobilize a campus is breaking invisibility. By developing awareness, contingent faculty leadership was created. Through networking, the number of leaders and activism increased. By breaking invisibility, contingent faculty leaders were able to develop allies among other groups on campus such as tenure-track faculty and the administration. A powerful mechanism for breaking invisibility was to distribute data, and make other people aware of the sheer number of contingent faculty on campus and the extremely low pay. Most tenure-track faculty were unaware of these facts. The second important mechanism was selling the expertise that contingent faculty have to offer. As one contingent leader noted:

> We have been very active in publicizing and promoting the incredible expertise among the contingent faculty. Our arts faculty have received many awards in the community, our business, science and technology faculty are known leaders in their fields. We make sure that people see the value we have to offer and that we might be worth fighting for [regarding] better working conditions.

Visibility was critical for getting other faculty, who had more time and leverage, involved (like tenure-track faculty). If contingent faculty had to shoulder the whole burden, the process would be slow and could falter. Campuses that institutionalized change sometimes had tenure-track faculty who played a leadership role. However, tenure–track faculty leadership was also a point of contention, because if these faculty did not understand contingent faculty work conditions well enough, sometimes they misspoke or made errors that hampered the mobilization and caused bad feelings.

## CONCORDIA UNIVERSITY (CANADA)

This campus collected data on their non-tenure track faculty to demonstrate the pay inequity to tenure-track colleagues as well as the salary of their non-tenure track colleagues on other campuses. A non-tenure track leader notes that U.S. institutions need to get better at collecting and sharing data, which is a key tool for mobilizing. In Canada, salary, term of employment, and other data from every institution are routinely collected, shared, and available for analysis.

There was one tactic used by the five campuses that moved toward institutionalization that was not used by others in the mobilization phase. This tactic is important to point out as it might be a key step toward institutionalization. In the mobilization phase, these campuses focused more on underlying values, assumptions, and stereotypes held by tenure-track faculty, administrators, and among contingent faculty themselves. Rather than focus on policies and practices, they focused on values and only pursued policies and practices once they achieved some baseline changes in consciousness. They emphasized values over overt practices. For example, on one campus, the first step was reducing the hierarchy amongst faculty in as many ways as possible: invitations to events, inclusion on web pages and directories, and uniform recognition of years of service. This created some unity and understanding among faculty that eased the introduction of new policies and practices. Once the mobilization phase is finished, a campus is poised to implement policies and move toward better working conditions.

## FASHION INSTITUTE OF TECHNOLOGY

The faculty on this campus realized the importance and power of being a single and united faculty working to improve working conditions. Early on they addressed and tried to dispel any two-tier mindset or second-class citizenship that had been created toward adjunct faculty. The union leadership examined their own views and held each other accountable for a perspective of respect toward non-tenure track faculty. Over time, they worked to create a unified faculty that then developed a wall-to-wall contract. But, before working on negotiations or working conditions, they worked on their own views and stereotypes.

## Challenges to Mobilization

Mobilizing contingent faculty was extremely difficult and involved significant challenges that have gone undocumented until this study. For example, some contingent faculty members had absorbed the negative messages spread by tenure-track faculty and believed in their own lack of self-worth. (Chapter 7 in this book, focused on Cal Poly Pomona, addresses the challenges of negative messages absorbed by non-tenure track faculty and offers more in-depth advice.) As a result, many may have felt unmotivated to fight for their rights. At Cal Poly Pomona, awareness and challenging the status quo were vital. On other campuses, contingent faculty were extremely fragmented—there was a lack of unity between tenure-track and non-tenure track faculty and even among groups within the contingent faculty. In addition, contingent faculty in composition and the arts experienced poorer treatment than those in the professional areas. Even within the same department, contingent faculty often did not interact with each other due to different teaching schedules and lack of a communal workspace. Interviewees noted how full-time non-tenure track and part-time non-tenure track faculty often saw each other as "the enemy," and competed for courses and resources. They noted how the administration often, either by design or accident, furthered this animosity and drove a wedge between groups so that they did not develop collective momentum. For example, on some campuses, the administration did not establish a part-time to full-time faculty ratio, so groups of contingent faculty saw themselves in direct competition for course assignments. Contingent faculty lacked time to be involved as they were often teaching at multiple institutions, had a second job, or had incredibly high workloads; it was not uncommon for them to teach around 12 classes a year. All these elements of contingent faculty work made mobilization difficult. Because contingent faculty tended to be isolated, creating a network was particularly important. Moreover, contingent faculty were largely invisible on many campuses. Practices that made them and their experiences more visible were critical.

## Implementation

The literature on institutionalization notes how the implementation phase creates infrastructure and capitalizes on momentum to support the change.[3] However, we found implementation to be difficult because of challenges that emerged and tended to blindside change agents. Furthermore, change agents were overwhelmed by a myriad of barriers; with the long time frame for instituting new policies, many lost energy. Also, while mobilization followed a clear path of strategies and tactics, implementation was a scattershot of many different actions that needed to be used in combination to be successful. Many people focused too narrowly on a few activities. We present the strategies and tactics in the order they were typically used, as some needed to occur before others. These include:

1. developing a rationale;
2. using data, benchmarks, and model institutions to guide policies;
3. creating a regular meeting, task force, or committee charged with contingent faculty work conditions;
4. being included in governance;
5. garnering outside pressure from unions, media, students, and accreditors;
6. utilizing allies and departments to leverage changes;
7. creating a plan of action.

Campuses that reached the institutionalization phase used two practices (developing a rationale and creating a plan of action) that did not appear to be present at institutions where the process had stalled. We ask readers to pay particular attention to these strategies. Not all strategies address a particular challenge, but when they do, we note the challenge.

## Developing a Rationale

While calling attention to inequities was sufficient for mobilization, in moving toward implementation, contingent leaders realized that they needed a more complex and multifaceted rationale for why it was important to create better policies and practices for contingent faculty. All the campuses that moved toward institutionalization made a clear connection between contingent faculty work conditions and the educational outcomes and learning environment for students: "Momentum really developed for changing contingent faculty policies when we could connect it to how it was impacting students, that was when the tenure-track faculty noted they were willing to sacrifice part of their pay." Leaders were able to demonstrate how unpaid office hours, lack of office space, or lack of job security would affect the experience of students. These inequities made it difficult for contingent faculty to meet with students regularly, mentor them, or write letters of recommendation. Contingent faculty leaders also described the way that low morale compromised the community and student educational outcomes. They acknowledged the challenge of finding funding for changes and engaged in discussions about ways to lower expenses so that greater equity could be created for contingent faculty.

## Using Data, Benchmarks, and Models

Data collection was critical to mobilize people for change, and it became even more important in the implementation phase. Almost every campus that we spoke with had identified some model campuses found through various listservs.

If they were unionized, the Higher Education Contract Analysis System (HECAS) database was available for collecting data from contracts. They used the data to develop an action plan for implementing changes:

> For every policy we have in place now, we found a campus with the kind of policy we wanted in place. These models helped us imagine much better policies than we would have come up with ourselves. And we did not look to any one campus, we pulled the best from several different campuses.

One contingent faculty leader talked about the use of benchmark data:

> Our institution is very prestigious and always likes to compare themselves to Star institution (pseudonym). Star institution actually has strong policies for contingent faculty as it is in one of the few strong union[ized] states. We were able to use the institution that they use as their reputational peer to convince them to create new policies on campus around salary, multi-year contracts, governance, professional development and seniority.

However, one major challenge was that data was often hard to obtain:

> In Canada all the staffing information is public and available. Here, it is hard to get data. The administration controls it and is often unwilling to share statistics on numbers, salary. States do not collect data. Data could be so helpful to our cause, but it is hard to come by.

Some campuses obtained the data they needed through important partnerships with individuals or groups who knew how to gain the necessary information and were willing to share it.

---

### NEW FACULTY MAJORITY

New Faculty Majority (http://www.newfacultymajority.info/national/) is working to develop data such as pay scales and benefits so that individual campuses can have data and models to use to facilitate their work to achieve better working conditions for non-tenure track faculty. The organization and its listserv can also be contacted for best practices and models. In general, non-tenure track faculty listservs provide invaluable resources for data and models.

## Creating a Regular Meeting Time through Task Forces or Committees

One of the vehicles that was important to starting off implementation was the creation of regular meetings of faculty (often both non-tenure and tenure-track) through a task force or committee charged with contingent faculty work conditions. This strategy was most used on four-year campuses and it was often set up through the faculty senate. However, on unionized campuses, the union leadership set up meetings with union membership to discuss regularly how to move policies and practices forward. A tenure-track faculty member commented on a major challenge: "Contingent faculty have little if any venue to meet in. They are not organized in any way and this task force has been extremely important in bringing them together as well as getting them in contact with tenure-track faculty members."

## Being Included in Governance

We labeled some campuses as early implementers because they had fewer policies and practices in place for contingent faculty members; late implementers had many more policies and practices in place. A defining feature of late implementers was that these campuses included contingent faculty in governance, which tends to propel more and broader changes. There was also a difference in how contingent faculty were included in governance. Early implementers had token members on the faculty senate with no vote or only a partial one granted. Invitations to departmental meetings were made, but with little follow-up or compensation. Campuses that had more policies and practices in place increased the number of contingent faculty on the senate to be proportional to their percentage within the faculty (or at least much closer), which guaranteed contingent faculty representation on key committees (e.g., curriculum), and ensured them a vote. As one contingent leader noted:

> You will always be a side order of fries unless you participate in governance. Some contingent faculty think governance is a luxury and we should just focus on rights like benefits. But, if you are going to be a real member of the community, treated as a professional, and included, you must participate in governance.

Several contingent leaders even pronounced that governance was the most important factor in implementing and institutionalizing change. One challenge to participation in governance—even for the late implementers and campuses that were institutionalized—was creating a system that encouraged participation rather than making participation a burden. Only two campuses had compensation for contingent faculty who participated in governance, or included governance within evaluation and promotion.

## CLACKAMAS COMMUNITY COLLEGE AND MOUNT SAN ANTONIO COMMUNITY COLLEGE

Clackamas Community College is an example of a campus that saw the potential of governance and has capitalized on it for creating change. Part-time faculty are involved in the college council that meets with the president of the college. While not all individuals involved in governance get release time, leaders on various groups and committees do get course release. They negotiated to have participation in governance compensated. Plus, there is a general invitation to participate in governance and there is a great deal of participation. The reason for strong involvement is that the adjunct leaders make people aware of how their involvement in governance has led to positive changes such as a seniority clause, pay increases, professional development funds, and the like. At Mount San Antonio Community College, contingent faculty realized the benefits of governance participation but could not get the state to pay for it. They realized that in order to create the right learning environment for students, it was critical that their voices be heard. Therefore, they felt it was important that the union pay for part-timers to participate in governance.

### Garnering Outside Pressure

Some campuses became stalled in the implementation phase—they could obtain only minor salary increases and marginal health benefits (that they had to pay for) and then were unable to move forward. Others had mobilized, but were stuck in long-term discussions about policies or could not get the institution to engage with them in discussions. In these many instances, garnering outside pressure from unions, media, students, parents, and accreditors was a way to push forward the implementation. In the words of one contingent faculty member:

> We use[d] the opportunity of our accreditation visit to meet separately with the review team and give them an earful about the problems we were experiencing. This resulted in a poor accreditation report. But, that may not have been enough, we also got an op ed [opinion piece] in the paper, and this created some community pressure as well. I think getting lots of outside concern can get the attention of people you need to start implementing policies.

Using outside pressure was characteristic of late implementers.

## Utilizing Allies

Another way in which the campuses got stalled was that campus-wide policies and practices did not translate down into departments. In fact, one of the most common problems that we heard was that policies and practices were unevenly implemented, and there was no enforcement of the policies uniformly throughout the campus:

> So you can have a policy that says contingent faculty members should receive funding for professional development, but that doesn't mean that it happens in the departments. You can have a campus-wide policy that says each school will have orientation for contingent faculty members, but that typically doesn't happen either. Even policies such as salary or benefits, which you think would be harder to circumvent, are often subverted in the departments.

One of the ways to overcome this challenge to implementation was utilizing allies in departments to leverage changes. While many contingent faculty leaders pressed administrators to hold departments accountable, the strategy was often unsuccessful. Instead, they worked to generate tenure-track faculty allies (often who were or became department chairs). By creating five or six model departments on campus, with good policies and practices, it became harder for other departments to ignore the issue. In addition, these tenure-track faculty members started to discuss the problem at the faculty senate more vociferously, pressuring departments that were not following the policy.

## Creating a Plan of Action

One of the distinguishing characteristics of campuses that had moved toward institutionalization was that they created a plan of action. Most campuses' leaders emphasized a specific issue or a policy they were trying to get in place, such as seniority rights (policies that provide preference for class assignment based on having taught the class for multiple years). They tended to have an incremental approach and were using data and models to help them improve the policies they either wanted or had already put in place. However, campuses that were moving toward or had institutionalized change, conceptualized all of the changes that they wanted, and worked toward a grand plan. They did not give their future vision short shrift by only working toward small gains. As one faculty member noted:

> We recognize we are likely to obtain more changes if we have an agenda that we present to the administration and [make it clear] that we seek a gamut of changes over multiple years. That has proven to work each time we have negotiated for changes.

They also were realistic about their plans of action, and knew that without utilizing many of the other strategies listed above, such as getting external pressure or full participation in governance, their plans had little chance of success. Having a plan provided a blueprint for their actions as part of governance, for what data to collect, for what allies to target, and for union negotiations.

---

## MOUNT SAN ANTONIO COMMUNITY COLLEGE

Mount San Antonio Community College was one of the campuses that developed a plan of action. While they could have moved forward on negotiations like other campuses that survey their union membership and then recommend the top two or three items, they decided to develop an entire agenda of items that represented lots of different interests across disciplinary groups and units. Rather than just ask for a salary increase and paid office hours, they developed a long-term plan that they knew might take 10 years to enact. It was bold and they ended up achieving most of their long list of improved working conditions.

---

## *Institutionalization*

As we established in the last section, creating a rationale for the change and having an action plan were essential to move toward institutionalization. Also, earlier we noted that starting with underlying values in the mobilization phase appears to be something shared by campuses that have successfully institutionalized changes. We described these in the sections on "Mobilization" and "Implementation." These issues are also clearly connected to institutionalization, but occur earlier. The institutionalization phase is characterized by campuses that move beyond typical "mainline" union contract issues such as salary, benefits, and job security to the less visible, but equally important, issues of professional development, mentoring, socialization, and inclusion. This phase is characterized by valuing contingent faculty members and establishing practices and policies reflecting this commitment.

There are four main strategies used during institutionalization:

1. addressing the climate of the campus;
2. moving beyond mainline union policies and pockets of departments to the entire campus;
3. creating a single faculty;
4. taking leadership on major campus issues.

However, it should be noted that many campuses became too focused on main-line union issues such as salary, benefits, and job security. They had difficulty seeing the value of issues related to inclusion and climate, which they viewed as a luxury and potentially even an unachievable goal. This lack of vision was an obstacle for these campuses, impeding them from moving forward toward institutionalization. We should note that many of the contingent faculty leaders interviewed were preoccupied more with mainline union contract issues than an overall vision for an inclusive campus. We realize that such mainline issues are important, especially in this economic climate. However, these mainline issues should not be the sole focus of change agents, at the cost of a long-term vision for an inclusive campus.

## Addressing Climate

While the mobilization and implementation phases certainly influence the climate of the campus to be more favorable toward contingent faculty members, addressing climate became a focus within institutionalization. Also, because of advances made in changing the climate during the mobilization and implementa-tion phases, climate concerns moved beyond combating antagonism toward contingent faculty; instead they were focused on examining campus policies and practices to make sure they were more inclusive and not unintentionally unfair toward contingent faculty members. With active animosity gone, most of the poor climate was residual from institutional practices and policies that simply ignored or excluded contingent faculty. At this point, contingent faculty members talked about scanning the host of campus practices for inequalities: invitations to events, access to funding and resources, evaluation and assessment processes, curriculum development, administrative support, leadership opportu-nities, and the like. One critical aspect for addressing the climate and the remaining inequitable policies and practices was being able to have discussions about sensitive issues. These included the growth of contingent faculty members as a challenge to the institution of tenure; the importance of protecting tenure-track and full-time jobs (while also obtaining parity for contingent faculty); that absolute parity in pay or benefits may not be a final outcome; and viewing contingent faculty members as good teachers, but realizing that their working conditions impact quality. If people cannot openly discuss these types of issues, they can create tension and block institutionalization, leaving campuses at the implementation phase.

## Moving beyond Mainline Union Policies and Pockets of Change

Campuses that institutionalized change shifted from a focus on mainline union policies to a broader set of issues related to a positive climate. These broader issues included creating a process for full-time or part-time contingent faculty to move onto tenure-track lines, intellectual property issues, academic freedom, paid office hours, tuition remission, and the like. For faculty with union contracts, they started to hone language in each area to be more precise, and cover a broader set of issues related to climate that might better protect contingent faculty:

> We just overlooked lots of areas earlier like academic freedom or intellectual property, areas that are often easier to change than salary or benefits because we held those to be the key issues for equity, but inclusion and digging deeper into other fairness issues should not be ignored.

Institutionalized campuses had policies and practices that reached all departments and were no longer exceptional policies or practices. One contingent faculty member described this issue:

> The difference now is that every department has professional development opportunities, every department socializes contingent faculty members into the life of the department, and every department recognizes the value of and looks toward contingent faculty for leadership. It used to be that only happened in pockets.

## Creating a Single Faculty

Institutionalized campuses had a single faculty.[4] There was no longer talk about tenure-track versus non-tenure track, full-time contingents or part-time contingents, or adjuncts who teach only a single class. In addition, faculty contributions to campus were more similar in nature. All faculty were expected to participate in governance in some way. All faculty were considered equal and competent teachers, and participated actively in curriculum development. All faculty were scholars who should keep up on changes in their field and should participate in professional development. While we only had a few universities in our sample, research was not considered an obligation for contingent faculty members, but was certainly valued among contingents who made this a part of their role. Therefore, full institutionalization of policies and practices that were positive toward contingent faculty made the faculty a single community with relatively similar expectations, and supported the faculty to meet those expectations. Part of becoming a single faculty was also establishing contingent faculty lines as career paths: Therefore policies and procedures addressed issues of promotion, evaluation, and faculty development. Contingent faculty who felt part of the professoriate on campus focused more on their responsibilities and less on their rights. We heard faculty on institutionalized campuses talk more about the teaching and learning environment rather than their working conditions. In the words of one faculty member: "When you are treated with respect, as a professional, you think more about your obligation to the institution and students. When you are not, it is easy to forget obligations." This result does not necessarily mean there were no distinctions among faculty roles, but there was equal respect when distinctions in the role did occur. The hierarchy did not exist. One tenured faculty member spoke about becoming a single faculty again:

> For years we were a divided faculty. At first, we actually didn't even realize we were divided (at least the tenure-track faculty) because we were not aware of the other faculty members. Then we went through a real period of animosity toward each other and the administration. I wish that animosity weren't part of our past. I think that happens on many campuses. But now we really treat each other with respect, non-tenure tracks have full participation in governance and there are no distinctions among us.

### Assuming Leadership

On campuses that had moved to institutionalization, contingent faculty took leadership roles with major issues on campus. A contingent faculty leader talked about the significant leadership roles that they now play:

> We are really looked to now for our expertise on a set of issues. Since we were doing much of the online courses, we developed a template for how courses should be offered and assessed. The same process is now used with tenure-track faculty and it was our model. We've also been active in reducing class size on campus, which is getting out of control …We have also worked to create the student outcomes assessment measures that are used on campus because of our familiarity with pedagogical theories, which made us the likely experts on campus.

As this interviewee suggested, campuses that moved toward institutionalization had strong contingent faculty leadership, were rewarded for this leadership, were respected by their colleagues, and had their suggestions implemented.

---

## CONCORDIA UNIVERSITY AND CAL POLY POMONA

Concordia University's part-time faculty play a prominent role in the leadership of the campuses and have increasingly played that role. The union encourages part-timers to take on leadership roles so that it demystifies their ability to contribute to the overall learning environment and demonstrates their expertise. Also, see Chapter 7 in this volume on Cal Poly Pomona, which highlights how lecturer leadership helped to transform tenure-track faculty views of lecturers, and began to change the climate on campus.

Institutionalization is still quite rare in higher education. While implementation is usually affected by the unwillingness of administrators or tenure-track faculty to change, ironically, the failure to achieve institutionalization at this point appears to be shaped by the contingent faculty leaders themselves. Contingent faculty leaders tend to focus on a narrow set of rights such as salary and benefits, and tend not to focus on deeper issues such as climate and inclusion. They have not begun to stress the responsibilities of contingent faculty and emphasize how those responsibilities contribute to the teaching and learning environment. The campuses that institutionalized change had a broader vision and used a key set of tactics to activate that vision, such as a rationale for their change, addressing climate and underlying values, and a plan of action. The process of institutionalization we identified mirrors the literature of accepting and valuing contingent faculty members, as well as having positive practices and policies as the norm for the institution. The outcome of institutionalization results in a unified faculty and a new status quo. It is also important to emphasize that campuses which moved toward institutionalization focused on values over policies and practices. They recognized that changing policies to alter attitudes is less likely to be effective. This follows what we know from organizational theory about changing cultures—that starting with values is more effective (Schein, 1992). Figure 2.2 provides a summary of our study findings.

## Some Factors of Institutionalization to Consider

Across the three phases of institutionalization, there are some factors that shape the process and that leaders should be aware of as they develop a change agenda and process. Because the change process really is context-dependent, it is possible that some of the above strategies may be easier to apply than others. Depending on institutional type and institutional culture, there are some factors that advocates may want to keep in mind when determining if certain strategies or tactics are more applicable than others: leadership, focus, external environments, and partnerships. As the reader thinks about the changes she wants to advocate and the strategies and tactics she may use (see Figure 2.2 for a breakdown of stages and strategies/tactics), she may want to see to what extent these factors exist on her own campus. Throughout this book, we try to highlight these different contextual factors in each of the cases and show how they may impact the institutionalization process for contingent-friendly policies and practices.

### *Leadership*

Researchers have identified leadership as one of the key levers in institutionalizing organizational change and innovation into the culture (Boyce, 2003; Curry,

| MOBILIZATION | IMPLEMENTATION | INSTITUTIONALIZATION |
|---|---|---|
| • Develop awareness<br>• Create network<br>• Break invisibility | • Develop rationale<br>• Use data, benchmarks, models<br>• Create task force/establish meetings<br>• Participate in governance<br>• Garner external support<br>• Utilize institutional allies<br>• Create action plans | • Address campus climate<br>• Move beyond mainline policies and pockets of departments to the entire campus<br>• Build a single faculty<br>• Take key leadership roles |

FIGURE 2.2 Overlay of three-stage model with study findings about institutionalization of policy development

1992; Kanter, 1983; Kezar, 2007). This was clearly a major finding within our study (Kezar & Sam, in press). At the 30 institutions we studied, on campuses where leaders left or burned out, we saw stalling of their progress toward change. Leadership provides direction, motivation, inspiration, vision, skills, role-modeling, and support for implementation (Boyce, 2003; Curry, 1992; Kanter, 1983; Kezar, 2007). Because change for contingent faculty is happening from the bottom up among faculty leaders, we highlight two important findings in the recent research on faculty leadership. First, faculty leaders/activists who are not in formal positions of authority need to use unique strategies or tactics different from those in positions of authority (Hart, 2005, 2007; Kezar, Gallant, & Lester, 2011; Kezar & Lester, 2009). While they cannot change reward structures or mandate change, bottom-up leaders can hold dialogs, write concept papers, lobby the media, partner with students to help influence the administration, and collect data and create a research base to support the type of change they envision (Kezar et al., 2011; Kezar & Lester, 2009). Our findings in this study (Kezar & Sam, in press) support these broader findings about faculty change agents and how they create change from the bottom up. Second, tactics for change vary based on institutional context (Hart, 2007). For example, faculty have used external contacts with the media or state legislators to create pressure for institutional change on campuses where there is a more adversarial relationship between faculty and the administration. In contrast, on a campus with more collegial relationships between faculty and the administration, the faculty leaders created prestige networks—getting close to people considered influential and persuading them to their cause. Thus, grassroots leaders needed to adopt approaches different from leaders in positions of authority. Also, varying contexts may require specific leadership. Our study identified institutional differences that are highlighted within the case-study chapters.

## Focus

Leaders will find it difficult to encourage change and innovation in a culture when the actual goals are vague or ambiguous, or when priorities are in disarray (Murray, 2008). Numerous scholars have noted that part of a successful initiative is clarity of vision—the tenets of the reform can be clearly explained and communicated (Kezar, 2007; Massey, Wilger, & Colbeck, 1994). Clarity can be enhanced by models and benchmarks (Eckel & Kezar, 2003; Kezar & Eckel, 2002), through member values being in congruence (Litzler, Clairborne, & Brainard, 2007), and by aligning resources with the change effort (Boyce, 2003). As the innovation enters different phases, maintaining focus on the desired end result becomes both a necessity and a challenge for change agents (Murray, 2008). This study (Kezar & Sam, in press) also found that campuses had difficulty mobilizing when they could not define a shared interest and focus. Contingent faculty leaders often could not decide on a focus. There was often dissent about how far they should take the campus and they typically compromised at minor changes; for example, many campuses had conflicting and unresolved priorities, some focusing on salary and others wanting governance. Unresolved divisiveness amongst faculty prevents institutionalization and deeper change. Also, institutionalization was often compromised by leaders making too much compromise and not developing a bold enough long-term action plan that incorporated the broad interests of non-tenure track faculty of varying contracts or disciplines.

## External Environments

When looking at organizational reform, leaders often focused on the institutional level rather than the external environments, which may also play a role in the success of a reform (Datnow, 2005). In the K–12 literature on institutionalized reforms, scholars have argued that supportive infrastructures must exist at the various levels: state, district, and community (Anderson & Stiegelbauer, 1994; Fullan, 1989; Moffet, 2000). Eckel and Kezar (2003) have demonstrated how accreditation processes, disciplinary societies, professional associations— such as the American Association of University Professors (AAUP)—and other external groups can shape change processes in higher education. Crises such as the recent economic collapse can also affect how policies and practices are institutionalized, as well as determine the priorities of the campus (Levin, 1980). In our study, external pressure and groups clearly played a role in the implementation phase to keep change moving forward. Accreditation teams, community groups, the media, policymakers, and students were all used to generate support and awareness for the changes and put pressure on administrators to negotiate.

## Partnerships

Leaders should attend to internal and external groups or partnerships to aid the institutionalization of an innovation. Osa and Schock (2007) discussed the use of both networks and influential allies to begin mobilizing and supporting people for change. Networks help facilitate communication, as well as providing additional means for both information and resources. Influential allies supply credibility and social capital that can move the change to the next stage, as well as providing links to the external environment (Lueddeke, 1999). Among contingent faculty, several networks currently exist, including COCAL (Coalition for Contingent Academic Labor) and the New Faculty Majority— two groups created to link contingent faculty members with those who are at different campuses or locations, exchanging information and offering support. There are also professional groups such as the NEA (National Education Association), AAUP, and AFT (American Federation of Teachers) (all unions) which often lend support in terms of resources and experience concerning enacting for change.

COCAL, the New Faculty Majority, and union groups were major sources of support for faculty in this study. It is doubtful that the leaders would have emerged on these campuses without the support from these external networks. A single contingent faculty leader on a campus can feel like she is in a hopeless situation without the external social networking. Also, contingent faculty leaders leveraged information from listservs and other multimedia sources to mobilize people and show others that they are not alone fighting for these issues. The external groups also provided ideas to propel campuses through implementation. Therefore, one of the most important findings is that contingent faculty leaders should connect to broader networks to help institutionalize changes. Again, technology played a pivotal role in creating networks. Most faculty network virtually; there is no money or opportunity for contingent faculty to meet in person. Technology enabled virtual relationships and support, and sharing of information on promising policies, and practices, and strategy. Virtual communities play a significant role in forwarding change and as the media advances, it provides greater potential to fuel such movements. For example, graduate students' unionization web fora have advanced sites where they catalog union language, share campus statistics, and create active blogs. These practices will likely become more prevalent among contingent faculty over time.

## Conclusion

The framework offered in this chapter provides leaders with a way to think about their change process—in distinct stages, with different challenges within each phase, and with core strategies for moving forward. We suggest factors (focus, leadership, external pressures, and partnerships/networks) that can also affect the pathways to institutionalization of policies and practices that are positive for contingent faculty. As readers continue through the chapters on the various case studies, it may be important for them to keep in mind how these factors may influence the change process on different campuses, as well as how these factors may influence their own campus-change efforts. This chapter provides a way to visualize and plan a path toward institutionalization and the deep change that becomes part of the fabric of the campus. The chapters that follow give examples of specific campuses and describe how they did indeed move forward, and provide depth and further explanation of the concepts reviewed in this chapter.

## Notes

1  For further detailed information on this study, please see Kezar and Sam (in press).
2  For examples of positive policies and practices, please see recommendations by American Federation of Teachers Higher Education (2002), and American Association of University Professors (2005).
3  Readers may be interested in the way that implementation looks different from institutionalization. The implementation phase entailed addressing the "mainline" concerns among contingent faculty that tend to be those addressed by unions: salary, job security (multi-year contracts or seniority), benefits; and only sometimes addressed secondary issues such as office space, pay for office hours, and governance. Secondary issues were more fully addressed when campuses moved to institutionalization.
4  When we speak of a single faculty, we are not speaking of bargaining units. Rather we are speaking of a change in faculty mindset. Of our institutions that reached this stage, some faculty were in separate units, while others were wall-to-wall (tenure-track and non-tenure track.faculty in the same unions).

## References

Alexander, E. R. (2005). Institutional transformation and planning: From institutionalization theory to institutional design. *Planning Theory, 4*(3), 209–222.

American Association of University Professors. (2005). *Inequities persist for women and non-tenure track faculty: The annual report on the economic status of the profession 2004–05*. Washington, DC: American Association of University Professors.

American Federation of Teachers Higher Education. (2002). *Fairness and equity: Standards of good practice in the employment of part-time adjunct faculty*. Washington, DC: American Federation of Teachers.

Anderson, S., & Stiegelbauer, S. (1994). Institutionalization and renewal in a restructured secondary school. *School Organization, 14*(3), 279–293.

Baldwin, R. G., & Chronister, J. L. (2001). *Teaching without tenure*. Baltimore: Johns Hopkins University Press.

Boyce, M. E. (2003). Organizational learning is essential to achieving and sustaining change in higher education. *Innovative Higher Education, 28*(2), 119–136.

Curry, B. K. (1991). Institutionalization: The final phase of the organizational change process. *Administrator's Notebook, 35*(1).

Curry, B. K. (1992). *Instituting enduring innovations: Achieving continuity of change in higher education*. ASHE-ERIC Higher Education Report No. 7. Washington, DC: The George Washington University.

Datnow, A. (2005). The sustainability of comprehensive school reform models in changing district and state contexts. *Educational Administration Quarterly, 41*(1), 121–153.

Eagan, M. K., & Jaeger, A. J. (2009). Part-time faculty at community colleges: Implications for student persistence and transfer. *Research in Higher Education, 50*(2), 168–188.

Eckel, P., & Kezar, A. (2003). Key strategies for making new institutional sense. *Higher Education Policy, 16*(1), 39–53.

Fullan, M. (1989). Managing curriculum change. In M. Preedy (Ed.), *Approaches to curriculum management* (pp. 144–149). Milton Keynes: Open University Press.

Gappa, J. M., & Leslie, D. W. (1993). *The invisible faculty: Improving the status of part-timers in higher education.* San Francisco: Jossey-Bass.

Hart, J. (2005). Activism among feminist academics: Professionalized activism and activist professionals. *Advancing Women in Leadership, 18.* Retrieved on July 12, 2009, from www.advancingwomen.com/awl/social_justice1/Hart.html.

Hart, J. (2007). Creating networks as an activist strategy: Differing approaches among academic feminist organizations. *Journal of the Professoriate, 2*(1), 33–52.

Jaeger, A., & Eagan, M. K. (2009). Unintended consequences: Examining the effect of part-time faculty members on associate's degree completion. *Community College Review, 36*(3), 167–194.

Kanter, R. M. (1983). *The change masters: Corporate entrepreneurs at work.* London: Allen & Unwin.

Kanter, R. M. (1990). *When giants learn to dance.* London: Allen & Unwin.

Kezar, A. (2007). Tools for a time and place: Phased leadership strategies for advancing campus diversity. *Review of Higher Education, 30*(4), 413–439.

Kezar, A., & Eckel, P. D. (2002). The effect of institutional culture on change strategies in higher education: Universal principles or culturally responsive concepts? *The Journal of Higher Education, 73*(4), 435–460.

Kezar, A., Gallant, T., & Lester, J. (2011). Everyday people making a difference on college campuses: The tempered grassroots leadership strategies of faculty and staff. *Studies in Higher Education, 36*(2), 129–151.

Kezar, A., & Lester, J. (2009, March/April). The importance of external influences in the promotion of grassroots change in higher education: The promise of virtual networks. *Change*, 45–51.

Kezar, A., & Sam, C. (in press). Institutionalizing equitable policies and practices for contingent faculty. *Journal of Higher Education.*

Levin, C. H. (1980). *Managing fiscal stress: The crisis in the public sector.* Chatham, NJ: Chatham House Press.

Litzler, E., Claiborne, C., & Brainard, S. G. (2007). *Five years later: The institutionalization and sustainability of ADVANCE.* Washington, DC: American Society for Engineering Education.

Lueddeke, G. R. (1999). Toward a constructivist framework for guiding change and innovation in higher education. *Journal of Higher Education, 70*(3), 235–260.

Massey, W., Wilger, A., & Colbeck, C. (1994). Departmental cultures and teaching quality: Overcoming "hollowed" collegiality. *Change, 25*(4), 11–20.

Mishler, E. G. (1991). *Research interviewing: Context and narrative.* Cambridge, MA: Harvard University Press.

Moffet, C. A. (2000). Sustaining change: The answers are blowing in the wind. *Educational Leadership, 57*(7), 35–38.

Murray, G. (2008). On the cutting edge of torpor: Innovation and the pace of change in American higher education. *AACE Journal, 16*(1), 47–61.

Osa, M., & Schock, K. (2007). A long, hard slog: Political opportunities, social networks and the mobilization of dissent in non-democracies. In P. G. Coy (Ed.), *Research in social movements, conflicts and change* (Vol. 27, pp. 123–153). London: Emerald Group Publishing Limited.

Schein, E. H. (1992). *Organizational culture and leadership* (2nd ed.). San Francisco: Jossey-Bass.

Schell, E., & Stock, P. (2001). *Moving a mountain: Transforming the role of contingent faculty I composition studies and higher education.* Urbana, IL: National Council of Teachers in English.

Schuster, J. H., & Finkelstein, M. J. (2006). *American faculty: The restructuring of academic work and careers.* Baltimore: Johns Hopkins University Press.

Umbach, P. D. (2007). How effective are they? Exploring the impact of contingent faculty on undergraduate education. *The Review of Higher Education, 30*(2), 91–123.

# PART II

# Case Studies

# 3

# AN INSTRUCTIVE MODEL OF HOW MORE EQUITY AND EQUALITY IS POSSIBLE

## The Vancouver Community College Model

*Frank Cosco and Jack Longmate*

Emerging from the amalgamation of three pre-existing institutions, Vancouver Community College (VCC) was founded in 1965. It is the largest and oldest public college in Vancouver, British Columbia (BC), Canada. Vancouver Community College offers more than 140 programs and serves nearly 25,000 students a year (see Table 3.1). The Vancouver Community College Faculty Association (VCCFA) was originally certified as a trade union in 1951. It represents faculty, librarians, and counselors at VCC and currently has about 730 faculty on its seniority list. The VCC/VCCFA collective agreement has become recognized across North America as exemplary in its equitable treatment of all faculty, whether full-time or part-time, permanent/regular, or probationary/ contingent. Through bargaining and vigorous contract administration, the VCCFA has successfully institutionalized change for all faculty at VCC. For the great majority of faculty—be they full-time, part-time, librarian, counselor, teacher, or curriculum developer—being treated either equally or equitably is the norm.

Since 1990 the VCCFA has been Local 15 of the Federation of Post-Secondary Educators of British Columbia (FPSE), a federation of 19 post-secondary faculty unions at colleges and universities throughout the province. The federation does not bargain or directly administer collective agreements, but it does support that work and it has established clearly progressive goals and policies such as "regularization of the person" to guide the work of its member unions (www. fpse.ca).[1] Although many of its characteristics may be found in other BC workplaces, especially those at other FPSE locals, the Vancouver model does not necessarily represent other higher education workplaces in BC or in Canada generally.

**TABLE 3.1** Institutional Snapshot of Vancouver Community College

| | |
|---|---|
| *Institutional type* | Public community college |
| *Student population* | 25,000 |
| *Unionized* | Yes |
| *State* | British Columbia, Canada |
| *Institutionalization phase* | Institutionalization |
| *Main changes* | Only one salary scale; pro-rata workload; no overtime; automatic regularization of the person; workload allocation by seniority; ensuring transparency; rights to benefits and entitlements; full participation in institutional governance, departmental processes, and union business |

In this chapter, we first give a detailed review of the workplace provisions of the employment contract at VCC. Next we look more closely at how this system came about and how the changes were made, and how the Vancouver model compares to the U.S. system. Then we discuss the usefulness of the VCC model and the role of the union and union leaders, along with some suggestions for instituting best practices when an institution does not have a union. In conclusion, we highlight the *Program for Change: Real Transformation over Two Decades*, a schema that itemizes incremental, concrete steps to move to equal treatment over a generation (http://www.vccfa.ca/program-for-change/index.html). Our purpose in showcasing the Vancouver model is to give readers examples of how inequity can be reduced.

*For key features of the employment system at Vancouver Community College, see the collective agreement at* http://www.vcc.ca/deptUploads/faculty-collective-agreement.pdf.

## Overview of Main Features of Faculty Employment at VCC

Unlike community colleges in the United States (US) where faculty are classified as full-time tenured or part-time non-tenured, the primary distinction for VCC faculty is either "regular" status, which is the functional equivalent of tenure, or "term" faculty, which is probationary. Much greater fluidity exists between regular and term than between tenured and non-tenured.

At VCC, faculty normally go through only one hiring process to start their whole career. Most commonly, term faculty become regular through the regularization process as established by the VCCFA, whereby after two years of teaching at least 50 percent of the full-time load, with a satisfactory evaluation (or no unsatisfactory evaluation per the collective agreement), the probationary or term faculty member is elevated to regular (permanent) status. This is not the exclusive route to regularization: A faculty member may be hired full-time and may be initially hired as a regular. But with regularization, virtually all faculty can be said to be on track to becoming regular faculty with the job security it confers.

(This contrasts with the U.S. system, where adjuncts can work for decades with little hope of gaining job security and have dismal prospects of winning a tenure-track job.)

The key provisions of VCC are described below. It is our contention that the Vancouver model can serve as a useful template for other faculty employment systems seeking to achieve greater equity and equality.

## VCC Has Only One Salary Scale

Vancouver Community College faculty, whether full-time or part-time, term or regular are paid according to a single salary scale. For part-time faculty, the salary scale of annual faculty wages is completely pro rata, down to the hourly rate. It has 11 steps, with the lowest, step 11, at C$51,797; and the highest, step 1, at C$83,231 (as of 2011). An instructor's initial placement is determined through a formula negotiated into the collective agreement. Neither the length, nor the time status (i.e., full- or part-time) of that appointment affects placement, which can be at any step. Because VCC does not use a semester/section system, the annual salary is then prorated to determine an hourly salary based on 1,010 hours (202 days x 5 hours per day) of potential annual assigned duty. Using that formula, the hourly salary at step 11, the lowest step, is currently C$51.29 (rounded). Similar amounts are determined for those at other steps. Being fully pro rata, these amounts are used for all work. For example, on one's first ever call-in as a substitute instructor (which has to be for a minimum three hours even if the class is shorter), the pay is at least 3 x C$51.29, or C$153.87. See Table 3.2 for all salary amounts.

**TABLE 3.2** VCC Faculty Salary Schedule (Applies to Full-time and Part-time, Regular, and Term)

| Step | Annual salary | Per diem Annual/202 days | Hourly Per diem/5 hours |
|------|---------------|--------------------------|-------------------------|
| 1 | C$83,231 | C$412.04 | C$82.41 |
| 2 | C$77,970 | C$386.00 | C$77.20 |
| 3 | C$72,628 | C$359.55 | C$71.91 |
| 4 | C$69,655 | C$344.83 | C$68.97 |
| 5 | C$67,104 | C$332.20 | C$66.44 |
| 6 | C$64,553 | C$319.57 | C$63.91 |
| 7 | C$62,002 | C$306.95 | C$61.39 |
| 8 | C$59,450 | C$294.31 | C$58.86 |
| 9 | C$56,899 | C$281.68 | C$56.34 |
| 10 | C$54,348 | C$269.05 | C$53.81 |
| 11 | C$51,797 | C$256.43 | C$51.29 |

*Source*: Vancouver Community College/Vancouver Community College Faculty Association Collective Bargaining Agreement.

The same type of prorating is in effect at other colleges and institutions in BC that use a semester/section system. It simply means that for faculty at institutions with an annual eight-section full-time load, pay is prorated per section, so the annual salary (there is essentially one common pay grid for all FPSE units) is divided by eight, resulting in pay of C$6,475 per section at the bottom step and C$10,404 at the top step.

## Pro-rata Workload, Consistent with Departmental Practice

Within certain parameters, each VCC department can determine how the full-time weekly load of 25 hours of assigned duty is divided between direct instruction and other duties. If it is a 16:9 hour mix, then every instructor with an appointment, no matter their seniority, no matter their time status, gets that ratio of assignment. In this case, a half-time instructor would be responsible for 8 hours of class time and 4.5 hours of other duties such as office hours, and be paid for 12.5 hours of assigned duty. It is noteworthy that while the full range of job functions are prorated for part-time faculty at VCC, in U.S. colleges, assigned duty for part-time faculty is generally to "just teach" and rarely includes non-teaching duties. A by-product of the Vancouver model of equal pay and equal work is a community of interests and solidarity among faculty that is difficult to achieve in the stratified U.S. two-tiered faculty system.

## No Overtime

Overtime assignments are essentially prohibited by the collective agreement. A rare exception is for programming reasons, such as government requirements in apprenticeship programs. In these cases, the college negotiates a variance with the union. Any such variance results not in extra pay, but in extra time off—time in lieu of the overtime worked. The VCCFA will also permit a temporary overtime situation in the case of a medical emergency. This prohibition of over-time teaching contrasts with common practices in the U.S. community colleges, where full-time tenured faculty are often allowed to teach overtime or overloads; whenever they do, they take work from contingent faculty and undermine initiatives seeking job security and greater equity for contingent faculty.

## Automatic Regularization, Conversion from Term to Regular Status

Individual term faculty at VCC who teach at half-time or more for any two-year period with satisfactory evaluations are automatically converted to regular status which lasts, without further summative evaluation, for the rest of their career. Regular status is the functional equivalent of tenure. Regularized faculty and the college presume their jobs will continue and are not subject to being cut without due process. If they are part-time regulars, they have the further right by seniority to ratchet up to full-time status if work is available. In contrast, the community college part-time or adjunct faculty in the US may teach for decades with no job security and small or dismal hope of ever becoming full-time. Also, in many U.S. states, like California, part-time faculty workload is limited to a percentage below full-time; for example, no more than 67 percent of a full-time load. It should be emphasized that at VCC, this regularization applies to the *person*, not his or her *position*. For example, the person is converted to a new status, instead of the position being opened up to competition between faculty. It is based on the principle that if a faculty member maintains a half-time level of term appointments for most of any two-year period, then he or she will change status automatically and become a regular.

It remains the case at some other BC colleges and universities within the FPSE orbit that the right of conversion is limited to the *position*, and not applied to the *person*. At such institutions, the accrual converts the work from "term" to "to-be-posted regular," which is then up for competition. The person whose work created the spot is then required to compete for the work. In some other situations in BC, the right of the person to convert is limited because there has to be what is deemed "ongoing" work (i.e., work that is considered to be not temporary and transitory in nature). Also, at some institutions, service by replacing those who are on leave or in department leadership positions may be overlooked by institutions disinclined to grant regularization. These restrictions do not exist at VCC.

At VCC, given satisfactory evaluations (or the lack of an unsatisfactory evaluation), the person changes status from term to regular and the change happens automatically on the first of the month following the requisite accrual levels being met. There is no other posting process and there is no restriction such as the establishment of ongoing work. In the rare case when there actually is no ongoing work, the newly regularized person receives an immediate notice of layoff and all the attendant rights conferred by regularization, such as those of transfer and full or partial recall. Because the full notice period lasts for four months, such faculty are assured of four months of pay, and work is found for them.

## Workload Accrual from Half-time to Full-time

Since "regular" or "term", not "full-time" or "part-time", are the key status indicators at VCC, many regulars have half-time workloads or fractional workloads between half-time and full-time. When work is available within a department or teaching area for which they are qualified, should they wish to work up to full-time, part-time regulars have the right by seniority of first refusal before term faculty. If they can maintain that additional level of work for an additional two years in the same manner as indicated above, then their regular time-status level is increased by that factor.

## Seniority

After their first "term" appointment, all VCC faculty accrue seniority, and seniority is the primary, though not the exclusive, determinant of workload assignment. Those with the greatest seniority generally have the first choice about teaching and other assignments. (See the "Workload Allocation by Seniority" section below.) Seniority accruals are transparent, rankings are public, and compliance is ensured through equal access to grievance processes. Term faculty accrue seniority on a pro rata basis from their first term appointment. After regularization, both full-time and part-time faculty accrue seniority at exactly the same annual rate of 261 full days per year. This protects the seniority ranking of those with part-time status. Indeed, a part-timer may be senior to a full-time colleague and will maintain that ranking for the remainder of his or her career. Seniority is meaningful and enforceable, and in addition to being used for assigning work, is key for job protection.

## Workload Allocation by Seniority

For newer faculty, after any six months of contracted work, at any time status, term faculty have the right of first refusal to available work by seniority. This collective agreement provision brings term instructors a significant measure of job security and confidence that, as they continue their work at the college and toward regularization, their rights are being upheld within a context of fair and transparent process. In contrast, in the U.S. system, full-time or part-time status is the chief determinant of workload assignment. Seniority for U.S. non-tenured faculty is usually informal and transgressions are not consistently addressed through grievances. Furthermore, rights to re-appointment for the non-tenured are rare.

## Ensuring Transparency

As noted above, seniority is a key provision in determining workload allotment. Also, reverse seniority is a key determinant in establishing transfer rights and the order of layoffs. The VCCFA web site offers several distinct seniority data search reports to make public the order for any of these eventualities. If, for example, a budget reduction should cause a general reduction of force in the faculty institution-wide, then a report of the seniority of all faculty members, institution-wide, would be instructive to allow the individual faculty member to see where he or she stands relative to others; that report is suggested by Table 3.3, which is an abbreviated version of the actual listing available at the VCCFA website. The status column contains either "T" to designate term or "R" for regular, along with the time status for the regular instructors. Seniority is measured by "service days," which is the common denominator for all faculty across term and regular lines, disciplines/departments, and teaching areas. If a cutback were to affect a

**TABLE 3.3** Sample of VCCFA Seniority List, College-wide, Sorted Alphabetically

| SURNAME | FIRST | STATUS | CALCULATION COMMENCEMENT DATE | NEW PRO-RATA SERVICE DAYS (APRIL 1/10) | DEPARTMENT | AREA | SCHOOL/ CENTRE |
|---------|-------|--------|------------------------------|----------------------------------------|------------|------|----------------|
| C | A | T | 2007 04 13 | 34 | Instructor Education | Instructor Education | School of Instructor Education |
| C | B | T | 2009 05 04 | 53 | Science | Anatomy & Physiology – University Transfer | Arts & Sciences |
| C | C | R100% | 1980 05 05 | 7190 | English Language Skills | ESL | Language Studies |
| C | D | R100% | 1989 05 01 | 5041 | English Language Skills | ESL | Language Studies |
| C | E | R56.25% | 1983 05 01 | 3150 | Outreach | ESL | Language Studies |
| C | F | R100% | 1983 09 15 | 6665 | Certified Dental Assisting/Dental Reception Coordinator | Dental Reception Coordinator | Health Sciences |

*Source:* Vancouver Community College and Vancouver Community College Faculty Association.

**TABLE 3.4** Sample of VCCFA Seniority List, Sorted by Department

| SURNAME | FIRST | STATUS | CALCULATION COMMENCEMENT DATE | NEW PRO-RATA SERVICE DAYS (APRIL 1/10) | DEPARTMENT | AREA | SCHOOL/ CENTRE |
|---|---|---|---|---|---|---|---|
| C | G | R100% | 1980 05 05 | 7190 | English Language Skills | ESL | Language Studies |
| C | H | R100% | 1977 05 03 | 7117 | English Language Skills | ESL | Language Studies |
| B | I | R100% | 1980 05 05 | 7024 | English Language Skills | ESL | Language Studies |
| W | J | R100% | 1980 09 08 | 6803 | English Language Skills | ESL | Language Studies |
| D | K | R100% | 1980 09 08 | 6160 | English Language Skills | ESL | Language Studies |

*Source:* Vancouver Community College and Vancouver Community College Faculty Association.

**TABLE 3.5** Sample of VCCFA Seniority List, Sorted by Area

| SURNAME | FIRST | STATUS | CALCULATION COMMENCEMENT DATE | NEW PRO-RATA SERVICE DAYS (APRIL 1/10) | DEPARTMENT | AREA | SCHOOL/ CENTRE |
|---|---|---|---|---|---|---|---|
| M | M | R100% | 1979 09 04 | 7799 | College & Career Access | ABE Computer Lab | Arts & Sciences |
| E | N | R60% | 1981 09 12 | 7182 | College & Career Access | ABE Computer Lab | Arts & Sciences |
| L | O | R100% | 1986 03 01 | 6231 | College & Career Access | ABE Computer Lab | Arts & Sciences |
| C | P | R100% | 1991 09 24 | 4845 | College & Career Access | ABE Computer Lab | Arts & Sciences |
| O | Q | R56% | 2005 09 06 | 1139 | College & Career Access | ABE Computer Lab | Arts & Sciences |
| Z | R | T | 2008 05 01 | 219 | College & Career Access | ABE Computer Lab | Arts & Sciences |

*Source:* Vancouver Community College and Vancouver Community College Faculty Association.

specific teaching department, the seniority report of instructors by teaching department is suggested by Table 3.4; and if a cutback should be scheduled for a more specific teaching area within a department, then Table 3.5 shows the seniority ranking of instructors per teaching area. These tables are part of VCCFA's effort at formalizing the employment process, and making personnel decisions as transparent and free of bias as possible. This is extremely important in the infrequent event of those facing layoff from a particular area invoking transfer rights to areas of determined competency; in such a case, college-wide earned seniority prevails over any department-specific seniority. All college work determines one's single seniority number and it outweighs one's length of service in a particular department or area.

The VCCFA publicly posts the seniority rankings of all VCC faculty, which is viewable from the VCCFA website (http://www.vccfa.ca/faqs/seniority. html). This transparency, of providing several different sets of data reports, in and of itself provides a sense of security to term faculty, as they know where they stand relative to other faculty. It is also a measure that is not costly to institute.

## Fair Evaluation

New instructors are subject to summative evaluation as one of the requirements for continued appointments and for conversion to regular status. Through many rounds of bargaining, the VCCFA has refined the language of transparent evaluation mechanisms and procedures in the corresponding series of collective agreements (see Articles 15, 16, 17, and related appendices in the collective agreement). Being in the collective agreement makes these provisions enforceable through the grievance procedure.

Normally, two successful evaluations are enough to ensure regularization. The onus is on the college to ensure that evaluations happen because a person can be regularized as long as there is no unsatisfactory evaluation.

## Rights to Benefits and Entitlements

Although there is a requirement to maintain a half-time workload for qualifying periods, all term faculty who satisfy those requirements have access to almost all the same rights and benefits as regular faculty. These include extended health benefits beyond those provided by the governmental healthcare system, professional development leave and funds, dental benefits, and paid vacation. The suite of benefits without vacation amounts to about an additional 12 percent of salary. After a salary threshold of about C$24,000 (less than half of the lowest annual salary) is met, all faculty, whether term or regular, are automatically enrolled for the rest of their career in the government-sponsored, jointly governed, defined-benefit pension plan. All premiums for all benefits except for the pension plan are solely employer-paid. The pension, jointly paid for by employers, employees (administration and faculty), and the provincial government, is based on shared employee/employer premiums of about nine percent of salary each.

## Full Participation in Institutional Governance, Departmental Processes, and Union Business

At colleges and universities in BC, there is a statutory right for faculty to be involved on college or university boards, and college education councils or university senates. All faculty at VCC have the right to run for governance positions and to vote for such candidates. All have the right to vote or stand for election in departmental matters, including the election of department heads and coordinators. In fact, term candidates who get elected automatically become full-time regulars and maintain that status after their term of departmental leadership (capped after six consecutive years) ends. Union by-laws reflect the same inclusiveness. There is a full entitlement to run for the union executive, steward, or bargaining committee positions and fully equitable voting rights. This system contrasts with the two-tiered faculty structure in U.S. colleges and universities, where it is rare for part-time faculty to participate in department meetings—they are rarely compensated to do so—and nowhere is being elected to a position in departmental governance a means of being awarded the equivalent of tenure.

## Contingency Kept to a Minimum

The net effect of the Vancouver model is that true contingency is kept to a minimum. A faculty member at VCC is normally interviewed for a job only once in his or her career. Given available work and satisfactory evaluations, they are on a career path to full-time work from their first "term" appointment. If only half-time work is available or if a person only wants to work half-time, that employment comes with a full benefit package. A part-time regular instructor accrues exactly the same annual seniority amount as a full-time regular instructor, so his or her rights do not diminish over time, nor will the seniority standing be overtaken by someone who happens to teach more classes.

Unlike some BC post-secondary workplaces, there is no quota for the "optimum" proportion of regulars versus non-regulars at VCC. The relatively organic process of regularization is allowed to take its course because, given enough work, everyone can potentially become regular. Table 3.6 breaks down the numbers of faculty in the various categories in 2001 and 2008.

The VCCFA does not have exact numbers on the proportion of work done by term and that done by regular faculty expressed either as numbers of individual faculty or in terms of full-time equivalent faculty (FTE). Given the nature of VCC's non-semester-based schedule, it is a number that changes constantly from month to month. In order to estimate the proportion, we have assumed a conservative estimate of the size of VCC's faculty complement as being 550 FTE

**TABLE 3.6** VCC Faculty, 2001 and 2008

|  | 2001 | % of individuals | 2008 | % of individuals | 2008 estimate of % of FTE work |
|---|---|---|---|---|---|
| FT Regulars | 402 | 56 | 373 | 44 | |
| HT+ Regulars | 48 | 7 | 47 | 6 | |
| HT Regulars | 66 | 9 | 57 | 7 | |
| All Regulars | 516 | 72 | 477 | 57 | 75% |
| Term + 80 days★ | 129 | 18 | 188 | 22 | |
| Term < 80 days★ | 70 | 10 | 174 | 21 | |
| All Terms | 199 | 28 | 362 | 43 | 25% |
| Total | 715 | | 839 | | |

Key: FT= full-time; HT+ = those part-timers above half-time; HT = half-time.
★ *The 80 days are 80 FTE days and refer to 80 days of FTE seniority. It is the equivalent of being employed full-time for four months, approximately one semester.*

faculty, an estimate used in a recent round of bargaining. One can calculate from the listings on the full seniority list that the average workload in 2008 for the 47 faculty in the HT+ category is close to 72 percent. Converting the three sub-totals for the number of regular faculty in 2008 to numbers of FTE faculty yields 373 FTE full-time, 34 FTE at more than half-time, and 28.5 FTE at half-time. Therefore, the FTE workload of the 477 regulars listed is a little over 435 FTE. Using the 550 FTE estimates that the VCCFA and VCC used in bargaining would mean that 79 percent of the 550 FTE workload at VCC is done by regulars. For these purposes, where exact figures are not necessary to make the point, we can reduce that estimate to say more reliably that in FTE terms, 75 percent of faculty work at VCC is done by regular faculty.

### Increasing the Normalization of Work

VCC has had the typical features of a corporatized workplace: a CEO-centered management structure, executive privilege, top-down management always seeking to maximize its flexibility to shape the college's budget in its own vision, and unprecedented growth in senior management. However, the strength of the union has provided a means and place for collective action and solidarity for faculty. Through principled militancy, it has enabled faculty resistance and struggle against corporate approaches to management, and has even allowed faculty the means to make progress during those times. Working at VCC as either a term or a regular faculty member is in many ways a normal job without arbitrary distinctions in pay, status, or rights. Because there is real freedom of speech and action within departments, it allows all to contribute to the issues of education. Increased solidarity between all groups of faculty is a result of transparent, solid rights of transition from term to regular status, and an ethos of equity and equality. This creates a foundation for collaborative approaches to the problems of the day.

## How Did Such a System Come About?

Canada, and especially BC, have a proud tradition of unionization. This history is not without its flaws, but it has always fostered strong themes of workplace justice, equity, and principled action. Since the late 1980s, through 10 rounds of principled bargaining, the VCCFA has achieved a workplace with a very high level of equity in pay and rights, and job security for the great majority of its members. It continues to bargain for improvements to its collective agreement. Assertive maintenance of rights by a resourced group of stewards protects and enhances what has been achieved. The VCCFA has not done this alone; as mentioned in the introduction, it belongs to the provincial federation of post-secondary faculty unions, the Federation of Post-Secondary Educators of British Columbia (FPSE), which since its inception has worked to bring principles of equity and equality to the post-secondary workplace in BC through strengthening and resourcing the work of its member unions.

The accomplishments of the VCCFA were hardly inevitable; nor did they come about simply because of persuasive argument or because management at VCC has been uniquely progressive. Principled militancy best describes the union's successful approach. In six of the last ten rounds of bargaining, the VCCFA has used the dynamic of seeking and attaining strike votes and occasionally going on strike. There have been three strikes in that period, one of five weeks in 1990, one of less than three days in 1994, which was taken in concert with other unions within FPSE, and one for only two hours in 1998. Strike votes in 1988, 1992, and 2011 led to settlements without strike action. As this is written as of May 2011, the VCCFA has completed bargaining for a new collective agreement for 2010–2012 with the advantage of having a recent successful strike vote. While the strike and especially the strike vote are significant, they are hardly the only explanatory factors. Faculty guided by labor movement principles of equity and the goal of leveling up those with the least rights came into leadership in the existing union at VCC in the 1980s and transformed it into an agent of change at VCC.

Transforming union leadership was not an easy process and required time. It entailed running for union positions without the support of the executive's nomination committee and often losing. Some of the necessary measures included caucusing with like-minded people in one's own department and within other departments, being prepared to go to the microphone at meetings dominated by those not in favor of a change agenda, and speaking against proposed collective agreements that were not equitable. Eventually individuals with an agenda for change started to get elected. That led to further difficult processes, serving as minority members of executives that were hostile to change. This clashing of interests, while a difficult phase, did contribute to building solidarity across all faculty.

The VCCFA used, and continues to use, all the means available within the labor and collective bargaining context, including education of leaders and stewards, seeking solidarity with like-minded groups, providing training in collective bargaining and grievance handling, to name a few discrete strategies. Wherever possible, the VCCFA sought and fostered alliances with the student union, staff union, broader union federations, and other community groups. In 1990, the same year that it joined FPSE, VCCFA also joined the Vancouver and District Labour Council. Later through FPSE, it became part of the British Columbia Federation of Labour, the Canadian Association of University Teachers (CAUT), and the National Union of the Canadian Association of University Teachers (NUCAUT). Its membership in FPSE provides legal and defense fund support, as well as fora for collective action and training.

In the 1980s, VCCFA started deliberately to address issues of inequality in rights and entitlements, especially the growing number of term faculty who had no rights to re-appointment and could remain essentially contingent at the discretion of management. Change in this area has come incrementally over 25 years and 10 rounds of bargaining. It is a continuous process; failures in one round can set up goals for the next. The incremental progress in the conversion of work-status provisions over 10 bargaining rounds provides an illustrative example (see Table 3.7). In the recently completed 2010–2012 round, the VCCFA was not successful in reducing either the required time-status level for regularization below half-time nor the required number of days below 380 in 24 months, but it will try again in the next round.

While the conditions described herein might seem enviable to U.S. contingent faculty, the VCC faculty workplace is not without issues. The VCCFA is still working to bring more equity to those part-timers below half-time who have pro rata pay and have a first-refusal right to work, but who cannot access some of the other benefits and rights.

## How Does the Vancouver Model Differ from U.S. Systems?

The accomplishments of the VCCFA were first circulated to the U.S. contingent faculty community in 2000 after the TESOL Convention, which that year took place in Vancouver. Since U.S. contingents have become aware of the VCCFA provisions, the Vancouver model has provided a paradigm for change. These provisions have helped U.S. contingents and faculty leaders to rethink possibilities and to recognize that there are other options (June, 2010; Longmate & Cosco, 2002; Nelson, 2010). While some might think that the differences between the United States and Canada make the Vancouver model less relevant, or otherwise

**TABLE 3.7** Chronology of VCC/VCCFA Bargaining Achievements on Conversion of Work Status

| Collective Agreement | Conversion to regular status provisions for faculty at half-time or more time-status |
|---|---|
| 1987–1988 | – regularization of the person<br>– if employed for 20 months of a continuous 24 months<br>– if appointments expected to be "ongoing"<br>– subject to administrative approval |
| 1988–1990 | – 20 months changed to 410 duty days out of any continuous 24 months<br>– automatic conversion to "three-year" regular status, need for "ongoing" expectation of available work and administrative approval eliminated<br>– "three-year" status is the same as fully regular status except not eligible for severance in the event of layoff<br>– after three years then subsequent automatic conversion to fully regular status (if needed, severance accruals backdated to include all service, whether term or regular) |
| 1990–1992 | – 410-day requirement changed to 380 days |
| 1992–1994 | – elimination of the "three-year" status<br>– 380 days in 24 months brings automatic regular status, but in event of layoff, access to severance delayed till three years after conversion<br>– right by seniority for part-time regulars to ratchet up their status to full-time through the same 380/24 accrual process<br>– in one school of the college (the one with the most term faculty), the right to re-appointment by seniority after first appointment, which makes the 380-day accrual process more fair |
| 1994–1995 | – no change |
| 1995–1998 | – some loosening of the 380-day requirement allowed if a department has a significant number of non-teaching days that prevent the required accrual |
| 1998–2001 | – no change |
| 2001–2004 | – right to re-appointment by seniority extended to all term faculty after any six months of appointment or cumulative appointments<br>– normal number of required evaluations during probationary period increased from one to two |
| 2004–2007 | – no change |
| 2007–2010 | – no change |
| 2010–2012 | – no change |

assume that it cannot function within or be integrated into the U.S. higher education setting, certain policies have already been integrated into U.S. institutions and there is nothing in the U.S. system that makes these policies unworkable. Reservations about the Vancouver model seem to be based on assumptions rather than an analysis of actual implementation.

By detailing the provisions of the Vancouver system and how they impact the professional lives of non-tenure track faculty, the differences between the U.S. system and the Canadian approach become starker. On a simple lexical level, the term "part-time instructor" means someone who happens to teach less than full-time in both Canada and the United States. But in Vancouver, since a part-timer can be more senior than a full-timer and can be granted assignments before a full-timer, the term "part-time instructor" has a different meaning than it does in the United States, where the term "part-time faculty" carries a host of connotations and presumes a non-proportional rate of pay, no job security, very rare seniority accrual rights, permanent probationary status with the threat of repetitive (and too often arbitrary) summative evaluations, a workload restricted to classroom instruction only, and limited involvement in campus activities (AFT, 2010; Gappa & Leslie, 1993).

The most obvious difference between the VCCFA and U.S. systems is salary. Faculty salary at VCC is straightforward: All faculty, whether full-time or part-time, whether permanent (regular) or probationary (term), are paid according to the same salary scale. Thus, part-time faculty who work 30 percent or 60 percent of a full-time load, receive 30 percent or 60 percent of the full-time pay. In contrast to this 100-percent pro-rata approach, U.S. part-time faculty are generally paid at a rate that is far below their full-time counterparts (e.g., 50 percent). Assuming a full-time faculty annual income as US$50,000 for illustration purposes, a U.S. part-timer teaching at 60 percent of a full-time load would not receive an annual income of US$30,000, as he or she would at VCC with its 100-percent pro-rata policy, but 50 percent of that US$30,000, or about US$15,000 annually.

Exacerbating the problem of low, non-prorated salaries for U.S. part-time faculty are caps that limit workload to some percentage less than the full-time load (e.g., no more than 67 percent of full-time). In VCC, by contrast, not only do part-time faculty receive prorated pay, they have the right by seniority to increase their regular workload status up to full-time without restrictions.

Contributing to this job security of part-time faculty at VCC is the very important VCCFA provision that full-time faculty may not teach additional sections above their full-time load (course overloads), which, as noted in the "No Overtime" section above, is at variance with U.S. community colleges that generally have no parallel restrictions. Whenever full-time faculty are allowed to teach course overloads, they take work from part-time, contingent faculty. This direct conflict of interest over workload may help to explain the lack of interest on the part of U.S. tenured-faculty-dominated unions to bargain for job security for non-tenured faculty, as protecting the jobs of part-time faculty could interfere with the ability of tenured faculty to teach overloads at will. Because VCC has avoided this conflict of interest, there is a greater chance for the development of solidarity and all faculty pulling together for common collective bargaining or legislative goals.

Probably the most significant difference is VCCFA's regularization system, whereby after two years of teaching at 50 percent of the full-time load without an unsatisfactory evaluation, the probationary or term faculty member is elevated to regular (permanent) status, with its better layoff protection. This contrasts sharply with the U.S. system, where adjuncts can work for decades with little hope of gaining job security and dismal prospects of winning a tenure-track job.

As mentioned in the "Automatic Regularization, Conversion from Term to Regular Status" section above, a key feature of the VCC regularization is that it is the *person*, not the *position*, that is regularized. By respecting the professionalism and dignity of the individual faculty member, VCC rewards individual initiative. Elsewhere, too often, regularization of the *position* occurs after a new faculty member has done a job successfully, but instead of the person being converted, the position is converted and then opened up to competition. VCC's respect for the individual instructor contrasts sharply with the sense of expendability that U.S. part-time faculty may sense from their employer. In U.S. colleges, far from the job security conferred by regularization, layoffs of part-time faculty can be remarkably impersonal and can be effected by simple non-renewal at the next semester or session, with no explanation or due process and generally no grounds for grievance.

Regarding work assignments, U.S. collective bargaining agreements typically delineate a differing set of job functions based on full-time or part-time status. At VCC, by contrast, workload assignment is comprehensive. It includes all forms of work, whether in the classroom or not, and does not distinguish between full- and part-timers; all are expected to participate fully in the work of the department according to their individual competencies and interests.

Seniority and its uses provide another clear delineation between the Vancouver and U.S. models. At VCC, faculty accrue seniority on a pro-rata basis from their first "term" appointment. After regularization, whether full-time or part-time, faculty accrue seniority at exactly the same annual rate of 261 full days per year. This protects the seniority ranking of those with part-time status. Indeed, a part-timer may be senior to a full-time colleague and will maintain that ranking for the remainder of his or her career. This contrasts with the relatively arbitrary and too often callous U.S. treatment of contingents and part-timers, rarely conferring formal seniority, much less making it meaningful or enforceable (Gappa & Leslie, 1993; Hollenshead et al., 2007).

Leaves provide another example of a difference between the Vancouver model and the prevailing system in the United States. While it is rare for U.S. contingent faculty to be granted leave of any sort, at VCC, all faculty earn vacation entitlement through a pro-rata calculation. Part-time regular faculty who work at half-time or more have an equal right to other leaves, including paid education leave. Faculty continue to accrue seniority while on any sort of leave, paid or unpaid. Of particular note is the extraordinary application of maternity leave that the VCCFA and other FPSE locals won through arbitration, which extends maternity-leave rights to term faculty. It protects their regularization accrual relative to their term colleagues during their leave. This is unheard of for non-tenured faculty in the United States.

Militancy is the final and possibly the most noteworthy example here. A key difference is the use of the strike vote to support union goals. Strikes within U.S. higher education are so rare as to be virtually non-existent. Strikes by unions of public employees are prohibited in many states. By contrast, the strike vote is a tool that the VCCFA has employed as a deliberate strategy with favorable results. Like a bell, the strike vote resonates. Its effects spread from the local where it occurred and reach out and help other FPSE locals that may not be able to be as militant, by assisting them in making progress toward workplace goals that they might otherwise not be able to achieve. In the United States, by contrast, since neither the strike nor the strike vote is part of the active strategies of higher education unions in most U.S. states, the complexion of faculty unionism is decidedly less militant and arguably less effective.

## How Can the Vancouver Model Be Useful?

### *An Alternative Set of Principles to Corporatization*

Corporatization of the world of higher education and post-secondary work has run rampant for decades, especially in the United States. Its principles are manifested in the disparity of rights and entitlements between the tenured and tenure-tracked on the one hand, and the majority (the adjunct class) on the other, to say nothing of grossly unfair pay structures. Implicit principles of collegiality and cooperation in the academic world are, however, no match for corporatization, which has transformed post-secondary education into a sphere of contradiction, inequity, and stratification. Perhaps an idealized academy left to its own devices might have created an equitable workplace system. The corporatization of post-secondary education has meant, however, that while one may speak of the idealized culture, policies, or practices of an institution, in reality those cultures, policies, and practices are driven and controlled for the most part by an administrative group. This is a group that, while paying lip service to traditional values, finds itself driven by the needs of any corporate business: bottom-line financing, maximizing flexibility in its workforce, and ensuring that management views trump those of faculty employees. Corporate management works hard to ensure that this model stays the dominant way of approaching the issues of the day.

Given the power imbalance, it is quixotic to expect corporate institutional leadership to initiate changes that would create and sustain greater equity. As it occurred in BC, change is not likely to come from the current power base of institutions; it is more likely to come from the collective power of faculty, and that change is more likely to be guided by the best principles of unionism. The establishment in BC of a college system in the 1970s, which was outside of the traditional university workplace, gave the faculty of that day the opportunity to create their own principled view of the ideal workplace. They shaped a borrowed mechanism—the separately organized and independent labor union established under the Labour Relations Code of the province. To enhance their strength and professional development as union leaders, they devoted a sizable portion of their members' dues to a provincial federation of unions, FPSE, which then hired professional staff, created a defense fund for grievance handling and strike pay, created an effective provincial lobbying mechanism, and conducted educational and skills enhancement activities.

For BC faculty, unionism—having a set of principles based on equity and workplace justice—has been vitally important. While the principles came from the union in our situation, alternative principles could conceivably be adopted from any source. Furthermore, the means to achieve and maintain change was established and resourced. Otherwise, the corporate model—competition for scarce resources, maximum workforce flexibility, and management privilege—could not have been effectively challenged. It has been the union movement, holding most closely to the principles of equity and workplace justice, that has demonstrated ways and means of achieving and maintaining change.

## *Tenure*

We advance that a primary value of this model is that it offers an alternative to tenure as the solution to the problem of contingency. Some may criticize the Vancouver model for not having true tenure. For this discussion, we restrict ourselves to defining tenure as "true" tenure—a situation where no layoff is possible unless the institution demonstrates financial exigency or absolute proof of redundancy, normally through a third-party examination. When viewed from outside the academic milieu, and leaving aside the variations in teaching workload that come with the status, being truly "tenured," with its attendant full-time, lifetime security, and good salary, amounts to a very special employment status. This extreme job security is laudable. The pursuit, however, of only that level of "purity" has, after decades of stratification, contributed to the current apartheid-like system where the majority of academic work is done by contingents at near-poverty levels of pay. Academic freedom is too often restricted to those having tenured status. While it is often asserted that academic freedom and tenure go hand-in-hand as protections and rights (Rhoades, 1996), in our view that statement alone is overly restrictive. Academic freedom can also be fully protected by having provisions in collective agreements that provide it to all faculty. Inclusion in collective agreements provides the consequential protection of due process and grievance rights under the corresponding legislation. This is the case in many BC colleges and universities that may not have true tenure provisions. If collective-agreement rights are not attainable, then while it is nowhere near as strong, institutional policy may include academic freedom for all. Some BC institutions have both. True tenure is unique to the academic world. To return to a situation where the great majority of faculty have tenure, and others have a realistic hope of tenure, would take a massive transfer of resources. It is unlikely that those in power will agree to such a transfer, let alone agree to a broadening of the extreme job security of true tenure.

The form of job security at VCC, regularization, offers a much more attainable model. From governmental and societal points of view, regularization is more consistent with the kind of job security that exists outside of post-secondary institutions. A job-security system that relies on regularization does not mean there is no protection against layoffs, nor that one cannot levy a high political cost on administrations or governments that might want to target faculty through layoffs. Such a system does not mean that anyone need go without academic freedom protection—it can be made an issue for grievance within the provisions of the collective agreement. Neither does it mean that the status of tenure would need to change. A minority deemed worthy by their peers could be granted the extraordinary job protection of being truly tenured. Those so tenured would, however—and this is laid out in the 2011 FPSE Principles and Policies for University Bargaining—not have any unique pay status. Tenure would be unlinked from special salary levels significantly above those of non-tenure—only the single scale would remain. There would seem no compelling argument for retaining the current multiplicity of salary scales; nor for tenure, which is supposed to be about academic freedom, being tarnished with the task of being the key to access to financial well-being.

Under the Vancouver model, the great majority of faculty enjoy good, family-supporting, satisfying careers with high levels of security, benefits, rights, due process, and good incomes. This model demonstrates that faculty in union situations can apply principles of equity to the post-secondary world with great success. They do not have to, and in fact cannot, rely on traditional collegial mechanisms such as senates or a presumed spirit of collegiality. Moreover, those in non-union situations can find examples of workplace rights where they can usefully target their efforts. The model demonstrates that achieving and maintaining change is not a question of trying to have better, more effective administrative policies and practices at an institution. There has been too much history of administrations exercising their right to interpret and unilaterally change policy and practice. Where unionization is possible, it is the statutory enforcement of collective agreements that ensures that standards and rights remain intact and are carried out, especially in times when it would be easier or financially expeditious for the college not to adhere to the negotiated rights.

## Progress toward Equality, with and without a Union

### Unions Can Stop Reinforcing Barriers

Where unions represent both tenured and non-tenured faculty, they have a special responsibility and opportunity to build solidarity and create numerous paths to equity. However, if they do not, if they wash their hands of their adjuncts, of working for better evaluation procedures, of extending and strengthening grievance rights, of advocating for rights to equitable workload, and ignore other opportunities for equity, then union memberships have collectively created a situation more morally fraught than even that where unionism is not possible. Those in union leadership positions bear even more responsibility. It falls to them to develop platforms and action plans based on equity; and to challenge, lead, and educate their members toward joining in the struggle for true union principles of equity. If this does not happen, then meaningful progress toward equity will continue to be rare. It is not enough just to advocate solely for pay increases, which are in themselves based on an arbitrarily unfair structure. When all-inclusive unions do not make improving the rights of their most discriminated-against members one of their top priorities, they are reenforcing corporatism.

### Union Strategies Can Be Used Outside Unions

The VCCFA workplace was achieved using the classic tools of unions: resourced bargaining, the right to take strike votes and to strike, grievance processes up to and including independent arbitration. These tools exist in a legislative and social environment in BC and Canada, which is relatively progressive and respectful of the rights of labor. However, in jurisdictions without those advantages, progress is still possible. Faculty working together can themselves choose to make their work world fairer in many different ways, even without the full suite of union rights. Any area of work where management leaves faculty with a measure of control can, and should, become an area of increasing equity, solidarity, and progress. This is where higher education has advantages which do not exist in other sectors with a high incidence of contingency, such as the service industry. Post-secondary work is an area of work where there is still a good measure of activity behind the classroom door and the department-office door that is beyond the direct control of managers. All faculty have many areas of agency and choice.

The best principles of unionism and the concrete examples of the Vancouver model can provide a guide to other institutions, whether or not an academic workplace is supported by a faculty union. Those interested in real change toward equality could start by reckoning with the following questions: Why should scrupulous attention to the best practices as set out in the evaluation literature not be used to evaluate adjuncts? Why should class allocation controlled by departments not be done on the basis of either very limited overtime (a right that should be eliminated with the passage of time) or no overtime at all for tenured department members? Why can it not be done for adjuncts on the basis of seniority rights to work? Why should adjuncts not have academic freedom protected by enforceable due process? Why should senior tenured faculty act as if they were also corporatized managers when it comes to their dealings with contingent faculty? Everyone committed to reducing inequity can make progress based on principles similar to the best of union culture and make real improvements in the lives of faculty who cannot access the superior tenure-track. This is especially true in non-cost areas such as evaluation, work allocation, and inclusion in fair and transparent departmental processes.

### Faculty Should Change What They Have the Power to Change

Where unionization is not currently possible, and even where it is, there are many areas of faculty control where little except a lack of will and guidance prevents more equitable practices being implemented. Perfection should not be the enemy of the possible. Areas for change within faculty control (such as inclusion in departmental decision making or changes in hiring practice) can be targeted, best practices can be taught and learned, small gains can be celebrated. Gains will in turn create incentives for further change.

## Program for Change

Based in large measure on the system in the VCC/VCCFA collective agreement and throughout BC, the authors have devised a schema for progress on over 30 aspects of post-secondary work. It is called the Program for Change (either at http://newfacultymajority.info/PfC/ or http://vccfa.ca/program-for-change/index.html). It breaks down many aspects of post-secondary work, such as fair evaluation or the right to re-appointment, into attainable stages and marks them over four five-year increments so that any group has benchmarks for measuring what progress it has made over a 20-year period. Higher education institutions and change agents can use the Program for Change to implement incremental changes toward greater equity.

Benchmarks are grouped according to provisions that require either no cost or nominal initial cost, a sample of which is shown in Table 3.8. Those that would drive institutional costs, such as compensation, are shown in Table 3.9. Examples of what faculty unions and associations could do are given in Table 3.10. Potential legislative milestones are shown in Table 3.11.

Every and any aspect of work can be improved. It is not just a single-minded focus on true tenure and salary that can make a difference. The authors propose

**TABLE 3.8** Example from Program for Change:[2] Non-cost or Incidental One-time Costs

| | 2010 | +5 | +10 | +15 | +20 |
|---|---|---|---|---|---|
| | | **Non-cost or Incidental One-time Costs** *No reduction in Rights for any Tenured or TT Person* *All rights are subject to grievance or other dispute resolution processes* | | | |
| NC1 Human rights: No discrimination No harassment, personal or sexual | | Upon first hire. Protected by grievance procedures or due institutional process; not connected to time-status. | | | |
| NC2 Academic freedom | | Protected by grievance procedures or due institutional process; not connected to time-status. | From first hire for all | | |
| NC3 Hiring | | Departmentally-based processes; transparent, set procedures | One process for all | | |
| NC4 Reappointment rights during probationary period | | Reappointment by seniority, as long as no unsuccessful evaluation | Rights retained for set period after last appointment | | |
| NC5 Seniority rights | | Right to seniority from first hire Right to seniorityaccrual Seniority retention between appointments Seniority List published annually | For regularized/normalized, equal part-time seniority accrual to full-timers' accrual Retention after layoff | | |
| NC6 Summative Evaluation | | Fair, tranparent process At most once a year during probationary period Only two needed for regularization | Summative evaluation done during probationary period; afterwards only if serious complaints | | |

*Natural rights*

*Rights during hiring and probationary period*

*Source:* Program for Change.

**TABLE 3.9** Example from Program for Change: Cost Issues

| | | 2010 | +5 | +10 | +15 | +20 |
|---|---|---|---|---|---|---|
| | | **Cost Issues** | | | | |
| Recog of Exp / Training | C1 Initial placement | | Fair criteria and formula for determination | Reduction in barriers to placement on scale | Continued reduction of barriers | Removal of barriers |
| Right to Equal Pay and Equal Work | C2 Step accrual | | Establishment of pro-rata increment equivalents | Pro-rata progression on scale | | Year-by-year progression |
| | C3 Scales | | Reduction in number of scales and numbers of steps | Continued reduction | | One scale with as few steps as possible |
| | C4 Compensation | | At least 50% of lowest TT or tenured rank (No contingent rate lower than 50% of the lowest TT or tenured rank) | At least 60% | At least 80% | One scale |
| | C5 Workload | | Include office hours & meeting times | Include options of research and service; with flexibility of choice | Fully pro-rata | |
| Rights to Professionalism | C6 Professional development time | | At least one week of paid time for all, pro-rata for part-timers | Up to two weeks | Up to one month | |
| | C7 Professional development funds | | | Spending allowance for those getting PD time | | |
| | C8 Education leaves & sabbaticals | | | | Equitable access to all, including part-timers | |

*Source*: Program for Change.

**TABLE 3.10** Example from Program for Change: Union and Association Rights and Support

| | | 2010 | +5 | +10 | +15 | +20 |
|---|---|---|---|---|---|---|
| | | **Union and Association Rights and Support** | | | | |
| Union and Association Rights | U1 | Union or association equity | Equal union or association membership by person with voice and vote, part of election processes | | | |
| | U2 | Union or association support | Establishment of contingent rights committees with majority of contingent members; up to 0.5% of total budget dedicated to contingent committees and advocacy (e.g., travel, registration, research) | Between 0.5% and 1.0% of total budget. | | |
| | U3 | Right to strike | Establish procedure of legally recognized collective bargaining agent to file to hold a strike vote | Enable ability to call for strike votes and conduct strikes | | |

Source: Program for Change.


**TABLE 3.11** Example from Program for Change: Legislation

| | | | | | | |
|---|---|---|---|---|---|---|
| | | **Legislation** | | | | |
| Legislation | L1 | Legislation: unemployment insurance | Breaks between contingent workeligible for UI, with institutional support and advocacy | Unfettered UI eligibility | | |
| | L2 | Legislation: pensions | | Equitable access to plans | Fully pro-rata inclusion | |
| | L3 | Legislation: remove restrictions on strikes | Legalized right of legal unions to call strikes | | | |

Source: Program for Change.

making any workplace better aspect by aspect, incrementally getting closer to the best features for all employees so that the gap between unfairness and equality becomes more and more narrow and therefore more bridgeable.

The approach undertaken by the Program for Change differs from the predominant approach proposed to reform U.S. higher education, which has for years relied on proposing new full-time tenure-track appointments as the cornerstone of improvement. That goal, while worthy at face value, does little to help the majority of educators who are teaching off the tenure-track. It fails to deal with the reality that employers, whether public or private, are unlikely to agree to start change by extending tenured job security to the majority of their employees with the significantly higher salaries and reduced teaching loads that come with tenured status. The Program for Change proposes realistic ways to improve the working conditions of non-tenured faculty so that their working lives will actually start to improve. Change needs to start; it will take decades to accomplish. (See Figure 3.1 for a diagram of VCC's change over the years.)

| MOBILIZATION | IMPLEMENTATION | INSTITUTIONALIZATION |
|---|---|---|
| • Unionization<br>• VCCFA through 10 rounds of principled bargaining | • Set of policies advanced over time through VCCFA and constituents | • One salary scale<br>• Pro-rata workload<br>• No overtime<br>• Automatic regularization<br>• Workload allocation by seniority<br>• Ensuring transparency<br>• Rights to benefits and entitlements<br>• Full participation in institutional governance, departmental processes, and union business |

FIGURE 3.1 Overlay of three-stage model with Vancouver Community College's progress toward change.

## Key Points:

1. We need a new paradigm for non-tenure track faculty to bring about change. The Vancouver model provides one such model for shifting our paradigm.
2. Long-term planning is essential and an overarching change agenda such as the authors' Program for Change. In the United States, we have not had sustained staffing or faculty plans.

3.  Union strategies of data collection, consciousness raising, agenda building, creating fora for collective action, identifying allies, leveraging outside groups can all be used outside the union context.

4.  Tenure-track and non-tenure track unions should support each other and united faculty potentially have more power together. Meaningful solidarity can be advanced through workplace provisions like those established at VCC.

5.  Principles and values can be powerful drivers of change. The Vancouver model was first based on defining a set of principles to guide action and policy. But the VCCFA example reminds us that actions speak louder than words, and values need to be translated into new policies and practices.

6.  Non-tenure track faculty policies are just as important as trying to fight for more tenure-track lines. But in the United States, most of the energy is focused on trying to obtain more tenure-track lines, which is becoming decreasingly possible or even normative. There needs to be more balance and focus on non-tenure track equity.

7.  In the United States, tenure is widely considered key for academic freedom, yet some feel that tenure has resulted in an apartheid-like bifurcation of faculty into "haves" and "have nots." In the British Columbian FPSE practice and policy and in the proposals contained in the Program for Change, tenure is retained but disassociated from compensation, while job security and academic freedom provisions are bargained independently of tenure.

8.  At VCC, almost all faculty are either regularized or on track to become regularized.

9.  Full-time and part-time status does not determine the workload one is assigned. Faculty may be assigned the same work; the part-time non-teaching workload (e.g., office hours) is prorated.

## Key Questions:

1.  Is our campus thinking about non-tenure track faculty work in a dramatically different way or just tinkering with existing policies? How might a bolder vision or model create better possibilities for a successful model?

2.  Are we thinking about non-tenure track faculty policies and practices within a long-term scheme and campus plan or merely looking at short-term needs?

3.  Are we looking at important changes that are not as all-encompassing as ending contingency, that might vastly improve the working life for non-tenure track faculty—such aspects as using more professional evaluation procedures, or using seniority for allocating and scheduling of appointments, or including contingents in the work of unions, associations, and departments?

4. If we are not unionized, are we considering union strategies that might still work even within our non-union context?

5. Are tenure-track and non-tenure track faculty working together to create change? If there are disagreements, what type of conversations might bring us to working toward consensus about goals?

6. Have we developed a compelling set of principles and values to support our change effort? How might the VCC model help us in crafting our principles?

7. Are we focused enough on non-tenure track faculty policies and practices and not just on the erosion of tenure? How can we see the collective needs of faculty as one issue?

8. In the United States, non-tenure track faculty are not paid according to the same salary schedule as tenured instructors. What justification is there for this difference? Would the VCCFA agree with those reasons?

9. From the standpoint of institutions, a chief advantage of non-tenured faculty who can be hired and fired "at will" is the flexibility they offer, since the institution is under no obligation to rehire them, unlike tenured faculty. What explanation is there for how faculty at VCC, and other colleges whose faculty are organized by the FPSE of BC, were able to win job security?

10. How does VCC justify paying its full-time faculty and its part-time faculty according to the same salary schedule? How does that differ from the U.S. standard?

11. From the standpoint of the student, do tenured instructors and non-tenured instructors perform different work?

12. Employees such as custodians or clerical personnel, after a probationary period, become regular employees. Why are contingent faculty members in the United States not treated the same way?

13. Many faculty unions in the United States are dominated by tenured faculty interests. How has the VCCFA avoided this domination from its full-time regularized faculty?

## Notes

1 In 2011, FPSE ratified a new policy statement on Principles and Policies for University Bargaining which can be found on its website (www.fpse.ca).

2 Tables 3.8, 3.9, 3.10, and 3.11 are exact replicas of Program for Change documents, in terms of *content*: they have been edited for *style* with permission of the authors.

## References

American Federation of Teachers Higher Education. (2010). *American academic: A national survey of part-time/adjunct faculty*. Washington, DC: American Federation of Teachers.

Gappa, J. M., & Leslie, D. W. (1993). *The invisible faculty: Improving the status of part-timers in higher education*. San Francisco: Jossey-Bass.

Hollenshead, C., Waltman, J., August, L., Miller, J., Smith, G., & Bell, A. (2007). *Making the best of both worlds: Findings from a national institution-level survey on non-tenure track faculty*. Ann Arbor, MI: Center for the Education of Women.

June, A. W. (2010, July 25). A Canadian college where adjuncts go to prosper. *Chronicle of Higher Education, 56*(41). Retrieved from http://chronicle.com/article/A-Canadian-College-Where/123629/.

Longmate, J., & Cosco, F. (2002, May 3). Part-time instructors deserve equal pay for equal work. *Chronicle of Higher Education, 48*(34), B14. Retrieved from http://chronicle.com/article/Part-Time-Instructors-Deserve/23489/

Nelson, C. (2010). *No university is an island: Saving academic freedom*. New York, NY: New York University Press.

Rhoades, G. (1996). Reorganizing the faculty workforce for flexibility: Part-time professional labor. *Journal of Higher Education, 67*(6), 626–659.

# 4

# TAKING A MULTIFACETED APPROACH TO CHANGE

## Madison Area Technical College

*Nancy McMahon*

Madison Area Technical College (MATC), a two-year technical and community college in south central Wisconsin, operates at 10 locations and offers more than 140 associate degree, technical diploma, short-term certificate and apprenticeship programs, liberal arts transfer classes, basic skills and high-school completion options, and many adult continuing education opportunities. The college enrolls 40,000 total students annually with 24,000 students in degree programs. A surprising 96 percent of graduates remain in the state after graduation. The district includes about 726,000 residents in 12 counties, 40 school districts, and 224 cities, towns, and villages (see http://matcmadison.edu/facts-glance for more information). The college employs about 1,500 part-time faculty and around 465 full-time faculty.

In the early 1970s, most MATC faculty were full-time teachers who were represented since the 1930s by a union, the American Federation of Teachers (AFT) Local 243, part of the AFT in Wisconsin. As the college grew from the 1970s to the present, very few full-time faculty positions were added. Additional courses were taught by ever-increasing numbers of part-time faculty which led to the organization in 1996 of the MATC Part-Time Teachers' Union, AFT Local 6100. Prior to the development of the AFT-Local 6100 collective bargaining agreement (CBA), most college departments and campuses operated as isolated fiefdoms with inconsistencies in hiring part-time faculty, assigning courses to part-time faculty, providing teaching support, and paying part-time faculty. Working conditions for non-tenure track faculty varied markedly. As the part-time faculty union negotiated an initial contract (starting in 1996), some administrators privately appealed to the union to request certain language for much-needed uniformity across the college. For example, the phrase "part-time teachers' working conditions are the students' learning conditions"

**TABLE 4.1** Institutional Snapshot of Madison Area Technical College

| | |
|---|---|
| Institutional type | Two-year technical college |
| Student population | 40,000 |
| Unionized | Yes |
| State | Wisconsin |
| % of non-tenure track | Over 50% (But "tenure" is not a term used at technical colleges. On the AAUP survey information, for example, it may say there is no tenure; however, full-time faculty have union contracts for several years at a time and cannot be fired without cause once they pass probation of three years.) |
| Institutionalization phase | Institutionalization |
| Main changes | Orientation; mentoring; course documentation prior to teaching; multi-year contracts; governance; professional development; pay for office hours, service, and training; evaluation; office space |

(used throughout the United States in adjunct/part-time/contingent faculty support efforts) helped MATC acknowledge a need for change.

In this chapter, I review several critical aspects that led to needed changes as well as describing the changes we were able to accomplish. The main strategies I highlight are data collection, strategic planning, accreditation, best practices by model departments, and the union. The chapter is not organized chronologically, but divided into these key strategies. Collective efforts by the administration, faculty, and the union achieved several critical programs, such as mentoring, orientation, and better pay, through their comprehensive approach of working together. However, there are challenges to including initiatives involving part-time faculty that MATC experienced as well. Teaching at the college since 1973, I have had the time and opportunity to view many different approaches and the pros and cons of each approach.

## Use of Data Collection and Strategic Planning to Change the College Culture

Administrators at MATC recognized the need for solid data in order to instigate change. To establish a baseline for measurement of the college environment, MATC began using The National Initiative for Leadership and Institutional Effectiveness (NILIE) survey and the Personal Assessment of the College Environment (PACE) in 1996. The college has repeated the PACE survey every three years in the spring from 1996 through to 2008. In this survey, the college climate can range from 1 to 5, with 1 representing a coercive climate and 5 representing a collaborative climate (see Table 4.2). The trend in MATC's overall PACE mean scores is shown in Table 4.3.

**TABLE 4.2** Personal Assessment of the College Environment (PACE) Survey Descriptors

| Range | Climate |
|-------|---------|
| 4–5 | Collaborative |
| 3–4 | Consultative |
| 2–3 | Competitive |
| 1–2 | Coercive |

**TABLE 4.3** MATC's PACE scores 1996–2008

| Year | 1996 | 1999 | 2002 | 2005 | 2008 |
|------|------|------|------|------|------|
| Overall Mean Score | 3.39 | 3.48 | 3.46 | 3.66 | 3.40 |

Madison Area Technical College experienced an upward employee satisfaction trend since 1996, but the score went down in the 2008 survey after an administrative reorganization at the college. Data provided a view of increasing employee satisfaction when the college administration embraced an attitude of increased inclusion for all faculty, staff, and administrators in establishing college policies and making college decisions. The PACE survey results reflected the faculty and staff satisfaction because their input was being valued by the administration.

The data collection set the stage for a strategic planning process. In November 1999, the MATC district board adopted three core institutional values of *excellence, respect, and integrity*. Strategic planning included the formation of Strategic Initiative Excellence Team 3 (SIET), which gathered information from many sources and developed the college's values statement. The college president, along with her team, organized a series of "values at work conversation sessions," held during in-service time in January 2002. These sessions included *all* college employees and provided a time and venue as an important part "of MATC's efforts to create and support the best possible work culture for our learning community" (Simone, 2001). The college core values are listed and explained in the following link: http://matcmadison.edu/madison-area-technical-colleges-strategic-values. These values were important as they launched the college on a reflective process about how we should work together. For example, the value of respect became important when looking at the culture between tenure-track and non-tenure track faculty. In addition, the value of excellence became a critical lever when highlighting non-tenure track faculty's more limited ability to perform based on their lack of access to key resources such as professional development, (paid) time to connect and align curriculum with other teachers of the same courses, and forming collegial bonds within departments.

## College Inclusion of Part-time Faculty Due to AQIP Accreditation System

Increased teaching support for part-time faculty has evolved due to the college's 2001 adoption and implementation of the Academic Quality Improvement Project (AQIP), part of the Higher Learning Commission of the North Central Association of Colleges and Schools (NCA—the accreditation agency in the Midwest). The Academic Quality Improvement Project consists of ongoing self-assessment with focus areas determined after a series of "vital focus conversations" with all parts of the college. Largely due to the 2002 spring-break schedule, no full-time faculty from the college, but rather three part-time faculty were included in the team that attended an AQIP conference in Chicago. Once those part-time faculty learned at the AQIP conference that *all* faculty, staff, and administrators of an institution of higher learning were to be included in the decisions about the college's self-assessment, there was no excluding them from the process.

The required input from everyone at the college in the "vital focus conversa-tions" resulted in a collection of 169 action-project ideas that were pared down to seven and then to four action projects for MATC. Fortunately for the part-time faculty, this resulted in an action-project goal titled "Equivalent instructional support for part-time instructors." The AQIP 4 project team was given *the goal to create and implement a systematic process of including all part-time instructors as valued partners in the work of the college.* A team of nine administrators, four part-time faculty, two full-time faculty, two support staff, one coordinator/ note-taker, and one outside facilitator worked through 2005. Year One estab-lished ground rules to encourage open, honest dialogue around sensitive issues. Use of an outside facilitator was essential because of the distrust within the faculty that the college administration would not be objective, or impartial, and possess the level of integrity to facilitate true change. Part-time faculty were not only included but were also paid for their committee time. Receiving compensation was significant: Prior to this time, part-time faculty who served on college com-mittees were unpaid volunteers, even though all others at the table were working as part of their salaried time.

There were bumps in the road. Part of the way through the first year of regular meetings, one part-time teacher noticed a decrease in his meeting pay. His resulting inquiry revealed that payroll staff had been instructed to compensate the part-time faculty on the team at a lower pay level. Heated discussion ensued at the next AQIP 4 meeting, especially when the rest of the team learned that the human resources administrator on their team had chosen to reduce the pay rate for the part-time teachers without consulting anyone. The administrator failed to justify his action, and this pay reduction incident provided a sterling example of typical unprofessional treatment of part-time faculty at the college, cementing the case for the necessity of this AQIP 4 team, and use of an independent facilitator. Dismayed by the behavior of the culpable administrator, others on the committee discussed the lack of professionalism, and the lack of the college's core values of excellence, respect, and integrity. Furthermore, the part–time teacher who had noticed his pay reduction was highly respected in the city and county for his professional and civic work, a senior citizen who also happened to be a former MATC board member. The human resources administrator did not live in the city or county and was unaware of the part–time teacher's civic record. Part–time faculty's local connections are often unknown or overlooked by administrators who could use this strength to MATC's benefit.

The first year of the AQIP 4 project resulted in articulation of the team's shared understanding of the professionalism of part–time faculty and the need—across the district and across disciplines—for equal support for them. Year Two of AQIP 4 formalized the cradle-to-grave concept in the life cycle of a part–time teacher. Six steps were identified in the life cycle of part–time faculty in order to attract, support, and retain them: recruit, hire, support, perform, assess and develop, and terminate or continue. As home to a Big Ten university, Madison has a large number of well-educated people, so recruiting and hiring were not difficult. Supporting teaching needed attention and has been addressed successfully by the college. Assessment did not exist, but now is in place. The "terminate or continue" step depends on the teaching needs of the college, so part–time faculty have no assurance that their investment of time and energy will be rewarded with ongoing teaching assignments. While fluctuating enrollment does have some effect, many of the part–time positions could be contracted for a number of years, providing for more stability and continuity. For example, a small number of continuing part–time teachers may have other responsibilities such as becoming mentors, improving the curriculum, serving on college committees, and/or professionally contributing to their disciplines, but many part–time faculty are simply not re-hired or become discouraged and take other employment. Madison Area Technical College has about a one-third turnover rate of part–time faculty each fall. To my knowledge, there is no exit interview policy and there never has been.

Many, many issues involving part–time faculty were examined by AQIP 4, but time and practicality led to the selection of the "low-hanging fruit." The result, at the end of two years of work, was distilled into *four policies* presented to the college council for approval and implementation. (Other more complex issues were saved for future attention.)

1.  *All college faculty will have the opportunity to attend an orientation session prior to the time they begin teaching at the college.* Implemented and now institutional-ized, orientation meetings are offered in both day and evening hours with much of the information available online as well. A general new-faculty orientation is provided by the Center for Excellence in Teaching and Learning (CETL), the various campuses hold orientation sessions, and some of the academic divisions like Arts and Sciences hold additional orientation

sessions, depending on the number of part-time faculty in various disciplines and programs.

2. *All newly hired college faculty will be offered a mentoring relationship with an experienced faculty member.* The mentoring program has been highly praised by new-faculty participants. Part-time faculty are mentored by experienced part-time faculty teaching the same courses, if at all possible. Both part-time faculty mentors and mentees are paid US$250 a semester after submitting documentation (CETL form, available online) of their mentoring activities. Full-time faculty may mentor full-time or part-time faculty as part of their "service" (a percentage of their workload), as defined in their union contract.

3. *All part-time faculty will be provided with available course documentation prior to teaching a particular course.* Envisioned as an online portfolio or DVD for each college course, this has yet effectively to take place with only a small number of course portfolios available to newly hired faculty. A 2009 *Course Portfolio Final Report* outlined all aspects of the project, explained the processes developed by the committee, and proposed a curriculum review day once a year to coordinate materials and post updates on department Blackboard (internet instructional) sites. In reality, however, ownership of the portfolio project is still struggling to take root in the culture of the college. Online data (see http://matcmadison.edu/in/course-portfolios-madison-college) indicate a number of available portfolios, but such information about many courses still does not exist, or portfolios are incomplete as of early 2011. Reasons range from faculty reluctance to share teaching materials to lack of time for course committees to collect and approve portfolio materials. Online maintenance is also an issue.

4. *The Center for Excellence in Teaching and Learning (CETL) will be responsible for the professional development needs of part-time faculty.* The Center for Excellence in Teaching and Learning is absolutely the stellar service at MATC. Blessed with a director possessing a multitude of "people skills" and administrative talents, CETL has grown to provide orientation (a component of policy No. 1), the mentoring program (part of policy No. 2), and most importantly, the professional development opportunities for faculty and staff. The Wisconsin Technical College System (WTCS) has faculty certification requirements (see http://systemattic.wtcsystem.edu/certification/default. htm). Technical college teachers must be state certifiable (yes, there are many jokes about this) or be certified, or there are financial penalties for the college. Part-time faculty are often hired at the last minute, so they are allowed to teach with the understanding that they will begin taking the necessary courses to become certified instructors. However, part-time faculty are paid too little to live on their income from their limited teaching (at any one college), so other employment restricts their ability to attend classes for certification. In response to the diverse scheduling needs of part-time faculty,

CETL offers courses in-house, online, by blended delivery, and in a variety of time formats—evenings, weekends, summer condensed sessions, etc.

After the college approved the recommended four policies, the administration disengaged, relegating many of the tougher problems itemized by the AQIP 4 team to some file for later study. Management disbanded the original team, replacing it with a learner success part-time faculty advisory council, and the independent facilitator was dismissed, so his objectivity and honest appraisal of the situation were lost.

The associate vice-president in charge of part-time faculty support services was named to chair the learner success part-time faculty advisory council to address the implementation of the four major part-time faculty policies recommended by the AQIP 4 team. Members included nine part-time faculty, including the president of the part-time teachers' union and two administrators. The council met six times a year, three times in each fall and spring term. The purpose, charge, and scope of the council were consistent with the AQIP 4 mission to garner increased institutional support for part-time faculty. However, this council stopped meeting during the 2010–2011 school year by order of the college president in response to the part-time teachers bargaining for a new contract.

In a related accreditation area, part-time faculty have served on review teams for the learning systems quality improvement process (LSQIP) within the college. This is a self-assessment of learning programs and college services that is aligned with AQIP principles. Several part-time faculty have represented their departments as reviewers of LSQIP portfolios, submitted according to a designated format with a variety of information about the services or programs in the college. Reviewers read the portfolios, write responses according to a specific format, and attend meetings between representatives of the programs or services and the LSQIP review team. The reading, writing, and meeting time is compensated at an hourly rate for the part-time faculty. Others on the review teams are salaried administrators and full-time faculty who serve on the committee as part of their service to the college. Inclusion of part-time faculty on college accreditation committees has led to better understanding of teacher-scheduling difficulties and consistency-of-instruction issues in the programs under review. The college changed the LSQIP to a revised system in the summer of 2011.

## Arts and Sciences and English Department Best Practices

In this section, I highlight how certain units were helpful as change agents by adopting key practices and making these visible to others on campus. Prior to 1996, the Arts and Sciences Division (now called the Center for Arts and Science) and the English department were helpful to part-time faculty in marked contrast to some other areas of the college. Arts and Sciences (A&S) serves about 10,000 students a year, many in entry-level courses taught by part-time faculty.

With a one-third to one-half turnover of part-time faculty in some areas of A&S, the deans established an orientation for new part-time faculty. Arts and Sciences developed a faculty handbook, provided orientation each semester, and even supported (or reluctantly allowed) part-time faculty to attend conferences in the early 1990s. These best practices were then encouraged across the college, but some departments and disciplines resisted when directed to provide professional inclusion. Without continual institutional support, the culture change is difficult. An example of the difficulty in spreading best practices through the college occurred a few years ago with "critical literacy" and "writing across the curriculum" initiatives supported through A&S. These initiatives were very helpful to students and ran throughout the college for several years as funding and release time permitted. Unfortunately, as funding shifted to other areas and the faculty who participated in those initiatives retired or left the college, those programs, though still needed, have disappeared.

The English department, which is part of A&S, has about 25 full-time and over 50 part-time teachers listed on the department email list. Only one campus has a majority of full-time faculty; seven campuses have almost all part-time faculty. The increasing numbers of English part-time faculty, along with the turnover rate, led to the need for measures to provide uniform instruction across the discipline, resulting in part-time faculty inclusion on departmental committees for course areas taught by both full-time and part-time faculty.

The English department adopted a 2007 constitution that establishes proportional voting rights for part-time faculty. The department has some funds for conference attendance each year, so when the full-time faculty indicate their intention to attend conferences, one spot is set aside for part-time faculty. If the funding is US$500 per person toward conference attendance, part-time faculty have US$500 to split among those who wish to attend conferences. This has sometimes resulted in the money being split two ways, or into very small amounts if several part-time teachers request funds. However, the mere recognition of part-time faculty has been better than nothing, which was the previous practice. Another more recent practice has been for A&S to pay for membership (US$5 annually) to the Two-Year College (English) Association Midwest (TYCA), for all the part-time English teachers who wish to join. For a number of years, several part-time faculty have attended TYCA conferences and presented sessions.

Another full-time/part-time English faculty endeavor is a monthly *Best Practices* meeting. One Friday per month, an hour and a half of paid meeting time is devoted to best practices of teaching with a focus on a particular aspect like grade norming, combating plagiarism, certain teaching techniques, etc. Full-time faculty who helped to establish and maintain this group have received some service credit toward the service percentage of their CBA agreement. The English department also sponsors a *Faculty Excellence Workshop (FEW)*, another monthly meeting for part-time faculty (and full-time faculty if they choose to attend).

The FEW meets for three hours one Friday each month, with time to check papers and/or work on class preparation individually, followed by discussion of classroom management issues or other teaching-related matters. This workshop provides some paid time for checking the many papers that part-time faculty must assign when teaching their many sections of entry-level writing courses. The heavy paper load required of writing teachers has never been adequately compensated, but the FEW is at least a small acknowledgment that this workload disparity exists within the discipline. Several of the full-time faculty began at MATC as part-time faculty, and they are sympathetic to the part-time faculty who teach identical courses to themselves, but receive a fraction of the compensation. (Salaries of all employees at the college can be found at the following website: http://intranet.matcmadison.edu/salary-report/.)

## Part-Time Teachers' Union Role

The union provided a pivotal strategy for creating a stronger faculty voice which helped initiate the changes obtained through strategic planning, accreditation, and data collection. As wages stagnated and the numbers of part-time faculty increased in the early 1990s, the need for a voice was increasing, so with the help of the Wisconsin Federation of Teachers and the MATC Full-Time Teachers' Union (AFT Local 243), our stand-alone Part-Time Teachers' Union (AFT Local 6100) was organized. (A certain faction of the full-time union faculty worried about being outvoted by the many part-timers, so did not want a blended union.) Before the organizing vote, the college board chair sent all part-time faculty a letter asking that they "keep in mind the things that Madison Area Technical College has done voluntarily for you…It has always been our policy to be fair and equitable and to provide excellent working conditions" (Magnuson, 1996). Since the college had done nothing voluntarily for part-time faculty, and pay and working conditions were far from fair and equitable, the vote was 301 in favor of the union with 145 against. Relations were strained.

The next two and a half years were spent negotiating the first collective bargaining agreement (CBA). Prior to having a contract, each division, department, and/or campus operated with little uniformity across the college regarding treatment of part-timers as exemplified in the model departments. Prior to the first CBA, part-time faculty were asked to sign a one-paragraph agreement to work for the college for the school year. Signers could have been directed to drive the van, mop floors, or teach. Now teachers receive letters of agreement stating specific course assignments, dates, location(s), and compensation. The CBAs have been for a time span of two or three years, and none have been ratified before the expiration dates of previous agreements. The college separately bargains with three Locals, the full-time teachers, the support staff, and the part-time teachers, who have routinely come last in the scheduling of negotiations. Part-time faculty have the last spot on the bargaining calendar after the other unions have their contracts completed. Part-time faculty receive whatever funds are left to be distributed after the full-time faculty, administrators, and support staff have their pay and benefits approved by the MATC board.

Local 6100 conducts surveys of all part-time faculty in the bargaining unit several months prior to the expiration date of each CBA. Only once has the college worked on a joint survey, and that was not with the current administration (i.e., since the new president in 2004). After ranking the issues of importance according to survey results, the bargaining team (a group representing the campuses and disciplines with large numbers of part-time faculty) develops proposals for negotiation. Initially, there was nothing for the union actually to "bargain" because the union had nothing, but over the years, the contract has grown from pamphlet to booklet size. The Local 6100 CBA, however, is still just a fraction of the size of the full-time faculty CBA.

Since 1996, CBA advances have codified and unified language about salary/ wages and working conditions across the college. As previously mentioned, some administrators would meet with team members individually and off the record to promote some language that would make both parties' lives easier. Fearing for their own reputations (and perhaps job security), the administrators wanted the union to propose the language. Now the CBA defines probation as six semesters, provides a grievance procedure, and addresses absences and leaves along with many other items.

Additional work for the college—that is, work beyond classroom instruction—is now defined and compensated according to CBA language. As the college has grown in terms of student enrollments and few full-time faculty have been hired, there is a need for part-time faculty to serve on committees, develop the curriculum, and perform other professional duties. Salaried full-time faculty have 20 percent of their workload defined as service and 10 percent allocated for professional development. Prior to CBA language, many part-time faculty were expected to donate their time to the college in these areas. The union president appoints/approves all part-time faculty who serve on college councils or committees. There is a bimonthly meeting between the union leadership and management to discuss issues before they become official grievances.

The 2007–2009 CBA established a professional development fund for use by part-time faculty who often were excluded from departmental or center funding. A CETL committee of part-time faculty now reviews and approves part-time faculty applications for professional development funding of up to US$500 a year for continuing education tuition, professional conference participation, or professional examination fees or other activities.

With the offering of more diverse methods of course delivery, the college has assigned more online and blended-delivery courses to part-time faculty. As regards technology training and compensation for it, CBA language is continually in review due to ongoing problems of uneven and insufficient technical support for part-time faculty. Full-time faculty are provided with MATC computers and phones, while part-time faculty are generally expected to supply their own laptops, software, and phones.

Pay has improved since the union was formed. Compensation for teaching academic courses is now paid by the course instead of hourly rates based on face-to-face contact time. However, the difference between the pay for full-time instruction and part-time instruction has grown at an alarming rate. Faculty teach identical courses, but are paid very different amounts. See Figure 4.1 for full-time and part-time faculty pay comparison. Such disparity has been in the fore-front of the most recent negotiations and mediation. The last CBA expired on July 1, 2009 and the next CBA has yet to be ratified as of February 2011.

## Institutional Inclusion of Part-time Faculty: Becoming Part of the College Culture

The various strategies described above are leading to a culture change on campus that allows for new changes to happen that would not have been fathomed in

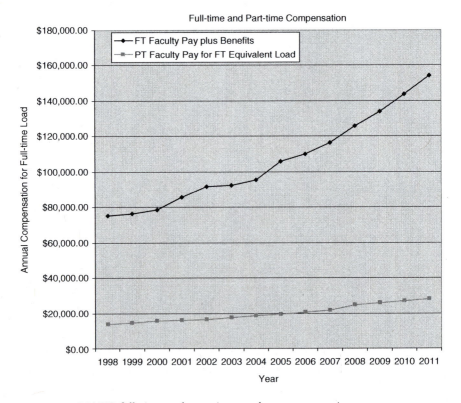

**FIGURE 4.1** MATC full-time and part-time teacher pay comparison
*Source*: Mike Kent, president, MATC Part-Time Teachers' Union.

earlier years. Prior to 1996, there was little or no institutional inclusion of part-time faculty. Gradually, with some administrators showing more foresight and wisdom than others, part-time faculty have increasingly become part of the fabric of the college. Students deserve equal education from all faculty, so the campuses with almost all part-time faculty strive, with some difficulty, to provide services and retain quality faculty. There is some scant progress. From formerly having no office space, part-time faculty now have limited communal office space provided at most college locations. The sheer numbers of part-time faculty with nowhere to work have necessitated the college finding or developing shared office space. More than 400 part-time faculty teach at the main campus which provides office space with 13 desks with computers. The downtown campus with over 100 part-time faculty provides an office with half a dozen spaces. The (newest) South Madison facility has seven desks/computers for over 50 part-time faculty in a room that also serves as storage and catch-all for that campus's supplies and equipment. However, by providing even this limited office space, the college at least acknowledges the needs of part-time faculty.

In the pursuit of "excellence," the college had to address part-time teacher evaluation. New 2007–2009 CBA language about part-time teacher evaluation (no system existed previously) led the college to establish the human resources office of part-time faculty support and services with four full-time administrators to observe teaching by probationary part-time faculty and to help them develop lesson plans and presentation skills (see http://matcmadison.edu/announce ments/part-time-faculty-support-and-services). A plethora of information for part-time teachers is now on the college website at: http://matcmadison.edu/in/ part-time-faculty.

As the college culture has moved toward the previously mentioned AQIP continuous quality improvement model, the part-time teachers' union president now has a seat on the college council. Part-time faculty member participation on college councils and committees has evolved, with a sample list below:

1. academic policy, planning, and implementation;
2. economic workforce development;
3. learner preparedness and success;
4. lifelong learning;
5. Madison College environmentally sustainable alliance;
6. learner success technology council;
7. intercultural council;
8. Americans with Disabilities Act work team;
9. learner success part-time faculty advisory council.

These committees and councils were each charged with college problems to solve or issues to address by working as teams, with specific time frames depending on the projects and type of project management. Projects ranged from college involvement in community efforts (e.g., environmental, or workforce development) to specific student issues.

The increase of office space, the implementation of professional review and assessment of part-time teachers, and paid inclusion of part-time teachers on college committees illustrate the college's culture shift toward recognition of part-time faculty as part of the permanent fabric of the institution.

## Ongoing Challenges

Culture shifts are possible, but follow-through and maintenance are the challenge. From 1996 to about 2009, Madison Area Technical College clearly was embracing the AQIP principles to improve the college environment. Students were receiving more uniform instruction than ever before, and part-time teachers were more fully included in all parts of the institution. However, the learner success part-time faculty advisory council ceased meeting at the direction of the college president when there were complications during collective bargaining in 2010. The current college administration has flattened the power structure and has reduced regard for the AQIP guiding principle of valuing people. The three core institutional values of excellence, respect, and integrity are still on the website, but are less evident within the college. Various college committees and councils that were established as part of AQIP efforts for more inclusion of all faculty and staff at the college have been suspended, reorganized, or have ceased to exist. The college council has stopped meeting. The current college president is not supportive of shared governance. The 2011 Personal Assessment of the College Environment (PACE) survey has been delayed, without a definite date for the next round. Until 2008, PACE results were shared with the employees while the culture was moving toward the top rating of *collaborative*. After a decade of improvement, the 2008 college environment score, however, was closer to the 1996 base score (see Table 4.3 above). Faculty and staff are distressed by college leaders who focus more on marketing than academic issues. Positions in the promotional areas have been added, but full-time faculty positions do not increase. While individuals within the college remain committed to the core values and strive for more faculty inclusion and the quality of the educational environment, the current top-down style of administration has imperiled the forward motion for inclusion and support of part-time faculty. However, the progress need not be lost; with the efforts of an active board of trustees, dedicated faculty, and progressive administrators, Madison Area Technical College will be able to overcome current difficulties.

More recently there have been additional challenges. On February 11, 2011, the governor of Wisconsin proposed a budget bill effectively to kill Wisconsin's public employee unions. Pressure was on the legislature to pass it within a week, without any meetings with the public workforce, but Democratic state senators left the state in order to take away the quorum needed to pass a measure that would end collective bargaining of working conditions and all items except base pay, which will be tied to the cost of living. The governor portrayed his union-busting tactics as part of a "state emergency" to give him power over things that are not directly budget-related. The governor and both houses in the Legislature are Republican. The draconian action of Governor Walker reminds us that labor gains of over 50 years can be quickly erased if citizens are not vigilant, if voters believe the corporate-funded campaign sound bites, fail to vote, or vote without being fully informed about candidates. While the Democratic state senators were out of state, the Republican leadership then stripped the collective bargaining language from the bill, changing their stance to assert that removing collective bargaining was *not* fiscally related, so the issue could be voted on by a simple majority. It was quickly presented and passed on a party vote, but has been challenged in court as violating the open meetings law, so that issue is now under judicial review, possibly going to the State Supreme Court.

In addition, MATC is facing huge budget cuts due to reduced state funding and a cap placed on property-tax levies. Student tuition cannot be raised enough to cover lost revenue, so the college has renegotiated contracts with all unions. In March 2011, the 2009–2012 CBA was stripped of any pay increases and returned to the 2007–2009 pay level. Also, members who are included in the Wisconsin Retirement System (WRS) must now pay 5.8 percent toward their retirement fund, an amount formerly paid by the employer, resulting in a reduction in take-home pay. On March 21, 2011, the CBA was ratified by members, and approved by the college board on March 24, in an effort to have the contract in place before the date on which the new state law was to take effect. The saga continues without any chance of positive resolution very soon. The full-time teachers approved an extension of their contract to 2014 with changes resulting in heavier course loads, larger class sizes, and smaller raises in pay. The gulf between full-time and part-time teacher pay per course continues to grow, even in hard times. The full-time faculty union worked with the administration to decide on measures to address the budget problems, while the part-time faculty union was never asked to be part of that process, even though part-time faculty teach half of the classes at the college. With no voice allowed, the part-time faculty disproportionately suffered the fallout from a loss of funding.

Leadership of the part-time faculty will continue to weigh all options for their members, whether continuing as a union, changing to some version of a cooperative or guild model, forming an American Association of University Professors (AAUP) chapter, or other possibilities as they present themselves. Although I had hoped to be able to leave MATC on a more positive note, this looks unlikely. I will soon be 65 and will retire as of June 30, 2011.

*Since my date of hire in 1973, administrators have come and gone, faculty has almost entirely turned over, campuses have been added, and enrollment has greatly increased at Madison Area Technical College in Madison, Wisconsin. My account of institutional changes in the support of part-time faculty (those with 50 percent load or less) is from my*

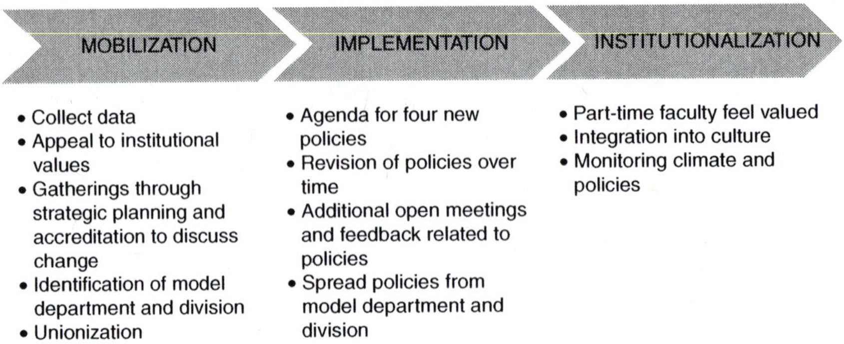

**FIGURE 4.2** Overlay of three-stage model with Madison Area Technical College's progress toward change

*perspective; others may hold their own views. Information is from my own files along with materials from college and union sources. Part-time faculty have moved from being invisible to shining a light on glaring workload and pay inequities, making the college uncomfortable. Although a next dark chapter seems about to unfold, many, many fine people have worked to improve the level of institutional support for part-time faculty, and I appreciate them all.*

## Key Points:

1.  Data collection is important for creating change. When data collection can be connected to other processes that have people discussing the data, like strategic planning and accreditation, it can become an even more valuable lever.
2.  Appealing to campus values (excellence, respect, integrity) is a helpful lever for change.
3.  Strategic planning processes are sites of collective action and lead to conversations where non-tenure track faculty issues can surface.
4.  Accreditation can be an external lever for change and a site for collective action, similar to strategic planning.
5.  Involving contingent faculty in governance and campus-wide processes ensures that non-tenure track faculty issues are raised regularly and as part of strategic efforts. Pay for involvement really makes a difference.
6.  Departments or units that can play a leadership role on campus and that understand non-tenure track faculty issues can also be key levers for change.
7.  The union is critical for pay and job security; working in tandem with faculty governance processes ensures that different issues are addressed. The climate for unions is becoming increasingly negative and other vehicles for change may need to be relied on more.

8.   Hard budget times constrain the progress of even changes hard fought for by unions. So it is critical to embed changes as deeply as possible so they become part of the culture.

## Key Questions:

1.   Have we collected data necessary to make arguments for change and to understand which ones are necessary?
2.   What values might we appeal to on our campus to support changes for non-tenure track faculty?
3.   Do we have an upcoming strategic planning process where non-tenure track faculty issues might be addressed?
4.   Can accreditation or other external levers be used for change?
5.   Are there any departments or units that might serve as a model?
6.   Are our union and campus governance working in tandem to create change? What is the current support for unions?
7.   How deeply embedded into the culture are the non-tenure track faculty changes we have fought so hard for?

## References

Magnuson, R. (1996). Personal communication, March 15.
Simone, B. (2001). Personal communication, December 10.

# 5

# INSTITUTIONALIZATION OF A POSITIVE WORK ENVIRONMENT AT A COMMUNITY COLLEGE

*Cecile Sam*

Mountain College[1] is a two-year public community college situated in a bucolic landscape in the western part of the United States. Because of its location, Mountain College is able to have the land necessary to support robust agricultural and animal-science programs, as well as the ability to expand its facilities. This expansion is important because Mountain College is one of the larger colleges in the nation, and needs facilities to meet a student population that is approximately 40,000, enrolled both part- and full-time, on credit and non-credit courses. This college is also home to over 1,000 instructional faculty, and the majority of them are part-time.

What makes Mountain College different from other community colleges is not just its size. Rather, a striking difference resides in the college's policies and practices for its adjunct faculty majority. Mountain College has implemented many of the recommendations made by scholars (see Gappa, Austin, & Trice, 2007; Gappa & Leslie, 1993; Kezar, Chapter 1 in this volume) and groups (see AFT, 2002). In Chapter 1 of this volume, Kezar highlights Gappa et al.'s framework (2007) for creating an effective faculty work environment and the general principles that fit within that framework. Many of the policies for part-time faculty of Mountain College are aligned with that framework.

In terms of professional growth, Mountain College provides professional development programs to part-time faculty, as well as compensation to attend those programs. Even though many of the workshops and programs take place on campus, there are also online programs available, for those faculty unable to attend. Part-time faculty are also able to apply for travel funds to attend conferences or other professional development workshops that are not held on campus. In terms of academic freedom and autonomy, with some exceptions (such as prerequisite courses), part-time faculty are free to create their syllabi or use ones

**TABLE 5.1** Institutional Snapshot of Mountain College

| | |
|---|---|
| *Institutional type* | Public two-year community college |
| *Student population* | About 65,000 |
| *Unionized* | Yes, wall-to-wall contract |
| *State* | California |
| *% of non-tenure track* | Approximately 65% |
| *Institutionalization phase* | Institutionalization |
| *Main changes* | Wage parity; professional development; compensated office hours and non-instructional hours; part-time faculty governance participation and leadership; medical benefits; re-hire rights |

provided for them, and as one part-time faculty member noted, "As long as I'm doing a good job, I'm pretty much left alone in my classroom." They are also invited to participate in departmental meetings as well as leadership groups such as the academic senate and the faculty association (the union group) with some compensation available to those in formal positions. Participation in departmental and school governance also relates to the element of flexibility, where faculty have some control to shape their work environment. Mountain College also has policies for those faculty in departments that only employ part-timers which allow them to take on more responsibility that is generally shouldered by full-time faculty.

Mountain College also has many policies that reflect employment equity. Though there is not full parity, part-time faculty receive 85 percent of full-time faculty credit salary, and are paid for holding office hours (for student contact). Even rarer is the fact that there are some health benefits for part-time faculty after a given number of semesters. In terms of workspace, part-time faculty have shared offices throughout the campus, with many departments having workspace for their own part-time faculty and often with open access to office supplies, computers, copier, and the like. Many of these policies contribute to the collegiality aspect of the faculty work environment, but other policies also play a part. For example, departments at Mountain College have orientation and mentorship programs for their part-time faculty. There is also an established seniority system to maintain re-hire rights for those faculty who have been teaching at Mountain College long-term.

All of these policies and programs are examples of the way Mountain College has created a work environment that can promote a positive culture for part-time faculty. Other practices, such as part-time recognition ceremonies, putting part-time faculty names and email addresses on department websites, and the visibility of part-time faculty in departments also reflect the overall positive work environment for part-time faculty. Though Mountain College still has room for improvement, and not all policies and practices have been implemented fully throughout all the departments or been accepted by all of the faculty, it is one of the few institutions that have made definitive progress for part-time faculty, and one of the few institutions that have reached the institutionalized phase.

The part-time faculty work environment at Mountain College was not always this way; nor did these policies and practices happen overnight. Numerous faculty, many who have been at the institution for over 25 years, note that this change took place over a couple of decades and was not always easy. This chapter examines the change process at Mountain College, and explores the various pathways and challenges that faced the people who wanted to change the institutional culture.

## History and Context

Mountain College opened over 50 years ago as a small community college, serving a predominantly Caucasian population. As time passed, the student population of Mountain College began to shift, moving toward a more diverse population of Hispanic/Latino, Asian-Pacific Islander, and Caucasian students. It is the only community college in its district, serving students from over 15 cities. Unlike many institutions, Mountain College maintains a surplus of revenue from each year and is able to save that surplus to use in case of budget cuts or deficits. This ability to retain some of its revenue from past years may allow Mountain College to have more leeway in determining its next course of action when other districts find themselves having to share funds among the other community colleges in the district.

## Faculty and Administration

Many of the faculty and administrators have long histories and/or ties to Mountain College and the location, going back over 20 years. Faculty and administrators have spoken of Mountain College as a "close-knit" community, with a commitment toward retaining faculty, both full-time and adjunct. "People who come here, come here to stay," said one faculty member. With numerous four-year master's- and doctoral-granting universities in the area, many of the faculty hail from the local area prior to working at Mountain College. Mountain College is also known for promoting administrators from within the campus community: As one administrator noted: "Most administrators were former teachers, and this is positive for the school." Another administrator stated that she was the first "outside" person to be hired for a leadership position in over 14 years. It is also important to note that more than a few faculty and administrators were actually once students of Mountain College.

This long history with the campus may account for the loyalty to it that is felt by the faculty and administration. There is a general desire to work to the benefit of the college. One part-time faculty member explained how working for the interest of the college also works in his interest: "You want to help the school develop and sustain itself, so you could keep your job and advance your career, but also so the school can get [a] better reputation in the community for quality education." An administrator talked about how he made the choice to be invested in Mountain College: "I really believed what Mountain College stood for and I wanted to add to it."

## Campus Organization

Like many community colleges, Mountain College maintains a mission to serve three goals: the first is academic (for transfer and matriculation of students to four-year institutions), the second is vocational (for associate degrees and certification), and the last is community (for community enrichment). Mountain College has two types of departments to serve these goals: credit-based departments and non–credit-based departments. The credit-based departments offer credit to students taking the course—these departments are the academic ones (e.g., English, sociology, or chemistry) as well as professional/vocational ones (nursing, welding, or aviation). Non–credit-based departmental communities deliver fee-based classes—like driver's education, or CPR training, or English as a Second Language (ESL)— that are offered for the enrichment of students or the community at large. Though there are many similarities between these two types of department, there is one striking difference: Non-credit departments are staffed entirely by part-time faculty. These non–credit departments are found in the Division of Continuing Education, a division composed entirely of part-time faculty with full-time directors who play the same role as department chairs. The Division of Continuing Education is one of the largest divisions on campus and is a strong contributing factor to the high population of part-time faculty at Mountain College.

## Institutionalization of Change at Mountain College

As noted previously, the changes for part-time faculty did not happen over a short period of time. Rather, they are the culmination of various events and contextual factors that had taken place over many years, and they began with establishing better working conditions for all faculty. The following section explores the changes that happened at Mountain College through the three phases of institutionalization: mobilization, implementation, and institutionalization.

### Mobilization

In the late 1970s, collective bargaining was introduced to Mountain College, so there were two faculty leadership structures instead of just one: the original faculty senate and the new faculty association. The first president of the faculty association saw collective bargaining as a way to improve Mountain College:

> In terms of collective bargaining, there is a gross misunderstanding both internally and externally about what collective bargaining is about. It's not about salary, it's not about what's in it for me, it's not even about what's in the best interest of the faculty. It's what's in the best interest of the college. And that's the way I saw it from the very beginning and I wanted to have a say in getting the process moving in that direction.

However, despite the potential of collective bargaining, the relationship between faculty and management was negative at first. As one faculty member explained: "The process was incredibly adversarial. It was an 'us–them' scenario and we almost went on strike in the mid 1980s." The conflict between faculty and administration at times was "mean spirited" on both sides; faculty felt powerless on their own campus, and they were at a loss as to how to make changes.

One of the lowest points for faculty occurred during the late 1980s to mid-1990s when morale was poor. One long-time faculty member stated: "There were days that I woke up and thought 'damn, I have to go to work.' I never thought that before, and after that time, I've never thought that. But for that time it was bad." There may be different reasons for the low morale: According to one faculty member, "Morale on the campus was awful, and it stemmed from the top. The president at the time was here too long. He was quiet, reserved, shy and he did not know the campus and did not want to take the time to know the campus." Another faculty member kept hearing that "the president and the trustees either hated the faculty or just didn't care."

Despite the challenges, there was the belief that:

> [I]f we did this right, we could head it in the direction so that ultimately we'd be sitting down at a table to negotiate a contract that everybody would be of the same mind. That this would be in the better interest of the college as a whole.

Faculty were unhappy with some of the executive leadership, but realized that in order to challenge executive leadership, "we had to be a unified front," which included the part-time faculty, who were included in the collective bargaining agreement. As one faculty leader stated, the "districts and administration use information to pit one against the other [speaking of full-time and part-time faculty], and this weakens the faculty as a whole." The faculty also realized that in order to create change, they could not do it alone; instead they had to "play the game and get faculty-friendly trustees who would listen to the faculty," and so they advocated strongly for those trustees that listened to them.

By the mid-1990s, both the faculty senate and the faculty association, under new leadership and with the support of new trustees, decided to take unilateral action and issued a vote of "no confidence" for the president, who retired soon after. At this point, the full-time faculty had found its voice and set into motion ways to strengthen the faculty contract.

Throughout this time, since the beginning of collective bargaining, it is important to note that by law, the faculty association had to represent the part-time interest all along, though in reality the association mainly focused on full-time faculty. It was not until full-time faculty realized that all faculty needed to be represented in order to gain support, that more attention was placed on part-time issues. There was also a distinct change in the new faculty leadership, both those in the senate as well as the faculty association. Unlike their predecessors, many of the new faculty leaders had once been part-time faculty and had experienced bias against adjunct faculty and negative work conditions either at other institutions or Mountain College. These experiences made the new faculty leaders cognizant of the challenges facing part-time faculty and sensitized them to part-time faculty issues. A philosophy began to develop which was "faculty issues are faculty issues," meaning that to take care of part-timers also means to strengthen full-timers as well.

With a new faculty leadership and a new college president, there were some positive changes for adjunct faculty. For the first time, two adjunct positions opened up on the faculty union, and the faculty leadership "formally acknowledged the importance of adjuncts to the whole campus community." The faculty association president at the time explained: "To make it more than lip-service we had to hear what they had to say and value their input." Establishing formal positions began a push to get part-time faculty more involved in the union process, and later the senate process. As one leader noted, "Once you get them engaged and show them that they are listened to, they're hooked. They want to be a part of something bigger."

Around the same time, there was another initiative happening with help from state funding. The state had started a program to incentivize those institutions with a certain percentage of adjunct faculty to close the hourly wage gap between full- and part-time faculty. Previously at Mountain College, full-time and part-time faculty were on two different pay scales and the union and faculty senate were working to bring those scales closer together. The state provided extra money to be able to meet the disparity, under the stipulation that the colleges eventually find ways to close the gap themselves.

## Implementation

With changes beginning to happen at Mountain College, new policies and practices were also being established, and all the faculty had to be ready to accept these changes. There were various tactics that Mountain College employed to move toward a more equitable work environment for all faculty.

To begin, both the faculty senate and the faculty association began to gather data about the needs of part-time and full-time faculty. They sent out surveys (in different colors to keep them organized) to understand better "what are the issues," and "how are they different for different groups," including the different types of part-time faculty. They used the data in different ways, first to dispel the myths that faculty had of one another, but also to use in contract negotiations. Once the survey results were made public to the faculty, they would vote on the issues of most importance and those issues would be taken into negotiations. The democratic process of voting on the importance of issues can be a fair way for faculty to be heard and to feel a part of the decision-making process.

For the part-timers, faculty at Mountain College realized that the largest issues focused on medical benefits, pay rates, re-hire rights, and office hours; then came faculty representation issues. Each of these elements provided their own particular concerns, but there were four main approaches that leaders used to try to meet the needs of part-time faculty. Within the following discussion of approaches taken by faculty leaders, the reader will see that the larger issues that adjunct faculty experience are ameliorated. After highlighting the approaches, a few challenges that were faced will be covered.

The first approach used by faculty leaders was applying solution-based thinking. For example, rather than take "no" as an answer to a plan or suggestion, it had to be replaced with an alternative suggestion that was equal to or better than the plan proposed. Faculty on all counts had to move toward a distinct destination and think of creative ways to meet the needs of part-time faculty. For example, Mountain College offers healthcare to their part-time faculty who teach at least one class for four semesters or more. The faculty negotiated that eligible part-timers would pay the healthcare premium through a tax-free payroll deduction. The district also contributes up to US$2,000 per year toward insurance premiums per part-time faculty member. At the end of the year, if the total amount of insurance premiums paid does not exceed the pool, then the money left over is redistributed among all the participating adjunct faculty, and "for the last few years, adjuncts have pretty much gotten all of their money back." The rest is returned to the district for the process to be repeated the next year.

In addition to creative and solution-based thinking, another approach that Mountain College took was applying existing policy. For example, they found ways to sustain some of the initial policy changes that benefited adjunct faculty and incorporate them into the permanent structures of the institution. For instance, the initial state incentive to minimize the gap between full-time and part-time hourly wages eventually led to the removal of two summer pay scales (full-time and part-time) and created one pay scale that pays all faculty during the summer session the same wage based on experience and degrees/credentials. Creating this single pay scale both sent a message to all faculty that "their work is valued equally," but also helped establish a precedent to garner more overall pay equity for part-time faculty. In addition, the administration at Mountain College made better use of the grants that provide faculty services such as professional development and orientation by adapting them to be in-house, so that future programs could be offered to all faculty at a much lower cost to the campus. This was an innovative way to use existing resources to support the part-time faculty better.

In their third approach, Mountain College faculty and administration really began to think about the overall learning environment of the college and what is best for the students. Numerous part-time and full-time faculty as well as administrators spoke about putting students first, and they emphasized the Mountain College community as one that "is shared responsibility for student learning." One faculty member explained: "It [student learning] includes all members in the college, beyond just faculty members, all units of college." This mindset established the reasoning to support practices like re-hire rights and paid office hours. One faculty member stated, "We want the best faculty for our students, that includes adjuncts. That means we have to be prepared to encourage them to come here and stay here." Numerous part-time faculty say that Mountain College has by far the best hourly pay rate and find the paid office hours gratifying. "It's not so much the money, though that's nice, it's also the acknowledgment of my work," said one part-time faculty member.

Even with the three approaches, many of these policies for part-time faculty were not initially accepted by all faculty. A fourth approach was used to help gain buy-in and alleviate concerns: conducting trial periods for some policies. These trial periods allowed Mountain College faculty to assess the success of policies and to determine if any changes needed to be made. For example, part-timers who were active on campus said "we're wall-to-wall, we're just as important." They wanted to be recognized in similar ways to the full-timers because they had the same degrees and training, taught the same courses, and the like. Mountain College began to open positions for part-time faculty on all of the major committees, and some positions were compensated. Some part-time union representatives were compensated using union dues, because to pay them "is to do the right thing, we want participation on every level." This representation extended to participation at all department meetings as well.

However, with regard to part-time participation in department meetings, not all the full-time faculty liked the idea. The original goal was to have it in the contract that all faculty, part-time and full-time, were to be invited to departmental meetings and would have an equal voice in voting. One administrator, who was a faculty leader at the time, explained, "There was this real fear that full-time faculty would lose control of their departments, that the adjuncts… would take over." Realizing that no headway could be made without addressing this fear, the faculty leaders asked department chairs to test the policy for one year, and re-evaluate its effectiveness. "In reality, it's kind of unfeasible to think that for example, all 60 adjunct faculty in the English department would show up to a departmental meeting and outvote the full-timers…that just won't happen, but we needed to see," noted one of the faculty leaders. After one year, full-time faculty realized that "the outcomes never really changed, adjuncts want the same thing for the departments as the full-time, to work for the students," and that their fears were unfounded. As a concession, the language in the current contract requires that all faculty be invited to departmental meetings, but how their input is received, either by full vote or advisory committee or the like, is determined by the individual department.

### Institutionalization

The campus climate at Mountain College has changed significantly over the last 30 years—moving away from a campus with a disenfranchised and divided faculty, to an overall faculty community that works closely with the current administration toward improving the student learning environment. The result of this work is something both faculty and administration explain as the "Mountain Way" or "Mountain Family." For example, one administrator stated: "There is something that we call 'Mountain Family' that is built on respect for faculty." A faculty member talked about her experience: "At Mountain College, you hear people talk about the 'Mountain Way' a lot. At first I thought it was a little scary, but I sort of get it now…it means being connected, being on the same page with respect to our student achievements, and it means supporting and encouraging others on campus and in our fields as well."

Currently, many of the practices and policies for part-time faculty have become part of the campus culture. Adjunct faculty have established representation on committees and leadership bodies. It is not unheard of for adjunct faculty to attend faculty meetings, apply for funding for conferences, and be compensated for non-instructional work. As noted earlier, with having departments and divisions made up entirely of adjunct faculty, in many cases in these departments, the adjunct faculty take on many of the responsibilities that are often the expectation of full-time faculty. The leadership realizes that in order for these departments to function, adjuncts have to help in terms of service, and since they are not salaried, they need to be able to offer them compensation. Mountain College leadership is also not limited only to the campus. Different faculty have taken on larger leadership roles in their union or professional state organization to help other institutions too, and change state legislation.

The "Mountain Way" that many faculty and administrators speak about creates a faculty ethic that seems to permeate throughout the campus. Currently, with the state in a budget crisis, public higher education institutions are expecting to reduce programs, enrollment, and classes. These cuts usually mean that at a campus, part-time faculty are the first to lose their classes. Already the administration is asking each department for a five percent program cut across the board. However, in a gesture that seems unheard of at many institutions, one administrator at Mountain College mentioned that "we want to be mindful of adjunct faculty and first will look to overload and see if people would be willing to give up some of their overload work to keep faculty." Already many faculty members and some entire departments have been responsive. The Mountain Way directs faculty into thinking about what is best for the school, which helps many of the faculty and administration maintain a long memory and a long-term plan. One chair noted, "we want to protect the people who have been here with us for a long time, who dedicated their time, and who need the work," recognizing that their part-time faculty had made long-term investments in the community. Another faculty chair thought about the future when he explained the need to keep adjunct faculty: "[W]hat happens when things get better again, but we've lost all of our good teachers to other places?"

## Lessons Learned

Understanding how change happens at Mountain College highlights various different "take-aways" that change agents may use at their own institutions. Some of them are similar to other case studies in this book: for example, collecting data to inform change as seen at the University of Southern California (Chapter 9), Villanova University (Chapter 10), and Virginia Tech (Chapter 6); and utilizing galvanizing moments as seen in San Francisco State University (Chapter 8), and Madison Area Technical College (Chapter 4). However, for this particular case, I would like to highlight three distinct lessons: recognizing context, long-term planning, and establishing a unifying goal.

### Recognizing Context

There are several factors about Mountain College that may make a difference to the way that the institutionalization of a positive work environment occurred. For example, Mountain College's ability to retain their yearly surplus is not common for most campuses. Mountain College also does not have to divide this surplus among other campuses within their district. This surplus of funds may allow Mountain College to approach the looming state budget cuts with a different perspective from those campuses that must make immediate drastic cuts to their programs and faculty. Currently, all faculty, including adjunct faculty, are kept informed of all the possible budgetary issues and the options available to the campus for the next few years, rather than just the next semester. Many chairs and administrators note that they will be able to stave off drastic cuts to the adjunct faculty (especially those who do not have re-hire rights) for longer than other institutions.

Another important factor in Mountain College's move toward institutionalization is its history. Because of the few years of strife between administrative and faculty leadership, faculty are very careful to maintain an environment that is supportive of all faculty. The campus is a very pro-faculty campus, with many of the administrative leaders being former faculty members at Mountain College.

One faculty member noted, "I feel that the faculty are empowered at this school." In addition, the relationship between faculty and administration is collegial. As one faculty member explained, "I know many of the administrators, because they were once faculty with us. There is a faith, I don't know if that's the word…yes, a faith that the administration will do what is in the best interest of the students." Thus, resources, history, leadership, and faculty culture all shaped their change process.

## Long-term Planning

The changes at Mountain College took place over a rather long time. Though it is true that most of the drastic changes for adjunct faculty occurred in the last 10 years, many of those changes were set in motion many years before. Faculty realized that they needed to support trustees and district leaders who wanted to build relationships with the faculty, and "even if they didn't agree with the faculty," both groups needed to "be willing to talk about why and come to some understanding." This move required mobilization that went beyond the campus itself to the existing community, to get people interested in what was happening at Mountain College, and to get the community to see that Mountain College was "their school." During that time, part-time faculty became full-time faculty, who became faculty leaders and chairs, and eventually became administrators. Even the faculty contract itself had come from a long line of revisions and changes and evolution to be the contract that it is now.

## Establishing a Unifying Goal

One overarching goal of Mountain College that helped drive policy-making decisions was that of student success. First and foremost, faculty and administration wanted to do what was in the best interest of the students; "we all had the same goal, it's just that we all may have different ways of achieving that goal." Despite the different approaches toward the goal, the idea that everyone had student success in mind eased possible tensions or bad feelings that would have arisen. As one faculty member explained: "Sure the discussion could get heated, but in the end it helps to know we all want the same thing." The goal of student success also allowed faculty to make reasoned arguments for certain adjunct faculty policies. For example, with the paid office hours, one of the arguments made was that "students need to have contact with their faculty outside of class to be successful—this means full-time and adjunct faculty." "As long as we can link it to how it can benefit the students, people find a way to make it [a program or policy] happen," was the thought of numerous faculty about how changes can be implemented on campus. There may be different reasons why the goal of student success is a powerful one. First, it is a goal that does not focus on the sole interest of either faculty or administration. Second, it is a goal that most people buy into, and it is prevalent throughout the organizational culture. The goal is physically visible throughout the campus, as well as expressed when faculty and administrators talk about past decisions and future plans.

Though there are still issues and challenges that Mountain College must work through, it is one of the few institutions that have made significant progress for their part-time faculty. They are proud of their faculty contract, which is described as "one of the strongest contracts because all of the faculty stand behind the issues...other contracts are good also, but Mountain's is best overall." There are next steps which faculty are working toward, such as ensuring that all departments really listen to the part-time faculty voice, and garnering more participation. The campus currently must focus on the upcoming budget cuts and try to maintain the services offered to the students and the community. From the first vision of how Mountain College should be one dedicated to student learning, to the ideal that Mountain College should be a place where faculty and administration could sit across from one another at the bargaining table and have the same goal in mind, "we're close to there now, we're 32 years removed from when it started and have made strong progress." Figure 5.1 illustrates the course of that progress.

| MOBILIZATION | IMPLEMENTATION | INSTITUTIONALIZATION |
|---|---|---|
| • Recognized the need for part-time faculty support<br>• Capitalized on state legislation<br>• Established part-time leadership positions<br>• Galvanized all faculty | • Encouraged and enabled more part-time faculty participation in governance<br>• Collected and used data<br>• Refined and revised faculty contract<br>• Implemented new policies on a trial basis and revisited them later<br>• Obtained stakeholder buy-in<br>• Policies and practices advanced over time through senate and union<br>• Developed a rationale for part-time faculty equity | • Acknowledged part-time faculty achievements and participation<br>• Faculty are predominantly unified<br>• Innovations of policy are now considered the norm<br>• Mutually accepted faculty and administrative goals |

**FIGURE 5.1** Overlay of three-stage model with Mountain College's progress toward change

## Key Points

1.  Administrative leadership at both the executive and district level can be changed through grassroots efforts and community support. Likewise, relationships with executive and district-level leadership can be built through the same efforts.

2. State-funded initiatives can provide colleges and universities with a good start toward making changes for non-tenure track faculty. However, campuses must think about the long-term sustainability of those changes once the initiatives have ended.

3. Having a mission or goal that receives unilateral support from faculty and administration alike can help support changes in policy and practices, especially when the reasons for the change can be clearly articulated in terms of the institutional mission.

4. It is possible to have top-down support for changes, especially when administrators and full-time faculty have had experience as part-time faculty. It is important not to discount possible allies.

5. Solution-based thinking is one way to move change efforts forward. Rather than focusing on what is wrong with policies, focus instead on how to make policies better than the ones suggested.

6. Trial periods for new policies can help convince reluctant faculty of the value of the long-term change. Trial periods can also help faculty determine if a change should be made.

7. Faculty need a venue to express opinions (even dissenting ones), so that once an agreement can be made it has the most faculty support.

8. The context and history of an institution can play a role in the options available to leaders of change. It may be that the context must be changed before other plans can be implemented. For example, change leaders may have to try to create a more invested community from the surrounding area, or mobilize to change executive and district leaders.

## Key Questions:

1. What are the prevailing values of the college and the department? Can the change initiatives fit within those values?

2. Have we linked changes needed among non-tenure track faculty (e.g., office hours) to improving student success?

3. What are the state or district initiatives that may help fund or incentivize any changes to policy or practices?

4. Who are the possible advocates and allies in among faculty and administrative leadership?

5. Are there ways for both the faculty senate and the faculty union to work together toward different changes and policies?

6. Have we surveyed the non-tenure track faculty to assess their main concerns?

7. What are the important concrete issues that we hope the change can resolve? If we were to rank those issues by importance, in which order would they be?

8. Have we used solution-based thinking when considering the direction to take when not all faculty agree?
9. Are there some initiatives that may be in conflict with the interest of others? Are there ways to reduce that conflict? Likewise, are there some initiatives that can have the most support from everyone?
10. Are there grants available to begin the change process? Are there initiatives that need to be made more permanent policies in the institution? Are there policies that are at risk of ending due to lack of external funding?

## Note

1   "Mountain College" is a pseudonym for the college in this study. College policy requires that any researcher who is not affiliated with Mountain College use a pseudonym for it in any published study. The researcher also promised school and personal anonymity before conducting interviews.

## References

American Federation of Teachers Higher Education. (2002). *Fairness and equity: Standards of good practice in the employment of part-time adjunct faculty.* Washington, DC: American Federation of Teachers.

Gappa, J., Austin, A., & Trice, A. (2007). *Rethinking faculty work: Higher education's strategic imperative.* San Francisco: Jossey-Bass.

Gappa, J. M., & Leslie, D. W. (1993). *The invisible faculty: Improving the status of part-timers in higher education.* San Francisco: Jossey-Bass.

# 6

# THE INSTRUCTOR CAREER LADDER AND ADDRESSING THE NEEDS OF RESEARCH FACULTY

## Evolving Policies at Virginia Tech

*Patricia Hyer*

Several important initiatives have been implemented over the last two decades for non-tenure track faculty at Virginia Polytechnic Institute and State University (Virginia Tech), and more are expected as a result of a task force on research faculty currently under way. In order to provide a background, this chapter briefly reviews the institutional context and the nature of faculty employment at Virginia Tech. Then a more detailed look at a recently implemented career ladder for non-tenure track instructors is given. Next, the author introduces a set of issues now being addressed for non-tenure track research faculty, a workforce that has increased by 50 percent over the last decade as Virginia Tech has aggressively expanded its sponsored research profile. To conclude, the author provides a summary of the lessons learned on supporting non-tenure track faculty at Virginia Tech.

## Institutional Context

Virginia Polytechnic Institute and State University is the official name, but the university is known to all as Virginia Tech. By Virginia standards, the university is large, with more than 30,000 students; about 2,200 are graduate students enrolled in degree programs in Northern Virginia and other locations throughout the state. The main campus is located in Blacksburg, a small rural town in southwest Virginia, several hundred miles from the state's concentrated population areas: Northern Virginia (Washington, DC), Richmond, and the Tidewater corridor. In contrast to urban institutions with large percentages of part-time and working adult students, Virginia Tech serves nearly exclusively traditional-age students at the undergraduate level, virtually all living in university residence halls or local apartments and enrolled full-time. Of the 28,600 students on the Blacksburg campus, 23,600 are undergraduates and 5,000 are graduate or

**TABLE 6.1** Institutional Snapshot of Virginia Polytechnic Institute and State University

| | |
|---|---|
| *Institutional type* | Public, four-year research university |
| *Student population* | 30,000 largely undergraduate |
| *Unionized* | No |
| *State* | Virginia |
| *% of non-tenure track* | 50% |
| *Institutionalization phase* | Mobilization |
| *Main changes* | Salary equity; promotion scheme; benefits; multi-year contracts; abolished policy where long-time full-time non-tenure track faculty were reduced to part-time; addressing policy for non-tenure track research faculty (mobilizing on this issue) |

professional students. A vibrant campus life, a beautiful setting, and the wide variety of strong academic programs make the university a popular choice for students and parents. Virginia Tech's history as a "polytechnic" and as a land-grant institution continues to be reflected in its programmatic strengths in engineering, science, agriculture, and architecture. However, virtually every field of study is offered through more than 65 undergraduate and 145 graduate degrees.

For more than a decade, Virginia Tech has been aggressively pursuing a plan to increase its profile as a major research university. Strategic investments, research partnerships, recruitment of new faculty with a strong orientation to research, and the successful efforts of senior faculty have resulted in an increase in total research and development (R&D) expenditures from US$232.6 million in fiscal year 2002 to nearly US$400 million in fiscal year 2009, an average annual increase of 10 percent per year. Virginia Tech is now 40th among universities with "very high research" programs as classified by the Carnegie Foundation. This critical shift in institutional agenda and profile has had important consequences for the faculty workforce.

Several waves of severe state budget reductions have also created constraints on faculty employment, challenging the university's capacity to staff the growing number of undergraduate course sections while building a research-intensive faculty. Thus geographic location, mission, institutional priority setting, and fiscal constraints have all played a part in both intentional and consequential employment patterns for faculty.

## Faculty Workforce Profile

While there has been a significant growth over the last 10 years in non-tenure track faculty hired to staff undergraduate courses and conduct research, the

Virginia Tech faculty workforce does not mirror the national faculty data with its predominance of non-tenure track hires. The profile in Table 6.2 reflects Virginia Tech's multifaceted mission as a research university, but it also reflects the realities of a rural location where the university is the primary regional employer and often the source of its own faculty talent. Virginia is a right-to-work state; there are no unions representing any group of public employees at the university.

The 10 percent reduction in tenured and tenure-track faculty members over the last decade reflects the loss of tenured faculty members due to retirement incentives offered to meet several rounds of budget reductions. While the university intends to resume hiring of tenure-track faculty members when budgets allow, it is unlikely to reach the level of 2001.

Non-tenure track instructional faculty on the Blacksburg campus tend to be full-time with longer-term employment histories than is commonly described in the literature on contingent faculty. Some non-tenure track instructional or research appointments are critical to dual-career hiring and help account for the longevity of employment at Virginia Tech for both partners. While the majority of faculty members included in the "non-tenure track instructional faculty" above are full-time *instructors*, a few carry a newly introduced rank of assistant professor of practice, associate professor of practice, or professor of practice; or clinical assistant professor, clinical associate professor, or clinical professor. Many of these faculty members have explicitly chosen a career focused on teaching; they do not aspire to a tenure-track position as defined by most research universities. The non-tenure track instructional category also includes visiting assistant professors,

TABLE 6.2 Headcount* for Tenure-track and Non-tenure Track Faculty Appointments at Virginia Tech, Fall 2001 and Fall 2010

| Type of appointment | Fall 2001 | Fall 2010 | Percent change |
|---|---|---|---|
| Tenured or tenure-track instructional faculty | 1418 | 1273 | -10.2% |
| **Non-tenure track faculty** | | | |
| Instructional faculty | 254 | 280 | +10.2% |
| Research faculty | 413 | 610 | +47.7% |
| Wage faculty (usually less than 50% appointment) | 261 | 414 | +58.6% |
| **Total non-tenure track faculty** | 928 | 1304 | +40.5% |
| Total full- and part-time faculty headcount | 2346 | 2577 | +9.8% |

*Table shows headcount and includes all full- and part-time faculty. It does not include administrative or professional faculty appointments. Instructional "wage" faculty are paid on a course-by-course or project basis and include retiree faculty members hired back to teach in their home departments.

Source: Office of institutional research and effectiveness, Virginia Tech.

whose appointments are short-term. Visiting faculty members are the most likely to desire a regular tenure-track position.

Those who are in full-time "regular" (ongoing) positions (regardless of rank title) receive the same benefits (health insurance, retirement, life insurance, sick leave, long-term disability insurance) as tenured and tenure-track faculty. Those hired on "restricted" contracts with a fixed ending date have full benefits, but more limited sick leave (regular faculty have an immediate six months of paid sick leave upon employment). Salaries among non-tenure track instructional faculty vary widely. For example, a significant number of instructors are employed in the English department where salaries are relatively low. Other departments may have only one or two instructors, whose salaries vary by discipline; some are relatively competitive. The minimum credential for instructors is a master's degree, but a significant number have doctorates.

A growing number of research faculty are specifically recruited in national searches from major research programs, and those faculty members often see their career path within the research faculty ranks (13 different rank titles are available, including research scientist, research assistant professor, or project director). Research faculty are usually funded by grants and contracts and they typically hold "restricted" employment contracts. Virginia Tech policy permits multi-year restricted contracts, allows "regular" (ongoing) appointments for some research faculty employed in larger-scale research programs with adequate resources to bridge gaps in funding, and provides full benefits to all full-time employees, including postdoctoral researchers. The faculty handbook describes a promotion process for the research ranks.

"Wage" faculty are typically employed on a course-by-course basis. There are no benefits, nor is there an expectation of longer-term employment. There is no university-wide pay scale, and the amount per course varies widely by discipline and by availability of departmental funding. Faculty "wage" employment on the Blacksburg campus certainly includes faculty members who desire a more permanent and/or full-time position, but it also includes previously tenured retirees whose numbers swelled in recent years because of retirement incentives used to address budget reductions, and a handful of full-time administrators who may be paid for teaching outside their administrative jobs. In contrast to the Blacksburg campus, highly credentialed adjunct faculty members are readily available to staff graduate courses at the Northern Virginia campus. That region of the state has one of the highest concentrations of PhDs in the United States, and the academic programs are enriched by the part-time involvement of experienced policymakers, corporate leaders, and scientists and engineers working in a variety of high-technology firms or government roles.

This detail is provided to make a point. The non-tenure track or contingent faculty at a research university is made up of widely varying roles, career paths, personal circumstances, and employment relationships with the institution. Disaggregation is essential in order to tailor meaningful and effective policies and practices.

## The Instructor Career Ladder

The instructor career ladder initiative builds on several previous policy and salary initiatives for instructors instituted over the previous two decades. In 1992, the university approved a major change eliminating a required termination of full-time employment for instructors at the end of their sixth year, a practice that had been codified in the faculty handbook to avoid any potential claims of de facto tenure. Continuing instructors were forced into part-time appointments denying them access to retirement and health benefits, which were not available to part-time employees by state law. However, the new policy initiative allowed unlimited contract renewals for full-time appointments. In addition, two-year renewable contracts were introduced along with several other related policy changes benefiting instructors.

In fall 2005, the provost committed funds to raise the base salary of instructors from US$28,000 in some departments to a minimum of US$31,000. A survey of regional public high schools documented that starting salaries for Virginia Tech instructors were below starting salaries for local high-school teachers. Additional funds were allocated to departments to address compression problems (when salaries of entering professionals are the same or even higher than those of colleagues with multiple years of experience) created by the base increase for entry-level instructors. In fall 2007, an additional base adjustment raised the entry salaries of all instructors to at least US$33,000 for a full-time academic-year appointment; additional compression funds were allocated to address inequities for more experienced instructors. Central funding for these salary initiatives was critical since department heads found it difficult, if not impossible, to make structural changes for instructors when also faced with pressing salary issues for tenured and tenure-track faculty. Low instructor salaries in some fields remain a challenge, especially since, as of 2011, there have been no salary increases for any state employees for several years.

These precedents reflected an institutional willingness to identify and address significant employment and compensation issues for instructors, some of whom have served their entire careers at Virginia Tech. In several departments—English, mathematics, and communication, for example—instructors also deliver a very significant portion of the undergraduate coursework, and they are critical in meeting the departmental teaching mission.

The English department at Virginia Tech has the largest number and most formally organized group of instructors on campus. There is a long history of their involvement in formal departmental committees related to composition coursework and undergraduate education in general, instructor evaluation processes, graduate teaching assistant (GTA) supervision, and peer mentoring. Thus it is not surprising that the issue of instructor promotions was first raised by the instructor concerns committee in the English department in February 2006. Early conversations among the instructors revolved around questions of whether they, as a group, even wanted a promotion process. Many instructors shared a strong sense of egalitarian solidarity with one another, and rank differentiation might set some apart, and above, others. Other issues concerned what criteria would be used to differentiate the ranks and where the resources would come from to implement promotions, if approved.

The first proposal was specific to instructors in English and included promotions based on time served in a specific rank. The concept of a promotion path was supported by the department, and then presented by the department head to the dean, and subsequently to the provost and associate provost later that spring. College and university administrators responded positively to the general goals of longer and more secure contracts, greater professional recognition, and salaries commensurate with experience and contributions. They suggested that the proposal include instructors university-wide, not just those in the English department, and that promotions should reflect accomplishments, not just time in rank. The associate provost (the author of this chapter) had been the champion of the earlier efforts on behalf of instructors, and she provided the leadership for the proposal development from that point forward in collaboration with the department chair, associate chair, and instructors in English.

In July 2006, the associate provost convened department heads from departments with significant numbers of instructors to determine their degree of support and possible concerns. While generally supportive, the department heads expressed some concern about how longer-term contracts would significantly reduce their budget flexibility. Department heads were invited to recommend one or more instructors to help shape and comment on the proposal.

Promotion processes for other non-tenure track appointments at Virginia Tech were reviewed as possible models, such as the promotion ladder for extension agents and for clinical faculty in the College of Veterinary Medicine. There was general agreement that some positive aspects of the promotion process for tenure-track faculty should be adopted, while reducing the burden of dossier preparation and the review process, since the stakes were not as high. A skeletal proposal was developed that included the stated assumptions that promotion was not an entitlement, and that no instructor was required to seek or be reviewed for promotion. Instructors could remain at the initial rank indefinitely if performing adequately; an unfavorable promotion decision would not be an up-or-out decision as it is for tenure-track faculty. Promotions would also be made on the basis of documented accomplishment beyond assigned course teaching, and would be rewarded with a title change, salary adjustment, and a longer-term contract.

In fall 2006, a forum for instructors and relevant department heads was held to discuss the skeletal model for an instructor career path. Self-introductions led to an awareness of the wide variety of roles that instructors played in different departments. While many taught undergraduate classes as might be expected, others also carried significant advising loads, provided administrative oversight for laboratories or a writing center, supervised graduate teaching assistants or internship experiences, provided one-on-one instruction in the math emporium (a mass online teaching facility), developed curricula, online courses, or assessment tools, and so on. This observation quickly led to a conclusion that promotion criteria may need to be department-specific. Some faculty members expressed concerns about differentiating among instructors who had previously felt class solidarity; they also worried whether the university would actually fund promotion adjustments if approved, and whether a process could be developed that would be fair but not excessively burdensome.

In January 2007, the associate provost and the department head in English introduced the career ladder proposal to the commission on faculty affairs, the governance body responsible for faculty policies. The commission members, the majority of whom represent the faculty senate, supported the general concept and offered suggestions to clarify aspects of the proposal. The career ladder had three ranks—instructor, advanced instructor, and senior instructor—and standard promotion adjustments for promotion at each stage received preliminary endorsement from the commission.

The next month, a second forum was held to introduce proposed policy language for the faculty handbook. The draft language included the new rank descriptions and the promotion process, but it also included employment policies for notice of non-reappointment, termination, multi-year contracts, and related issues. Some of this material had not been separately documented in the handbook, although it was an existing policy or practice. The new language stated the expectation that non-tenure track instructional faculty members would be eligible to participate in departmental, college, and university committees as appropriate to their assignments; that they should have meaningful engagement in program planning at the department level, especially as it related to aspects of the curriculum for which they assumed teaching responsibility; that they would be eligible to serve as voting members of the faculty senate (previously allowed by the senate constitution); and that they could participate on graduate advisory committees with appropriate credentials. (See Chapter 5 in the faculty handbook: http://www.provost.vt.edu/faculty-handbooks.php.)

Later that spring, the commission on faculty affairs approved the package and it was forwarded for subsequent review and approval by the university council and the board of visitors. While there were questions to be answered at every review stage, there was no significant or insurmountable opposition as the policy moved through governance channels. The policy became effective July 1, 2007—taking about 16 months from initial discussion among instructors to approval by the university's governing board, a relatively short time for a major policy change to move from concept to formal adoption.

But the work had just begun. Among the many questions that needed to be worked through and decided were:

- If the departmental tenure and promotion committees were responsible for the review, could the instructors be confident that they would not be held to the same standards as required for those seeking tenure?
- When and how would instructors have a say in the promotion of their peers?
- What happens for instructors who have been in position for many years? Can they skip to the highest rank? Would they receive the adjustment for each level or only the adjustment associated with senior instructor?
- What committees and processes are to be used in the case of departments and colleges that have very few instructors?
- What documentation is required?
- What flexibility is there to accommodate departmental differences in instructor assignments and priorities?
- How are the colleges with large numbers of instructors to handle the workload of dossier review at the department and college committee levels?
- How is the minimum service time to be calculated for faculty members with complicated and part-time work histories?

And many more questions were asked.

## Implementing the Instructor Promotion Process

The policy was to be implemented on the same cycle as promotions for tenured and tenure-track faculty, but that meant an enormous amount of work needed to occur very quickly for a fall start date. Waiting another full year was unacceptable since it would create an even greater delay in promotion adjustments, and hence more competitive salaries for the best-performing instructors. As soon as university-level approval appeared imminent in late spring, department administrators and the instructor concerns committee in the English department once again took the lead and began the difficult task of writing and negotiating the first set of departmental criteria and guidelines. A draft common dossier format (a variation of the format required for tenure-track faculty), and draft promotion criteria and departmental transition guidelines were reviewed in late August in a university-wide meeting of instructors, department heads, and deans, hosted by the provost's office. The associate provost subsequently revised the draft documents based on feedback, and continued to respond to the many individual and departmental questions and varying circumstances. A decision was made to allow promotions from instructor to the highest rank, senior instructor, for a transition period of two years; faculty members would receive the cumulative total of the two adjustments (US$2,000 for promotion to advanced instructor plus US$3,000 for promotion to senior instructor). After the transition period, promotions would only be considered from one rank to the next in sequence.

During early fall 2007, the English department instructors "workshopped" their draft candidate statements (a maximum of two pages) with each other, working through what accomplishments might be reported and where they would appear in the dossier, and the nature of the required attachments (CV, peer evaluations of teaching, annual evaluations from the department head, and so on). Departments typically adopted criteria for promotion requiring accomplishments in two or more areas beyond adequate performance in classroom assignments, such as exemplary teaching; extended professional development; course or curricular development; other contributions to instructional programs such as advising, mentoring, supervising student organizations, coordinating student conferences or internships; leading/supporting diversity efforts; conducting outreach activities; or scholarly/research publications (however, scholarship and publication are not *required* of instructor positions). Departmental transition guidelines addressed the issue of committee composition for the first and subsequent rounds of instructor promotion reviews (typically all tenure-track faculty at the outset, with increasing representation from promoted instructors in subsequent years in departments where there were sufficient numbers). Materials developed for the promotion process are posted at http://www.provost.vt.edu/instructor_promotion.php.

During the first cycle, 45 instructors were approved for promotion, and the university followed through on its commitment for the promotion adjustments, despite the lack of pay rises funded by the state. The dossiers attested to an accomplished group of faculty members with a remarkable commitment to undergraduate education. Indeed, making visible the contributions of the instructor corps was one of the most satisfying outcomes of the process. The most memorable dossiers were where the candidate statement turned a long list of activities into a compelling statement about the faculty member's career trajectory: how they changed their pedagogical strategies over time, reflections on their philosophy of teaching, the areas of their work that fed their passion for student learning and/or the discipline itself, and how they viewed their individual contributions to the mission of the department and university. While dossier preparation was more difficult for some instructors than others, the process allowed them to make meaning of their work and share their often hidden contributions with colleagues, not only in the department, but also in a wider college and university context. In this sense, the instructor promotion process succeeded in adapting and preserving one of the most important aspects of the promotion process for tenure-track and tenured faculty members. Newly promoted instructors were invited to the annual university promotion and tenure reception honoring all faculty members who were promoted and/or tenured during the previous cycle.

## Year Two and Onward

The associate provost met with instructors in the English and mathematics departments to debrief the first cycle and to seek ideas for improvement. Instructors and department heads in other departments were invited to submit comments as well. In general, the process went relatively smoothly, given the compressed timetable and the need to make up the rules as we went along. A number of minor suggestions were made, and changes incorporated in the common dossier format and department and college guidelines. In addition, a session was held for instructors considering submission of dossiers during round two; recently promoted instructors were invited to speak about how they compiled their dossiers and composed their candidate statements. Also, samples were put online to assist others.

No implementation is perfect, nor is a new policy equally well embraced or enforced throughout a large and complex institution. For example, consideration of promotion for the only instructor in a department remains very challenging; heads in those departments are often poorly informed about the career-ladder policy and the process for review. The department may not have adopted any criteria or worked through the process for review since they had no eligible candidate at the time the policy was approved. The situation frequently leaves the lone, often marginalized, instructor feeling that he or she is responsible for getting his/her own department up to speed. These departments are often more equivocal about instructor contributions. Even if the department heads realize that it might be more cost-effective to use instructors and better for students who benefit from faculty members solely focused on teaching, this does not mean that the tenured faculty fully value the contributions of their non-tenure track colleagues. Senior faculty in the department are often not focused on the career path and development needs of such instructors, who will have to do more than teach classes to be promoted. The provost's office continues to play a role in coaching departments in their responsibilities toward the professional development and promotion of instructors.

A second challenge is a direct result of budget reductions and continuing financial uncertainties. To target scarce and uncertain resources more effectively, the university centrally allocates some instructional funding to open additional course sections as needed for entering freshmen enrolling during summer orientation. While departmental allocations from year to year may end up about the same, they are not guaranteed, resulting in temporary or restricted appointments of instructors in departments dependent on last-minute, one-year-only allocations. (Previous efforts to allocate base funding for undergraduate instruction have been undermined by subsequent state budget reductions.) The result is more instructors on restricted appointments who will not be eligible for eventual promotion unless their appointment can be made more secure. (The policy does count service in a restricted contract toward the minimum years of service for promotion, but the employee must be in a regular appointment at the time of review for promotion.)

## Identifying the Needs of Other Non-tenure Track Faculty Groups

Research faculty present a very different set of policy challenges. (See Chapter 6 in the faculty handbook for current policies directly related to research faculty: http://www.provost.vt.edu/facultyhandbooks.php.) At Virginia Tech, the numbers of research faculty increased dramatically over a relatively short period, along with the level of talent of those faculty members, and the university's dependence on their contributions to the research mission. Research faculty are no longer viewed as easily replaceable employees with short-term contracts who move on as soon as a specific project is completed. Indeed, some are aggressively recruited and compensated at a high level, with the expectation that they will lead major research programs and that they will build a long-term career at Virginia Tech. In some cases, investment in research facilities and equipment for such faculty may cost millions of dollars. Hence, the satisfaction of such faculty members with their employment conditions and opportunities is critical to their retention, and a matter of serious concern to the institution.

Each research university starts at a different point in identifying the challenges that need to be addressed for this population. Job security in a high-risk funding environment is often at the top of the list for the research faculty members themselves. But so too are recognition as fully contributing members of the university community; and opportunities for promotion, participation in governance, and in teaching or graduate student supervision where desired. Some institutions may not have full benefits in place for some categories of researcher, such as postdoctoral researchers, although this is not a problem at Virginia Tech. Research faculty members may also be subject to poor or uninformed supervision by individual tenured faculty members, despite the fact that appropriate university policies and procedures are in place and publicized. Add to this mix the cultural differences and vulnerability of international scholars on employment visas that make them reticent about raising any concerns to departmental or university administrators, and you have the possibility for individual abuse or mishandling of the employment relationship.

The office of the vice president for research has convened a university-wide task force to identify and address a broad range of issues for research faculty. A benchmarking study of selected policies and practices at nine other research universities and a survey of Virginia Tech research faculty were done prior to formation of the committee. Subcommittees are discussing changes in policy and practice that range from assuring compliance with the increasing regulation of federal contracts to career development and recognition for research faculty. Here is a brief overview of the issues on the table:

- *Federal contract compliance*: The urgency of this topic emerged from the work of a previous task force. While some institutional funding is available for supporting salaries of research faculty engaged in writing new proposals, teaching, and other non-project-specific activities, such funds may not be available for all who are so engaged. (This is a particular problem in a few research programs supported by grants and contracts with very low rates of allowable overhead.) This could be an expensive issue to resolve, depending on how many faculty members need salary support, and how much of their salaries need to be charged to non-sponsored sources to assure compliance.

- *Access to international travel funds to present research papers*: Currently, funding for international conference travel is only available to tenured and tenure-track faculty members.

- *Consulting*: Historically, university policy allowed research faculty to act as consultants. Federal regulations suggest that research faculty who are fully funded on sponsored projects should not be able to consult on university time since they are being paid to work on the sponsored project only. The consulting policy needs to be revised to provide guidance on this matter.

- *Short-term disability*: Faculty on restricted (fixed-term) appointments are allowed 10 hours per month of sick leave without limitation on accrual; they also have long-term disability insurance. However, they are not adequately protected against lost income between the time when sick leave is exhausted and long-term disability begins after a period of six months' absence. This is a particular concern for those who give birth, since accumulated sick leave would not typically cover the entire period of childbirth recovery. (Employees on restricted appointments are covered by the Family and Medical Leave Act of 1993, but without pay.)

- *Opportunity to work with students and be compensated for overload teaching responsibilities*: Some career researchers seek opportunities to recruit graduate students for their laboratories, to serve on student committees, to interact more closely with departmental faculty, and to teach courses. Current policy does not allow additional pay for instruction, a considerable disincentive for the faculty member, and a difficult problem to resolve given federal regulations around effort certification (if a faculty member's time is charged 100 percent to a federal grant, they are not permitted to work on any other assignment). The availability of institutional funding to recognize contributions to the instructional program and non-project supervision of students will also be a major challenge if this activity is to be significantly increased.

- *Governance*: Research faculty members are not eligible members of the faculty senate, nor are their employment issues viewed as the ongoing responsibility of the standing commissions in the governance system. Is there an appropriate vehicle for research faculty involvement in governance? Which committees or commissions should be responsible for addressing issues for this growing population?

- *Job security issues*: Is there a way to provide bridge funding when there is a gap in project funding for researchers? Although current policy allows multi-year restricted contracts, this does not appear to be widely known.

- *University-level promotion process*: Research faculty may be promoted in rank and receive a salary increase at the time of promotion; however, the promotion process varies tremendously with written documents and timelines in some departments and institutes, and no guidance or formal process in others.
- *Postdoctoral researchers*: The number of postdoctoral researchers has greatly increased and the nature of their experience as a group needs thoughtful attention.

## Lessons to be Shared from the Virginia Tech Experience

While improvements in salary, policy, and conditions for non-tenure track faculty may not command the same attention as issues involving tenure-track and tenured faculty members, there is growing recognition of the substantial contributions that non-tenure track faculty members make to the complex mission of a research university. Successful attention to these issues over time has involved the engagement of many constituencies in identifying and implementing solutions, responsive leadership from upper administration, and persistence by advocates.

The instructor career ladder policy combined a bottom-up (initiated by instructors) and top-down (coordination and leadership by the provost's office) approach. Instructors laid out initial ideas and provided input on every stage of policy development and implementation. The conversations between instructors, their department administrators (especially in the English department), and upper administration were never adversarial, but rather, collaborative. The associate provost was instrumental in drafting acceptable policy language, negotiating support from key department heads, guiding the proposal successfully through university governance, and gaining the financial commitment from the provost. It is telling, perhaps, that the college deans played little part in this process. They did not oppose the career ladder proposal, at least in part because they did not have to find funds for the promotion adjustments, a cost that would have been a disproportionate burden on the college with the largest number of instructors. It may be an important observation that central administration needs to provide leadership to address issues for non-tenure track faculty, since they are unlikely to be a compelling priority for the deans whose attention is elsewhere.

The impetus for addressing employment conditions and policies for research faculty is driven primarily by central administrators at Virginia Tech. Research faculty are generally not organized. While there are several large institutes with significant numbers of research faculty (e.g., more than 50), many work in isolated laboratories with only occasional contact with other research faculty. Directors of the larger institutes and centers who are hiring in highly competitive markets have pressed for greater recognition and more flexible policies to support their faculty recruitment and retention efforts. They are strong advocates for change on behalf of their research staff. Supporting the evolution of this workforce is a fundamental strategy to achieve the university's goal of greater research productivity, and hence a priority for the office of the vice president for research.

Other strategies used in these two examples are common to the culture at Virginia Tech—engagement of a university-wide task force to collect and sift input from many constituencies; and use of data and benchmarking to inform the deliberations. These strategies take time and require careful staffing to ensure that the deliberations stay reasonably on target and result in usable recommendations. While faculty members with a strong data orientation may like to argue with the data presented, the university's culture supports analysis of problems through the use of both quantitative and qualitative data. Surveys and focus groups, for example, can be helpful when the voices of affected faculty members are not readily available. Intensive web research on policies at peer institutions and phone interviews with their relevant administrators have been extremely helpful. The practice of benchmarking recognizes that Virginia Tech operates in a complex national, if not international, faculty labor market and regulatory environment; learning from good models and/or the experience of others only makes sense. Medical-school policies at other institutions may help to pave the way as we address promotion paths and other issues for our growing research faculty, since they have dealt with these issues for many years. However the input is gathered, it is important from an institutional standpoint that the work of large, labor-intensive committees leads to some visible outcome. This will be especially challenging as the recommendations for research faculty come forth in an environment of highly stressed financial resources.

Another critical lesson is that one size does not fit all. Not only are differentiated policies and practices required to address non-tenure track faculty members in different roles (instructional versus research, for example), but some degree of differentiation may be needed even when the policy applies only to one group. The criteria for promotion within the instructional faculty ranks are not the same as the criteria for promotion within the research faculty ranks. Likewise, within the instructor promotion process, there are some differentiations by discipline or college. For example, instructor promotions in the English department require outstanding teaching, for all candidates, and significant accomplishment in at least one additional area (or a combination from several areas). By contrast, because a number of mathematics instructors do not work in a traditional classroom environment with traditional measures of teaching effectiveness, the College of Science opted for significant accomplishment in two or more areas, without specifying exemplary instruction in a classroom setting as a requirement for all. Allowing functional adaptation within overall university policy guidelines promotes acceptance in a decentralized university setting and significantly eases implementation.

Balancing concerns for equitable treatment with the recognition that faculty members come to their work with differing motivations and expectations (and often from differentially competitive job markets) is also important for successful recruitment and retention, and employee job satisfaction. While university surveys document the fact that research faculty members are among the most satisfied employees at Virginia Tech, and that many researchers do not seek opportunities for individual participation in university governance for a variety of reasons, it is still an institutional priority to address the overall needs of research faculty through official governance channels. The eventual solution may not be a time-intensive body such as the faculty senate or a formal commission, but a different, as yet undefined, entity where the faculty voice can be solicited and/or expressed, and relevant institutional policies developed and negotiated.

A final lesson to be drawn from the Virginia Tech experience is that policies must continually evolve. What may have been accepted practice a decade ago may no longer serve institutional priorities; adequately address external demands for documented and compliant policies and practices; respond to a more competitive job market; or satisfy an increasingly aware and involved employee base. Attention to policy evolution for non-tenure track faculty is difficult, but important to sustain, especially given our increasing reliance on their important contributions to the complex mission of a research university.

## Acknowledgments

The author wishes to acknowledge the contribution of Dr. Nancy Metz, associate chair and director of undergraduate studies, department of English, who provided insights and documentation of the career ladder process from the viewpoint of that initiating department. Instructors in mathematics and psychology provided additional documentation and observations. Ms. Sandra Muse, senior director for administrative services, office of the vice president for research, provided background on the goals and issues for the university-wide task force on research faculty.

| MOBILIZATION | IMPLEMENTATION | INSTITUTIONALIZATION |
| --- | --- | --- |
| • Non-tenure track faculty groups meeting together<br>• Leadership in office of the provost moving change forward<br>• Central administration advocate for research faculty<br>• University-wide task force | • Developed career ladder for instructional faculty<br>• Collect benchmark data on research faculty<br>• Appoint research faculty task force | |

FIGURE 6.1 Overlay of three-stage model with Virginia Polytechnic Institute and State University's progress toward change

## Key Points:

1. Departments with a long history of non-tenure track faculty or which have many non-tenure track faculty may be a source of ideas for change. Certain disciplinary groups have developed recommendations and models.
2. Different groups of non-tenure track faculty may need very different policies and practices, so work must be done with each group separately. A university is likely to have even more types of non-tenure track faculty, so this is a particular concern for this institutional type.
3. Many meetings and discussions can help to create greater focus, which can lead to institutionalization.
4. In multi-campus sites, the conditions for non-tenure track faculty might also be different, so policies may differ by site.
5. A data-driven environment can help facilitate change by seeing problems and inequities within data collected and through interest in looking at models and benchmarks and comparing to other campuses.

## Key Questions:

1. As a research university—what types of non-tenure track faculty do we have and are the policies needed similar or different for each type?
2. Do we collect good data and know what types of non-tenure track faculty we have?
3. If we have branch campuses, do they have special or different needs?
4. What level of leadership is there on campus to help create change?
5. What type of culture do we have (data-driven, social justice-driven, innovative)? Can any of these values be leveraged for change?
6. Will people on our campus speak freely at open fora? Do we have a political environment hostile to proposed change? Is it best to meet with groups individually?
7. Can you obtain a champion and utilize existing policy structures to build support among key constituencies so that shared leadership between the administration and non-tenure track faculty can lead to fast change?

# 7

# "LECTURERS ANONYMOUS"

## Moving Contingent Faculty to Visibility at a Master's Institution

*Päivi Hoikkala*

> *But just as we know that power tends to corrupt, we also know that powerlessness corrupts. We've got a lot of people who've never developed an understanding of power. They've been institutionally trained to be passive. Power is nothing more than the ability to act in your own behalf, to act for your own interest.*
>
> (Ernesto Cortés, cited in Rogers, 1990: 31)

In October 2000, I participated in a panel discussion on contingency as part of Campus Equity Week. This panel sought to draw attention to the multiple roles that contingent faculty play in higher education, and the very real challenges these roles present. As I introduced myself, "My name is Päivi, and I am a lecturer," reminiscent of the way Alcoholics Anonymous (AA) participants introduce themselves as they start on their road to recovery, it occurred to me that contingency often implies an internalized sense of inferiority. "I am just an adjunct," is something I hear frequently. Recognizing this internalized feeling of inadequacy is the first step on the road to "recovery from contingency" and to bringing issues of part-time academic labor to the forefront.

This chapter recounts my personal story of "recovery," as I have moved from the invisible margins of contingency to become a union activist. It is an account of the personal becoming political, to borrow the slogan from the feminist movement. Yet, I also place my experiences in the larger context of transforming contingent faculty roles in the California State University (CSU), the largest publicly funded university system in the United States with 23 campuses. While the collective bargaining agreement (CBA) between the California Faculty Association (CFA) and the CSU provides basic consistency in policies and the framework for lecturers' inclusion, the campus cultures are vastly different. My chapter outlines the centrality of the CFA as a vehicle for lecturer inclusion. I will then discuss the

**TABLE 7.1** Institutional Snapshot of California State Polytechnic University, Pomona

| | |
| --- | --- |
| *Institutional type* | Public four-year institution |
| *Student population* | Approximately 22,000 |
| *Unionized* | Yes |
| *State* | California |
| *% of non-tenure track* | 50% |
| *Institutionalization phase* | Implementation |
| *Main changes* | Salary equity; promotion scheme; benefits; multi-year contracts; grievance procedures; evaluation; professional development; non-tenure track leadership |

strategies for involvement and collaboration that have worked within the particular campus culture at California State Polytechnic University, Pomona (Cal Poly Pomona).

## Internal Revolution

Before describing the way we made changes for non-tenure track faculty at Cal Poly Pomona, it is essential to describe first my own internal changes to become an activist, as this process is often needed to spark the broader changes I will describe in the rest of the chapter. Many non-tenure track faculty will likely need to undergo a similar personal transformation in order to lead change on their own campus. I have come to understand this personal transformation through writers such as Ernesto Cortés, one of the most effective grassroots organizers in the United States, mostly because of his philosophy for organizing: Empower people to act on their own behalf (cited by Rogers, 1990). But many non-tenure track faculty do not feel such empowerment, and are often described as apathetic. What is often labeled apathy is really just a deep sense of powerlessness, an internalized feeling of inability to change what is. The first "revolution," or the first step to action, is thus internal: the recognition of one's value as an individual. Approaching contingent faculty organizing from this perspective places it in a larger context of struggle for social justice. It is also important to place part-time academic employment in the context of class, as contingent faculty activist Joe Berry (2005) points out in *Reclaiming the Ivory Tower*. While the reasons for contingency are structural, the reality is that contingency often becomes "personal," a perceived sign of professional failure which we then internalize.

My journey in contingency began long before I understood what was happening in higher education. After graduating from high school in my native Finland, I entered the University of Jyväskylä as an English major in the fall of 1979.

As I branched out into minors in Italian, art history, archeology, and adult education, I also began teaching English and Italian at the local adult education center—my first part-time position. Like so many of us, I was happy to have the opportunity to work in my field and believed that in the end, I would find the position that would carry me through my entire working life. What I had envisioned this position to be changed dramatically when, after receiving the master's degree, I decided to pursue a doctorate in Native American history.

Only a few lights flickered in the vast darkness below the Delta Air Lines flight from New York to Salt Lake City on a September night in 1987. The view was symbolic of my feelings as I was about to enter the graduate program at Utah State University and begin my foray into the world of American higher education. Two years later, the doctoral program at Arizona State University recruited me and I moved to Tempe. I worked as a graduate teaching assistant, receiving a meager salary, in-state tuition, and invaluable classroom experience at a research university. I also committed to a relationship that brought me to Southern California in 1993. While finishing my dissertation, I sought out part-time employment at a local private university and then at a community college, happy to get more teaching experience in preparation for my post-graduation career. Mine is a familiar story.

I received my doctoral degree in history in 1995 and entered a changing world of academic employment. The roughly three decades following World War II had seen a vast expansion of American higher education and, consequently, graduate education. The number of historians also increased during these years, while the professional historian became identified as a researcher, the presumed exemplar of the entire discipline. Although the conditions enabling this transformation of academia no longer exist, the legacies continue to shape the way we think of the profession. This legacy includes the assumption that all holders of a PhD seek and obtain permanent academic employment. Yet, while the number of positions has remained fairly steady, graduate programs produce far more individuals with PhDs seeking faculty careers than the academic job market can absorb. Furthermore, these programs overwhelmingly prioritize faculty positions at research universities (Bender, Katz, Palmer, & the Committee on Graduate Education of the American Historical Association, 2004).

This focus on research has marginalized teaching in graduate programs, while according to the Pew Charitable Trust survey of history graduate students (Golde & Dore, 2001), an overwhelming majority (84 percent) are attracted to the teaching aspect of an academic career. A further complication in the story is, of course, the radical change in the composition of higher education faculty, from tenured to contingent. Between 1979 and 2000, the percentage of tenured historians declined from 75 percent to 50 percent; at the same time, part-time faculty increased from seven percent to 25 percent (Bender et al., 2004).

The part-time stint in the private university in the Los Angeles area landed me a two-year full-time position, a decent salary with benefits, and confidence in my future career. I continued to send out job applications—being rejected, at times, in ways that were rather humiliating—while working on research publications to boost my resumé. In the fall of 1997, I joined the History Department at Cal Poly Pomona as a part-time faculty member. For the next two years, I remained the proverbial "freeway flyer," driving 35 miles from my home to Pomona in the morning; from Pomona, 60 miles to Santa Monica to teach evening classes at the City College; and finally, 28 miles back home. Driving along the 110 Freeway, I passed the lights of downtown Los Angeles two nights a week. They continued to hold a special mystique for me as I pursued my California dream.

My career did take a turn for the better when I was asked to take on responsibilities as co-director of a grant program in the History Department at Cal Poly Pomona. The department was short-handed, indicative of the changes in academe, and needed someone who could devote time to this program to provide professional development for elementary school teachers. This position allowed me to leave behind my freeway flying and work solely on the Cal Poly Pomona campus. It also gave me an entry into the campus in ways I could not even fathom at the time, giving me visibility as a professional, rather than "just a lecturer."

These experiences served as the backdrop for my participation in Campus Equity Week in the fall of 2000. It was a true moment of revelation. Listening to the other "testimonials," I realized that I, too, had internalized the standards of the profession that emphasize research and tenure while marginalizing teaching and part-time faculty. That moment helped me recognize the personal value in each faculty member, each staff member on campus, regardless of their position. It presented the internal revolution that Cortés (cited by Rogers, 1990) identifies as the beginning of the power to act on your own behalf, based on your personal values. The faculty union gave me the basic forms of protection for transforming this recognition into action.

## Power in Union

The instructional faculty members in the CSU are represented by the CFA, a wall-to-wall union that also includes librarians, coaches, and counselors, a total of nearly 23,000 faculty system-wide. The California Faculty Association came into existence after the California state legislature passed the Higher Education Employer–Employee Relations Act (HEERA) in 1978, enabling faculty to pursue collective bargaining. Faculty in the CSU voted for collective bargaining in 1982, and lecturers became part of the new union. This outcome resulted from the California Public Employment Relations Board (PERB) resolution arguing that all CSU faculty share a "common interest" and "perform functionally related services or work toward established common goals."[1]

The first CFA–CSU contract was negotiated in 1983, providing some basic rights for lecturers that derived from the California Education Code: access to the grievance procedure; health benefits and retirement through the California Public Employees' Retirement System (CalPERS); and the same salary schedule for all faculty members. More importantly, the contract laid the foundation for lecturer appointments in subsequent contracts. Yet progress was slow for lecturers within the union until the late 1990s; this is also when I joined CFA. Susan Meisenhelder, elected CFA president in 1999, had taught as a lecturer in the CSU and thus understood our issues. She hired an experienced union staffer as general manager, and the two of them—with the added funding from the agency fee (paid by non-members of the union to cover the cost of bargaining)—started implementing a new vision of a more democratic and integrated union. This vision embraced a central role for assuring the highest quality education for our students and addressing the concerns of a broad range of workers. The concrete result of these changes was the 2002 contract (Hoffman & Hess, no date), including significant gains for the contingent lecturer faculty.

The numbers of full-time and part-time temporary faculty in the CSU steadily increased between 1994 and 2008. These years saw increases in student enrollments, necessitating the hiring of new faculty. Since tenure-line positions remained fairly constant, contingent faculty became the "solution," as they provided a less expensive alternative to hiring permanent faculty while allowing the administration "flexibility." In the fall of 2010, 51.8 percent of the CSU instructional faculty held temporary positions. Of these appointments, 27 percent were at a time base (percentage of the full-time load) of 80 percent or more, while 42 percent of lecturers had a time base of less than 40 percent (California Faculty Association, 2011a).

The 2002 contract established the goal of moving lecturers into longer-term, more secure appointments with a higher time base, giving us the opportunity for a livable wage on one campus and the ability to focus on what we are hired to do: teach. The CBA thus includes language on annual and three-year contracts with entitlements to a certain number of teaching units. Article 12 on appointments spells out the details of how lecturers can get to this level of security. Although part-time positions (which are most lecturer appointments in the CSU) are still contingent on funding and enrollment, the article's order of appointment for work and its "careful consideration" language provide a framework within which departments are to operate. Careful consideration obligates a department to assign work based on the faculty members' evaluations and qualifications, rather than assigning work in an arbitrary or capricious manner. Also, Article 15 of the CBA offers policies on evaluation to support the "careful consideration" language. Finally, lecturers have access to the grievance procedure, outlined in Article 10 of the CBA.[2]

These basic protections and the environment of solidarity within the CFA, combined with good economic times, shaped my early experience of contingency and unionism. In 2001, Elizabeth Hoffman was elected associate vice president for lecturers at the statewide CFA level, also giving a boost to the statewide

Lecturers' Council. Each campus elected a lecturer representative to the CFA Assembly and the Lecturers' Council. On the Cal Poly Pomona campus, this representative also headed the campus lecturer support program. Having our own faculty development program surely gave legitimacy to lecturers while, at the same time, it segregated us into a category separate from other faculty. Yet the program addressed concerns particular to contingency, and I actively participated in the professional development activities it offered.

## Networking and Leadership

My position as a grant director gave me the luxury of making a decent living on one campus and allowed me to take advantage of programs that many of my lecturer colleagues could not. As a result, I began to weave a tapestry of personal relationships that benefited my professional career and provided venues for taking lecturer issues to various campus constituencies. One of the most important of these relationships in the larger campus context was with the Faculty Center for Professional Development (hereafter, Faculty Center). In addition to the lecturer support program, I regularly took part in the Faculty Center's workshops and other programming. This connection began in my first full summer at Cal Poly Pomona, when I signed up for a week-long workshop on classroom assessment, which involved a stipend for participants. The question arose as to whether or not lecturers were eligible for the stipend, implying questions about lecturers as faculty. Subsequently, the Faculty Center director concluded that there was no reason why I should not receive the stipend as a faculty member, establishing a precedent for full inclusion of lecturers in faculty development programs. The additional benefit of this exchange was my personal relationship with the director who then became an advocate for lecturer issues in other contexts as well. An added boost came from the fact that the associate vice president under whom the Faculty Center operated had started on campus as a lecturer, and thus understood our issues.

These contacts led me to a position as faculty associate, together with another lecturer, in the Faculty Center to develop teaching and learning workshops for all faculty including lecturers. Lecturer participation increased our presence and visibility on campus, helping to set aside the pervasive image of contingents as marginal to the campus community. In addition, it made clear our interest in pedagogy and our significant role as teaching faculty on campus. When the director of the Faculty Center left Cal Poly Pomona for another position, I was asked to take on his duties on an interim basis. This leadership role gave me direct access to the campus administration and to various networks at the state and national level. In these contexts, just being present as a contingent faculty member made the point that contingency is not indicative of personal failure or professional deficiency, nor does it imply a lackadaisical attitude about the life of the campus.

Of key significance was the solid support from the associate vice president. She had an understanding of, and compassion for, lecturer issues and she worked tirelessly to advocate for us at the administrative level. Once my interim position ended, she moved me to serve as interim director of service learning, another leadership role that allowed the continued development of connections with faculty and administrators. Finally, I had involvement with the International Center where I worked as editor of an annual campus publication. These leadership functions allowed me to meet faculty across departmental lines in a professional capacity. The personal relationships and networks then helped advance the notion of lecturers as active participants with an interest in the campus community.

It is obvious that campus and departmental cultures play a role in the ability of contingent faculty to insert themselves in leadership positions where they have the opportunity to develop networks of campus relationships. In my case, the department culture was collegial and there was support at the administrative level. The key, however, is to ask questions and look for opportunities for involvement, not to allow the internalized sense of inadequacy as "just an adjunct" stand in the way.

## Pedagogical Innovation

While full-time lecturers have responsibilities that include service and student advisory work, most contingent faculty in the CSU are part-time lecturers whose job it is to teach students. In addition, we often teach the high-volume general education classes that bring in the full-time equivalent numbers, and the funding, to individual departments. Teaching is therefore the one area where it is possible for lecturers to make a mark and thus to advance their visibility on campus.

Because the Faculty Center work involved me in pedagogical issues on a daily basis, I became interested in online teaching and learning. In 2002–2003, the Cal Poly Pomona faculty technology unit offered COLT (collaborative online learning and teaching), a year-long program for 12 faculty to study online pedagogy in preparation to teach online. This program involved a summer online course on pedagogy, and workshops and meetings throughout the year, culminating in teaching the first completely online course in the spring quarter. The university supported participating faculty by offering a stipend, a laptop, and a course release during the quarter of the online course.

Whenever money is involved, the status of lecturers as faculty is questioned, and this program was not any different. The dean of the college approved my application and that of another lecturer, yet questioned our eligibility for the laptops. She also argued that since both of us were part-time lecturers, there was no such thing as course release available to us. Personal connections again proved integral to resolving these questions in our favor, this time via the director of the technology program who had been a lecturer before assuming her position.

She successfully argued our case, with support from the associate vice president, and the two of us became full participants in the program.

This early foray into online pedagogy paved the way for my lecturer colleague and me regularly to teach courses that were completely online and hybrid ones; few existed at that time. We shared our teaching experiences at campus seminars and workshops as well as at statewide and national conferences. We became known on campus as early adopters of new technologies and "go to" people for other faculty interested in teaching online. The connections with the Faculty Center and the International Center also resulted in the two of us traveling to Armenia as part of a campus grant project to conduct two weeks of training in online pedagogy at the State Engineering University of Armenia in Yerevan.

Innovation in pedagogy thus proved an excellent tool for advancing lecturers' visibility, our inclusion in programs on campus, and understanding of our commitment to the work we do: teaching. It can also serve as a strategy for a modicum of job security, especially in situations where there are few other forms of protection. The key, again, is to ask for opportunities to be included and to promote contingent faculty commitment to our jobs as teachers. This strategy also places us at the core of the goal of providing quality education to our students.

## Faculty Collaborations

Awareness of internalized feelings of inadequacy among lecturer faculty members gave me pause and new insight into the realities of contingency to which I thought I was immune. In hindsight, it was the bugle call to activism in the union. My close involvement with the Lecturer Support Program and relationship with its director, who had a connection to the union, opened the door. She involved me in the CFA at the state level, and I also ran for a slot as elections officer on the campus chapter executive board. In 2006, I ran for and was elected as campus lecturer representative to the statewide CFA Lecturers' Council and the CFA Assembly. This role automatically seats me on the campus chapter executive board and puts me at the center of union functions on the campus level. Subsequently, I also chose to get involved in faculty rights issues, arguably the most openly confrontational position a union member can take. While at times daunting, union activism also functions as a security blanket: There is power in numbers.

The networks I have developed through my various leadership positions on campus have greatly benefited my union work. The strategy I emphasize in this work is collaboration, based on the Public Employment Relations Board notion that all CSU faculty share a "common interest" and "perform functionally related services or work toward established common goals."[3] Collaboration works best when dealing with individuals who are familiar with my professional experience in other contexts. These relationships operate on mutual respect, thus facilitating dialog outside the ubiquitous campus power relationships. So, discussions with individual department chairs have resulted in fair and contractually precise lecturer assignment procedures. Presentations to the campus-wide chairs' council have also helped to educate department heads about lecturer rights under the contract. While contractual violations and other irregularities certainly have not been eliminated, the collaborative approach at least facilitates dialog.

Another fruitful collaboration stems from the tenuous nature of probationary appointments. Faculty members with tenure-track appointments (but are untenured) have little certainty about their future, thus rendering them "natural" allies to contingents. While a step up from contingents on the status totem pole of higher education, probationary faculty also appear acutely aware of the abuses of these hierarchies. Therein lies the connection to lecturer issues. Another opportunity for collaborative relationships centers on classroom issues, especially workload. Probationary faculty—like lecturers—tend to teach more of the large general education courses than their tenured peers. Focusing on class-size issues as central to quality education offers an opening for genuine cooperation to benefit our "constituency": the students. And while reducing workload may be outside the purview of individual faculty members, dialog creates the space where respect grows and networks develop.

Working together with other lecturers campus-wide is evidently my most important faculty collaboration, and one in which support staff have played a key role. In my work across campus, the CFA administrative assistant and the support staff are integral to maintaining current email lists and communicating with lecturer faculty (sending them reminders for events and receiving replies, among other things). I have the good fortune of having such union support, but even on non-union campuses, administrative assistants at the departmental level can help individual instructors connect with other contingent faculty. Recognizing the role that educational support staff play in our campus work, and their personal value, is an integral element of developing collaborative networks.

Relationships with lecturers naturally take center stage in my work as union organizer and advocate for contingent faculty. Over the years, I have come to know colleagues across campus and departmental lines. Talking to them has opened my eyes to the variations in departmental cultures and the vastly different ways in which lecturers experience their roles. To communicate more effectively with Cal Poly Pomona lecturers, and with help from a colleague, I recently established a campus Lecturers' Council. Intending to follow up with personal contacts, I initially sent out an email to the lecturer email list, asking for volunteers to serve on the campus lecturers' council. To my astonishment, I received 16 immediate responses, including lecturers with whom I was not very familiar, and from departments with traditionally little participation. One lecturer reminded me of an important organizing principle when she responded by telling me how she had been wanting to get involved for a long time: You need to ask people. I was now in a position to ask because of the years of talking to lecturers, sending out emails, holding lunch meetings, and organizing workshops. Successful organizing takes time and effort.

Ideally, the campus lecturers' council will have a representative from each department whose role it is to maintain a list of contingents in the department, with contact information, as well as communicate with them on a regular basis. But even with partial representation, the approach has produced several benefits. First, instead of having to rely on a third party to send information—in my case, the CFA administrative assistant—I can now directly contact the campus lecturers' council members and get messages out instantaneously. Second, lecturers in the departments with representatives get communications from someone they know personally, making them more likely to read the messages. Third, the department representatives have a stake in the process and thus feel more connected to the union. I meet with the campus lecturers' council members regularly, with the focus on a particular issue each time. As they become more familiar with the contract and lecturer rights, they can take on more responsibility at the departmental level and thus help to build capacity. There is power, and security, in numbers!

This campus lecturers' council is modeled after the statewide CFA Lecturers' Council that meets during the spring and fall assemblies, and twice at other times during the year. In addition, there are monthly conference calls. This system-wide support network is extremely important in providing information and serving as a sounding board for issues on individual campuses. These lecturer activists also figure prominently as part of the CFA organization. We have representation on the CFA board of directors and committees; several lecturers also serve on the bargaining team, keeping our issues on the front burner and in the face, so to speak, of the CSU administration.

## Student Collaboration

The CSU is billed as "The People's University" with access, affordability, and quality as its core values. Cal Poly Pomona prides itself on its "student-centered" approach and the educational philosophy of "learning by doing." Yet these core values have been continuously compromised in the last decade. A wave of budget cuts first hit the system in 2002–2003, and they continue to threaten the integrity of the entire public higher education structure in the State of California. Student fees in the CSU have increased 242 percent since 2002, forcing many students to take on additional work or leave the system entirely. There have been periods of reduced enrollments, while the number of course offerings has also declined. For instance, there were 10,420 fewer course sections offered in 2009–2010 than in the previous academic year, a decline of eight percent; nine campuses experienced declines of between nine percent and 12 percent (California Faculty Association, 2011a). As a result, graduation in four years is just about impossible.

In response to these conditions, students in the CSU began to organize to oppose the budget cuts and fee hikes. They hold rallies, organize marches, and lobby state legislators and the state governor. On the Cal Poly Pomona campus, an impromptu demonstration was organized in 2008 practically overnight when the College of Science eliminated a large number of required science courses and let go a significant number of lecturers. The action was successful in restoring the classes and the lecturer faculty, and also prompting an inquiry into budgeting practices in the college. It is thus evident that student and lecturer interests are intricately intertwined, and a natural point of collaboration.

In the context of the growing economic crisis, new fee hikes, and course reductions in 2007–2008, student activists, with help from the CFA, formed Students for Quality Education (SQE) to build a student movement for educational justice in public higher education. While independent of the campus chapter executive board, the student interns involved in SQE report at executive board meetings and there is an effort to coordinate activities if possible. I have found this SQE collaboration crucial to lecturer issues. In the heat of the course reductions and lecturers "being disappeared"—not hired back—we held joint events to draw attention to the shared interests of students and lecturer faculty. Our focus was on how administrative decisions were compromising the mission of the CSU as "The People's University" of access, affordability, and quality. We also often share a table during events to provide information as part of statewide campaigns and elections, and the SQE students do classroom presentations on fee hikes, access, and quality education.

While not all students are organized in this fashion, connecting with their concerns helps to advance issues of contingency. Our interests are intertwined in the overcrowded classrooms and the budget cuts that threaten to reduce course offerings. To borrow a slogan from the last CFA bargaining campaign—"faculty teaching conditions are student learning conditions." We can connect with our students on a daily basis by talking about state budgets, the threats to public education, and rising tuition costs. This connection becomes yet another thread in the tapestry of personal networks to build power.

## Connections outside Academia

In April 2007, just days before what would have been the largest higher education strike in the history of the United States, CFA and the CSU administration reached accord on a contract. This agreement followed two years of negotiations and accumulating pressure that culminated in 94 percent of CSU union faculty voting to strike. It was an exciting time, and a time of great anxiety, especially for lecturers. The slogan "I don't want to strike but I will" appeared on T-shirts and posters, reflective of the anxiety about striking and reluctance to walk out in the first-ever such job action in the CSU system. What made the strike vote possible was the connection that CFA emphasized between faculty working conditions and student learning conditions. The campaign placed faculty demands in the larger context of quality education for California's students, thus reaching outside the narrow confines of higher education. The campaign was about students, access, and quality; not faculty salaries or workload.

My involvement in this campaign, and eventually in the strike vote, took place within the context of the National Education Association Higher Education Emerging Leaders Academy (NEA–ELA). I was accepted in a year-long leadership training program in 2006 and graduated in March 2007. The intensive training sessions focused on personal growth, unionism, and organizing. It was at the organizing session in Chicago in November 2006 that I experienced another "internal revolution." The training team surprised us with a "fish-bowl" session with the Honorable John Lewis, Congressman from Georgia—one of the key civil rights leaders in the 1960s. His testimony of his role in the movement, facing violence and constant intimidation, moved me at a very personal level and energized my union work. The contract campaign, moreover, made ELA immediately relevant. Even more important, it drove home the point about contingency as central to the struggle for the future of higher education. Essentially, ELA helped contextualize my own very personal experiences as a lecturer and make them political struggles.

The CFA, too, has continued to make connections to communities outside the campuses and the CSU system. The 2008–2009 budget process generated the Alliance for the CSU campaign. With the slogan "The Fight for the CSU Budget is a Fight for the State's Future!," CFA reached out to all the constituencies "who care about the future of the state and its state university system."[4] They include students and their families, alumni, faculty, CSU staff, administrators, employers, church leaders, and labor union members. Locally, we connected with our sister unions on campus, collected signatures from students and their families, went to our communities to talk with business leaders and others with a stake in having an educated future workforce. Personal relationships again granted access to a wide network of allies. Participating in these actions as a lecturer played a significant role in my widening awareness of contingency and its effects in higher education.

More recently, CFA has expanded its outreach to a nationwide alliance around restructuring and privatization in higher education. In January 2011, at the initiative of CFA, faculty leaders from 21 states met in Los Angeles for a discussion on how to assert the faculty voice in the national debate over the future of American higher education. One of the main organizers of the meeting, Susan Meisenhelder, stated: "Watching what is going on at our campuses and hearing from colleagues around the country, we have become convinced that we must act —together and quickly—for the good of our students, our profession, and our institutions" (California Faculty Association, 2011b: paragraph 2). Contingency is at the center of this fight as we continue to carry a lion's share of the teaching across the spectrum of academic institutions while remaining on the margins of academe. It is incumbent upon us to participate actively in these conversations about the future of higher education in the United States and worldwide.

## Conclusion

The fall 2007 CFA Assembly witnessed a grand celebration of our bargaining success that gave CSU faculty the first salary increases since 2002. This euphoria did not last long, however, as the State of California sank into the abyss of the economic crisis. The CFA held a somber furlough vote in the summer of 2009, ratifying an agreement with the CSU to implement the equivalent of a two-day-per-month furlough for the academic year 2009–2010. A total of 68 percent of CFA members voted in this election, with 54 percent of them voting in favor of furloughs (mandatory non-paid days off) and 46 percent voting against the furlough option.

> "The faculty vote to negotiate furloughs will help to save jobs, preserve employee health and retirement benefits, and ultimately, allow us to better serve students," said CSU Vice Chancellor for Human Resources, Gail Brooks, in response to the results. "We are facing a financial crisis, and need to move forward to reduce our employee costs."
>
> (California State University, 2009: paragraph 3)

The vice chancellor's comment highlights the administrative approach to "fix" the budget: reduce employee costs. It is thus evident that lecturer jobs take center stage in the debate over the future of the CSU as an educational institution. To a degree, the vote over furloughs was about saving lecturer jobs; it was also about maintaining solidarity among faculty. The year of the furloughs, unfortunately, heightened tensions and some faculty openly expressed their willingness to sacrifice lecturers' jobs to save their own. It has also become clear that furloughs did not improve the budget situation for the CSU: The system is facing another US$500 million, possibly more, in cuts. Lecturers' jobs are on the block again, and the shrinking resources are pitting permanent faculty against lecturers, and even some lecturers against each other, as they struggle to maintain a modicum of job security in their individual departments.

This environment of insecurity, coupled with the nationwide backlash against unions and public employee benefits, pose major challenges to efforts to fight back. Yet it is even more important now than ever to continue using established and new strategies of collaboration to build alliances. Of special importance are our alliances with the students, their families, and community groups to focus attention on the need for access to a *quality* higher education. The axiom "faculty teaching conditions are student learning conditions" still holds true. Specific to the CSU, and with leadership from Cal Poly Pomona professors Dennis Loo (sociology) and Dorothy Wills (anthropology), seven other CSU faculty

| MOBILIZATION | IMPLEMENTATION | INSTITUTIONALIZATION |
| --- | --- | --- |
| • Consciousness raising<br>• Union sets an agenda for change<br>• Leadership roles create visibility for non-tenure track faculty<br>• Collaboration with allies such as tenure-track faculty | • Create infrastructure and support for reform<br>• Lecturer support group<br>• Partner with administration to get non-bargaining items like professional development<br>• Build external network<br>• Student and community partners | |

**FIGURE 7.1** Overlay of three-stage model with California State Polytechnic University, Pomona's progress toward change

members and I contributed to a Master White Paper (MWP) to offer an alternative vision for the future of the CSU, a vision that emphasizes access, faculty control, and improvements in lecturers' job security. This collaboration among faculty of all ranks provides a blueprint for what we can do to mobilize people around the state. As the MWP executive summary states, "California stands at a crossroads. We face a choice between two radically different visions: those who uphold and celebrate private interests versus those who believe in the public interest and in public goods" (Loo et al., 2011: paragraph 1).

These trends are visible at other institutions of higher education in California and the rest of the United States. They are evident in other countries where students and faculty are also fighting back. In this chapter I have outlined a number of strategies that have worked for me, at my particular institution at a particular time in history, to include lecturers' concerns on the agenda of higher education institutions. While institutional cultures and the circumstances of contingency vary, these strategies offer some suggestions as to how we can continue to insert our concerns into the debates over the future of higher education.

## Key Points:

1. Individual non-tenure track faculty need their consciousness raised in order to organize and get involved. Leaders can facilitate this through finding mechanisms so that non-tenure track faculty can interact.
2. Relationship building with tenure-track faculty and administrators can help to create key alliances that lead to change.
3. Campuses that help to facilitate non-tenure track faculty leadership will benefit, as informed policies are created that make non-tenure track faculty more successful and enhance student learning. Leadership needs to be rewarded, incentivized, and compensated.

4.　Partnering with the community and students can help to facilitate change, and external and internal allies should be sought out.
5.　Non-tenure track faculty who can demonstrate their role as pedagogical innovators and leaders will help to demonstrate their assets and provide further rationale and justification for why change is needed.
6.　Networking with unions, NEA leadership, and state leadership provides non-tenure track faculty leaders with further ideas about how they can create change. They have access to models, benchmarks, and policies.

## Key Questions:

1.　Does our campus provide opportunities for non-tenure track faculty to interact and raise consciousness about problems?
2.　Have we built relationships with important campus stakeholders? Have we tried to leverage those relationships for change?
3.　Do we provide opportunities for non-tenure track faculty to become leaders with the necessary rewards and incentives?
4.　Have we considered students and the local community as partners in our change efforts?
5.　What external networks should we tap into? How can we collect resources more effectively from external groups as information to further our change efforts?

## Notes

1　California Government Code, Section 3579 (a) (1). Available at http://www.leginfo.ca.gov/cgi-bin/displaycode?section=gov&group=03001-04000&file=3579.
2　CFA–CSU Collective Bargaining Agreements, available at http://www.calstate.edu/LaborRel/Contracts_HTML/previous_cba.shtml.
3　California Government Code, Section 3579 (a) (1). Available at http://www.leginfo.ca.gov/cgi-bin/displaycode?section=gov&group=03001-04000&file=3579.
4　Alliance for the CSU. Available at http://www.allianceforthecsu.org/index.html.

## References

Bender, T., Katz, P. M., Palmer, C., & the Committee on Graduate Education of the American Historical Association. (2004). *The education of historians for the twenty-first century*. Urbana, IL: University of Illinois Press.
Berry, J. (2005). *Reclaiming the ivory tower: Organizing adjuncts to change higher education*. New York, NY: Monthly Review Press.
California Faculty Association. (2011a, January). *Research data for lecturers' council*. Sacramento, CA: California Faculty Association. Retrieved from http://www.calfac.org/sites/main/files/file-attachments/_lectcouncilpacket_for_dist.pdf.
California Faculty Association. (2011b, January). *Faculty leaders from 21 states launch national dialogue to save higher ed*. Retrieved from http://www.calfac.org/headline/faculty-leaders-21-states-launch-national-dialogue-save-higher-ed.
California State University. (2009, July). *Members of California faculty association vote to accept furloughs*. Retrieved from http://www.calstate.edu/PA/News/2009/cfa-furloughs2.shtml.

Golde, C. M., & Dore, T. (2001). *At cross purposes: What the experiences of today's doctoral students reveal about doctoral education.* Philadelphia, PA: Pew Charitable Trust.

Hoffman, E., & Hess, J. (no date). Improving the lives of contingent faculty while rebuilding the profession in the California state university system. [Unpublished manuscript.]

Loo, D., Wills, D. D., Karant, Y., Besosa, M., Hoikkala, P., Nagel, C., Stallones, J., von Glahn, N., Basu, R., & Westfall, R. (2011). *Cooking the goose that lays the golden eggs: California's higher education system in peril: A master white paper for the CSU.* Retrieved from http://defendthecsu.blogspot.com/2011/05/cooking-goose-that-lays-golden-eggs.html.

Rogers, M. B. (1990). *Cold anger: A story of faith and power politics.* Denton, TX: University of North Texas Press.

# 8

# LESSONS FROM LONG-TERM ACTIVISM

## The San Francisco State University Experience

*Shawn Whalen*

Founded in 1899 as a teachers' college, San Francisco State University (SF State) became part of the California State University (CSU) system of 23 comprehensive, polytechnic, and maritime universities in 1960. Located in the southwestern corner of San Francisco, SF State has evolved into an urban comprehensive university that offers baccalaureate degrees in 119 areas; 27 credential programs; 34 certificate programs; 95 master's degrees; and five doctoral degrees. San Francisco State University serves more than 30,000 students, including more than 24,000 undergraduates and nearly 6,000 graduate students. To serve its students, SF State employs more than 1,500 faculty. While there have always been contingent faculty over the years, the numbers have grown recently. In the fall of 2009, tenured and tenure-track faculty represented almost 58 percent of the institution's faculty; but as of the fall of 2010, the numbers of contingent faculty and tenured and tenure-track faculty were roughly equal, with contingents slightly outnumbering their tenured and tenure-track colleagues, and that trend seems to be accelerating.

The evolution of the role of contingent faculty at SF State has a rich history. Policy documents and initiatives that help define the role of contingent faculty go back nearly 50 years. Over that time, the campus has addressed the role of contingent faculty in governance, the fairness of hiring and evaluation practices, job security, initiatives to promote contingent faculty development, as well as efforts to establish collegial respect between permanent and contingent faculty. In this chapter, I highlight two formative elements of the culture of SF State and describe how they were used by contingent faculty leaders to advance the integration and employment rights of contingent faculty. With that context, I discuss the evolving conditions of contingent faculty including governance, hiring and evaluation standards, job security, and collegiality. Next I cover the roles of faculty

**TABLE 8.1** Institutional Snapshot of San Francisco State University

| | |
|---|---|
| *Institutional type* | Public four-year institution |
| *Student population* | More than 30,000 students |
| *Unionized* | Yes |
| *State* | California |
| *% of non-tenure track* | Ranged over years, up to 57%; currently 50% |
| *Institutionalization phase* | Implementation, moving into institutionalization |
| *Main changes* | Salary equity; promotion scheme; benefits; multi-year contracts; governance; grievance procedures; hiring and evaluation; professional development; non-tenure track leadership; respect |

governance bodies, the local union chapter, and contingent faculty leadership in forging change. Then I describe some of the lessons that we have learned along the way, and finally give a brief review of some of the work that remains to be done.

## Shaping a Unique Cultural Context

San Francisco State University's culture is unique and that uniqueness is reflected in its attitude toward contingent faculty. As a contingent faculty member, I am finishing my third term as the academic senate chair and I am not the first contingent faculty member to be elected to lead the SF State faculty. The first was Hollis Matson who served two terms from 1994 to 1996. Both Hollis and I have been amused by the reactions of our fellow senate chairs from other CSU institutions when they have learned of our faculty rank, but what may seem odd by institutional standards elsewhere seems quite normal at SF State. That is not to say that SF State is immune to the struggles that contingent faculty experience at other institutions, but my sense is that my status as contingent has not been the impediment here that it might have been elsewhere. So with that acknowledgment, it seems appropriate to provide a brief sketch of our institutional values and how they developed.

### The 1968 Strike

Between November 1968 and March 1969, SF State students and faculty engaged in a strike protesting the suspension of a graduate teaching assistant and Black Panther leader, George Murray, demanding the expansion of Black studies, and calling for the establishment of a School of Ethnic Studies. The strike at SF State lasted longer than any other academic strike in American history and has been well documented in both mainstream media and academic literature. Among the most notable features of the 1968 strike was the protesters' success in getting a department of Black studies and a School of Ethnic Studies established. Today's College of Ethnic Studies, along with each of its departments (including Africana studies, formerly Black studies), stand as an enduring legacy of the campus's grass-roots commitment to social justice and equity—themes that advocates for contingent faculty have capitalized on ever since. Though the strike occurred more than four decades ago, it remains a central component of SF State culture. The principles and values that underpinned the demands of the strikers continue to be echoed in the university's mission statement and in its strategic priorities. Indeed, knowledge of this history is a critical component of becoming oriented to the place. Without question, the interests of contingent faculty at SF State have been, and continue to be, served by the inclusive, democratic ethos of those times.

### Advancement in the Ranks

A second, fundamental component of the culture of SF State in regard to contingent faculty has been the ability of tenured and tenure-track faculty to identify with their contingent faculty colleagues. Though it has been far less common in the last decade, historically, SF State has had a significant percentage of tenured and tenure-track faculty whose initial appointments on the campus were as contingent faculty. In the 1980s and 1990s, many tenured senior faculty had once taught as contingents and were, therefore, far less likely to presume that contingent faculty members lacked a terminal degree (the highest degree one can earn in a specific field), or that they were somehow less equipped to contribute meaningfully to faculty discussions regarding curriculum or academic policy. As a result, the assumption of contingent faculty inferiority and the subsequent distancing of contingent faculty from critical academic decision-making were less common than they might have been at other institutions. Additionally, some who moved from contingent to tenured ranks went on to become respected academic administrators, providing even greater evidence that valuable talent existed among our contingent faculty.

With an institutional commitment to social justice and equity forged in a strike that turned traditional institutional authority structures upsidedown, combined with an uncommon awareness that contingent faculty often became as permanent as their tenured and tenure-track faculty counterparts, SF State was well positioned to address the emerging concerns of contingent faculty leaders.

### Evolving Conditions of Contingent Faculty

In 1960, San Francisco State College (as it was known then) became a part of the CSU system, thereby changing its name to San Francisco State University. At that time, contingent faculty lacked representation in faculty governance, faced ambiguous or non-existent hiring and evaluation standards, were afforded no job security, and confronted rigid rank distinctions in almost every aspect of faculty life.

## *Governance*

In 1960, the primary governance body of the campus was called the faculty council. Membership on the faculty council was restricted to tenured or tenure-track faculty and while contingent faculty had voting rights, they were not eligible to serve on the faculty council. Entry into the CSU system and the federation between a newly established statewide academic senate (ASCSU) and the individual campus senates required that the campus revisit its governance structure. However, rather than increasing the representativeness of faculty governance by including contingent faculty, the earliest changes resulted in excluding even more faculty from central university governance. By 1963, the faculty council had been disbanded and a new faculty constitution established an academic senate, but its membership was restricted to just tenured faculty—excluding probationary as well as contingent faculty.

The ineffectiveness of the academic senate during the 1968 strike highlighted its institutional weakness. Strikers demanded alternative decision-making structures that would afford greater access to contingent faculty members like George Murray, whose suspension initiated the strike. Moreover, after five months of questioning the authority of traditional academic hierarchy, faculty and students alike were eager to usher in a more fully democratic mode of governance. In 1971, two years after the strike ended, the faculty constitution was amended and all faculty, including contingent faculty, were eligible to serve on the academic senate.

But *guaranteed* representation of contingent faculty in the academic senate did not occur until 15 years later. The frenetic changes of the late 1960s and early 1970s had given way to a decade of relative stability in SF State's institutional structures. However, in 1978, California granted collective bargaining rights to its public employees, and in 1984, a campus chapter of the California Faculty Association (CFA) was established. In building its membership, the newly established union chapter highlighted the working conditions of contingent faculty and spawned awareness of the ways in which contingent faculty continued to be marginal university citizens. The early leadership of the campus CFA chapter included strong contingent faculty leaders. The warrants of the CFA's arguments resonated well on the campus and it should not be surprising that faculty who had been attracted to life in San Francisco might be predisposed to the political discourse of progressive labor. As union leadership embodied and espoused the importance of contingent faculty, the academic senate needed to adapt to ensure that contingent faculty perspectives were similarly included. As a result, in 1986, just two years after the union chapter was established, the faculty constitution was amended to require that each college elect a lecturer representative to the academic senate.

## Fairness in Hiring and Evaluation

A seminal moment in the history of contingent faculty at SF State occurred with the academic senate's adoption of a document called "Periodic evaluation of temporary faculty policies and procedures" (Academic Senate, 1986a) in the spring of 1986. At the system level, union advocacy had focused on the ambiguity in hiring practices and the tenuous nature of employment for contingent faculty. The union was successful in bargaining for measures that were designed to document the assessment of applicants for contingent work and the evaluation of contingent faculty prior to reappointment. These new requirements in the collective bargaining agreement (CBA) necessitated a campus policy document governing their implementation.

The union's CBA (described further under "Role of the Faculty Union") required periodic evaluation of temporary faculty, but the academic senate's new policy sought to ensure fairness and consistency in the evaluation procedures. This was the first academic senate policy that established expectations and standard procedures regarding the evaluation and retention of contingent faculty, and this served as a critical starting point for further discussions of importance to contingent faculty.

## Job Security

The progress made in the mid-1980s and the early victories of the union on behalf of contingent faculty generated momentum for contingent faculty leaders. Coincidentally, the percentage of contingent faculty rose substantially. In 1989, contingent faculty represented 57 percent of the campus faculty, the largest percentage in the institution's history. With momentum and numbers, it is not surprising then, that the academic senate revised and broadened contingent faculty protections provided by the "Periodic evaluation of temporary faculty policies and procedures" (Academic Senate, 1986a) in that same year.

In adopting a revised policy entitled "University policy on temporary faculty" (Academic Senate, 1986b), the academic senate established policies related to contingent faculty recruitment, appointment—including time-base minimums (the minimum level for part-time employment), rights to multi-year contracts, and credit for service time if contingent faculty were later hired as tenure-track faculty—evaluation, compensation, and further codified rights to participate in governance. The development of this policy coincided with union actions to incorporate similar protections within the CBA for all CSU contingent faculty, but the adoption of these principles by the academic senate reinforced our local institutional commitment to contingent faculty.

## *Forging Collegiality between Permanent and Contingent Faculty*

While policy documents inform the context of contingent faculty working conditions, they do not tell the whole story. To become truly integrated members of the faculty, contingent faculty need to be appropriately valued by their tenured and tenure-track colleagues. The evolution of SF State's policy from 1960 through to 1989 clearly illustrates a transition in the value placed on contingent faculty, but they do not fully explain the foundations of that transition.

As described above, the prevalence of former contingent faculty within the tenured and tenure-track ranks and the ethos that developed after the 1968 strike led to a campus culture that de-emphasized the importance of faculty rank. These cultural influences created a resistance to the traditional practice of routinely marking academic rank in university communication. As a result, typical communication practices generally avoid marking rank distinctions. The modes used to address fellow faculty in governance bodies and in internal documents, like committee rosters and other memos, rarely connect a faculty member to his or her rank. Consequently, a number of prominent contingent faculty report that their contingent status often goes unrecognized by colleagues outside their own departments.

## The Process of Advancing the Interests of Contingent Faculty at San Francisco State University

At SF State, the process of advancing the development of contingent faculty is the result of the union's collective bargaining activities and initiatives taken by the academic senate, as well as the impact of a few dynamic contingent faculty leaders.

## *Role of the Faculty Union*

California granted collective bargaining rights to CSU employees in 1978. Subsequent to this authorization, the CFA initiated collective bargaining on behalf of all faculty in the CSU system. Union interests in building membership led to a broad union platform advocating for both permanent and contingent faculty. Union outreach to contingent faculty helped to develop contingent faculty activism. As contingent faculty participated in union activities, they gained access to and awareness of university decision-making processes, and those faculty members quickly emerged as leaders not only inside the union, but also outside of it in department meetings, committee settings, or in the academic senate.

The union's ability to foster contingent faculty leadership was, by itself, an enormous contribution that enhanced advocacy for contingent faculty in both union and non-union settings. The union's organizational structure established parallel authority for tenured and tenure-track faculty and for contingent faculty, and ensured that contingent faculty leaders would shape the agenda and activities of the union. Additionally, contingent faculty serving in union leadership positions found that their influence in non-union settings was enhanced by the credibility that they had established in their union work (see also Chapter 7).

Among the most significant contributions of the CFA was Article 12 of the CBA. At its inception, it established contingent faculty entitlements and with them, the first forms of job-security protection for contingent faculty in the CSU system. Subsequent revisions have extended contingent faculty job security with the provision that contingent faculty with six years of service are eligible for three-year contracts, and that they have the expectation of re-appointment to subsequent three-year contracts "except in the instances of documented unsatisfactory performance or serious conduct problems."[1]

It is important to note that these advances were secured through union negotiations with the 23-campus CSU system and were therefore external achievements that became incorporated into our campus. However, these external negotiations necessitated campus involvement to implement these new requirements, thus creating a platform for contingent faculty issues at the campus level. Indeed, Article 12 of the CBA was the antecedent of the academic senate's "Periodic evaluation of temporary faculty policies and procedures" (Academic Senate, 1986a), the campus policy document that has served as the platform for advancing contingent faculty interests ever since.

Other important forms of protection for contingent faculty afforded by provisions in the CBA include criteria and procedures governing faculty evaluation, the right to apply for sabbatical leave, and the establishment of grievance procedures. The implementation of these forms of protection amplified contingent faculty interests on the campus and in the academic senate in particular.

### Role of the Academic Senate

If the union's CBA has been primarily responsible for ensuring the formal, structural protections of contingent faculty rights, the academic senate at SF State has been the venue where the day-to-day interests of contingent faculty have been integrated into university work. In addition to ensuring representation of contingent faculty within the senate and asserting the value of contingent faculty in its "University policy on temporary faculty" (Academic Senate, 1986b), the academic senate's diverse composition has ensured that the perspectives of contingent faculty are considered on all items brought before the senate. Among other things, academic senate policies afford contingent faculty the right to participate in the selection of department chairs, to take part in faculty development events, and to serve on committees of significance to contingent faculty. Academic senate policies also define orientation expectations and establish the right of contingent faculty to be considered for emeritus/a status.

Maybe more important than the policies themselves, by working together on these and other issues, contingent and permanent faculty in the senate have established a culture of respect for each other. A number of contingent faculty have served with distinction on the academic senate, and their influence has not been limited to items that are of particular interest to contingent faculty. Consequently the academic senate has been a site of real integration between contingent and permanent faculty, and it has established a culture based on merit as opposed to one based largely on academic rank.

A notable example of this phenomenon occurred when the academic senate was revising its policy governing tenure and promotion in 2005. A subcommittee of the senate spent the year developing a proposal that had been broadly vetted among the tenured and tenure-track faculty outside the senate. The proposal embraced greater emphasis on research and scholarly activity than the previous tenure and promotion policy, and while the tenured and tenure-track faculty were ready to embrace that shift, contingent faculty on the academic senate raised concerns. During the senate debate, two contingent faculty members argued that the relationship between the expectation for tenure and promotion and the values of the campus were deeply intertwined, and that while scholarly achievement should be appropriately emphasized, the proposal weakened the campus's commitment to its teaching mission. Based on those arguments, the proposal failed. The irony of having two contingent faculty members derailing a revision of the tenure and promotion policy was not lost on us, but there is perhaps no stronger example of the senate's willingness to concede to well-made arguments regardless of the rank of the advocate. That is not to say that distinctions between contingent and permanent faculty have been erased, but there is no denying that collaboration between contingent and permanent faculty in the public forum of the academic senate plays a significant role in modeling appropriate relationships in other settings.

## Role of Contingent Faculty Leaders

A number of contingent faculty have served many years in the academic senate, and some have played prominent roles in shaping university policy as a result. Contingent faculty members have served as standing-committee chairs and in every elected office of the academic senate. Two of us have served as chair of the academic senate. Despite never serving as chair, Jan Gregory, lecturer emerita in English, is perhaps the most important contingent faculty leader in our institutional history. Over the past two decades, she was a consistent advocate for contingent faculty and she was one of the most influential voices on the academic senate. She was instrumental in the evolution of the senate's "University policy on temporary faculty" (Academic Senate, 1986b), and she served as the chief recruiter of contingent faculty leadership for the union and for the senate for at least a decade. Jan's sophisticated understanding of the CBA and her work on the union's faculty rights panel ensured that the hard-fought policy victories for contingent faculty paid off in pragmatic terms. Despite her retirement a number of years ago, she is still sought out for her advice, and contingent faculty continue to benefit from her diplomacy on their behalf.

Despite the many contributions of my contingent faculty colleagues, perhaps the most enduring feature of their influence is the knowledge that significant leadership roles are not closed off to contingent faculty. While it is not typical for contingent faculty at SF State to serve in prominent university leadership positions, it is also not extraordinary.

## Lessons Learned from the San Francisco State University Experience

The challenges facing contingent faculty at SF State are not fundamentally different from those at other institutions. It is possible that overt activities addressing the concerns of contingent faculty have a slightly longer history at SF State than at some other institutions. While our history has been marked with some key victories, the work of protecting those victories as well as realizing the full integration of contingent faculty is not complete. That said, the SF State experience provides important lessons for contingent faculty here and potentially for advocates of contingent faculty elsewhere. Those lessons include the importance of understanding the significance of small victories, forging pathways for contingent faculty career development, focusing attention on institutional practices, and developing and maintaining contingent faculty leadership.

### Appreciating the Significance of Small Victories

Perhaps the greatest revelation stemming from my preparation for this project was the recognition of the significance of the academic senate's adoption in 1986 of the "Periodic evaluation of temporary faculty policies and procedures" (Academic Senate, 1986a). It should not be underestimated despite its content limitations. Indeed, the text of the document is largely unremarkable. Its provisions are primarily bureaucratic, and one might even read the document as devoted as much to establishing the university's rights with regard to contingent faculty performance evaluations as to establishing protections for contingent faculty. But it established a policy basis for contingent faculty interests and a platform for future advocacy.

Indeed, the achievement of that first policy document was grounding the existence of contingent faculty in university policy. Academic policy work at SF State is characterized much more by incrementalism than it is by revolution. In other words, it is much easier to strengthen an existing policy document than it is to propose sweeping changes in an entirely new policy. The broad forms of protection for contingent faculty—including establishing a minimum time base, rights to multi-year contracts, service-time credit (if contingent faculty were later hired as tenuretrack faculty), and the forms of compensation protection that followed three years later—were easier to accomplish when they could be presented as natural extensions of the principles established by the 1986 policy.

## Facilitating Career Advancement

An absolutely crucial component to advancing the integration of contingent faculty at SF State has been the institution's history of facilitating contingent faculty advancement to tenure-track, full-time positions or long-term part-time positions. Historically, SF State has allowed high-quality contingent faculty to increase their entitlement over time, and many achieved full-time status. That practice established a base of career contingent faculty who remained officially contingent, but who often had greater job security than some of their tenured colleagues. These "career contingents" were enormously important to establishing leadership among contingent faculty, and even if their involvement in contingent faculty issues waned in later years, they still provided their younger colleagues with a sophisticated understanding of the institution and the ability to forge alliances with other campus leaders.

Another important dynamic that shaped the evolution of the role of contingent faculty at SF State was the number of contingent faculty who moved into the tenure and tenure-track ranks. That transition has been far less common in recent years than it was a few decades ago, but the significance of having established campus faculty and administrative leaders who both appreciate the circumstances of contingent faculty and who personify the rebuttal of the inferiority of contingent faculty cannot be understated. An undeniable lesson of the SF State experience is that institutions which invest in the development and advancement of their contingent faculty will find it much easier to integrate them fully into the university community.

## Practice over Philosophy

The advancement of contingent faculty interests at SF State has been more of a pragmatic than a philosophical enterprise. It is fair to say that the campus has not given sustained attention to the abstract relationship between contingent and permanent faculty, nor to the distinct contributions and responsibilities that those categories of faculty might provide. That realization seems a bit odd and is decidedly inconsistent with typical proclivities in the academy, but it has probably helped to avoid more vigorous confrontations.

Pragmatism has proceeded on two fronts: development and maintenance of communication practices that complicate the ability of permanent faculty to assert undue authority *and* rectifying institutional practices that create indefensible disparities between contingent and permanent faculty. A combination of being vigilant to ensure that campus communication strategies avoid reifying hierarchical authority, while working to overcome institutional barriers that prevent contingent faculty from serving our students, has allowed contingent faculty to demonstrate that their interests and the university's larger interests are generally one and the same.

Perhaps the democratic impulses that permeated every corner of the institution during the 1968 student and faculty strike established an inherent aversion to hierarchical authority. Perhaps that aversion just stems from being located in the decidedly liberal political orientation of the San Francisco Bay Area. Regardless, our institution's contingent faculty benefit from a campus culture that, for the most part, resists overt connections between rank and authority. This affords contingent faculty the ability to be judged by the value of their contributions, and it can serve to level the playing field, at least somewhat, when contingent faculty find themselves opposing tenured colleagues.

While working to forge a climate that values the contributions of contingent faculty, contingent faculty leaders at SF State have focused their attention on improving institutional practices to serve contingent faculty more effectively. By focusing on institutional practices that undermine the integration of contingent faculty, they have advanced the rights of contingent faculty to vote in university elections, ensured contingent faculty participation in departmental and university decision-making, made sabbatical leave available to contingent faculty, and much more. Many of those individual achievements have served further to increase contingent faculty access to the next round of institutional decision-making, and, as a consequence, improve the integration of contingent faculty.

### Developing and Maintaining Leadership

A consistent barrier to the development of contingent faculty leadership is the lack of institutional structures that forge unity among contingent faculty. The campus union chapter does have regular lecturer fora, but they are not well attended, nor have they proved effective in creating contingent faculty unity. While permanent faculty regularly forge relationships in new faculty orientation, department and college meetings, committee work, faculty development workshops, and through scholarly collaborations, contingent faculty are much less likely to do so. Many contingent faculty are teaching at multiple institutions and their entire time on the campus is devoted to instruction and office hours (student contact). Without some effort devoted to forging contacts between contingent faculty members, one might have to be around for a number of years before getting to know other contingent faculty. What we learned is that there are certain areas where contingent faculty leadership had emerged and we needed to capitalize on those areas; we also needed to remove barriers to contingent faculty leadership—this is an issue we are still working on.

In terms of areas where contingent faculty leadership had emerged, departments housing basic-skills courses like composition, oral communication, critical thinking, and quantitative reasoning often serve as the exception to the isolation that might exist for contingent faculty in smaller departments. Contingent faculty working in these areas often have new faculty orientations and regular meetings of contingent faculty teaching introductory courses. At SF State, these groups have been powerful forces in advancing the interests of contingent faculty, and accessing them has been critical to identifying contingent faculty leaders. Not surprisingly, contingent faculty leaders from these departments have been critical agents of change. While departments with larger numbers of contingent faculty can help to foster solidarity among contingent faculty, smaller departments forced to rely more heavily on one or two contingent faculty members can provide different opportunities. Former academic senate chair, Hollis Matson, was a faculty member in a small department. Her ability to shoulder the departmental workload, teach broadly across the existing curriculum, as well as contribute to curricular innovation, facilitated her acceptance among her tenure and tenure-track colleagues. She reports that "eventually people just forgot that I wasn't tenured" (Matson, 2011).

In ideal circumstances, institutions would devote the same attention to the orientation of contingent faculty as they do to permanent faculty. Orientation for contingent faculty at SF State has largely been handled at the department level over the years, but the SF State's Center for Teaching and Faculty Development initiated university orientation sessions for contingent faculty a few years ago. The opportunity to meet contingent faculty from other disciplines and the development of cohort bonds among newly hired faculty can yield great dividends in contingent faculty leadership. However, recent budget cuts have weakened the center significantly and its ability to maintain these efforts is in doubt. But a strong orientation can help build contingent faculty leadership.

Another leadership challenge facing contingent faculty is somewhat inherent in the career trajectory of many contingent faculty. Unlike our tenured and tenure-track colleagues, who often devote their pre-tenure years to their teaching and research activities and their years after the achievement of tenure to university service, activism and university service among contingent faculty are more common in the early years. Contingent faculty activists report that it was easier to devote time to service projects and advocacy when they were younger, often single, and before family commitments created more constraints on their time. The challenges of managing larger teaching loads, teaching at multiple institutions, and compensating for lower wages make sustaining commitments to faculty leadership harder for contingent faculty. The consequences of this phenomenon are not insignificant. Even the most talented new faculty lack a sophisticated understanding of university decision-making processes, and they are unable to tap established relationships with faculty and administrative colleagues to advance a cause effectively. Without senior-level contingent faculty leadership, the enthusiasm and idealism of new contingent faculty can give way to a sense of frustration and futility (see also Chapter 7). Incentives for involvement in leadership is also another major issue essential to fostering contingent leadership;

this is addressed in the next section "Ongoing Concerns", as we have not made headway on this issue to date.

## Ongoing Concerns of Contingent Faculty at San Francisco State University

Current economic conditions pose the greatest threat to the pursuit of contingent faculty integration at SF State. The scarcity of resources and the uncertainty of stable funding increase divisions between contingent and permanent faculty. Tenured and tenure-track faculty hoping to secure funding for tenure-track hires are loath to commit resources to extending contingent faculty entitlements. The pursuit of tenure-track lines also provides the incentive for permanent faculty to dismiss the importance of contingent faculty while elevating the significance of tenure-track positions. These controversies run the risk of division and resentment between contingent and permanent faculty.

Smaller budgets also mean fewer classes for contingent faculty, and many have seen entitlements decline or vanish altogether. Recent years have seen an increase in the percentage of contingent faculty with time bases that are so low that they fail to qualify for health benefits. Additionally, frustrated and desperate contingent faculty are more likely to exploit every avenue to protect their livelihoods, including initiating grievance procedures. Those grievances often target the actions of department chairs or tenured faculty serving on hiring committees and, as a consequence, they risk the further erosion of collegiality between contingent and permanent faculty. In short, all of the factors that make the work of contingent faculty challenging are exacerbated by the erosion of institutional funding.

These conditions create even greater challenges for sustaining contingent faculty leadership. As career contingent faculty retire, there are fewer and fewer full-time contingent faculty to serve in leadership roles. For those remaining, barriers still exist to their institutional advancement as they are barred from roles in the retention, tenure, and promotion process, and from serving as department chairs. In addition, institutions interested in developing contingent faculty leadership should address the existing disparities in the incentives provided to permanent and contingent faculty to participate in department, college, and university service. At SF State, a full teaching load for contingent faculty is five three-unit courses per semester, whereas a full teaching load for tenured or tenure-track faculty is typically three three-unit courses. Accordingly, tenured and tenure-track faculty are compensated for having research and service obligations. Contingent faculty, while encouraged to participate in governance and service bodies, are not obligated or compensated to do so. The result is that contingent faculty service, for the most part, is volunteered, while tenure and tenure-track participation in service is financed and built into the institutional structure. The result is that contingent faculty leadership experiences greater fluctuation in intensity than does that of permanent faculty.

Another issue facing SF State is the impact of newly hired tenure-track faculty that do not appreciate contingent faculty. Some contingent faculty are concerned that the academic preparation of the junior tenure-track faculty has socialized them in their disciplines, but not socialized them as effectively in the academy as a whole. Those contingent faculty members report that newly hired assistant professors are more likely to feel threatened by contingent faculty assertiveness than their more senior colleagues, and they are more likely to dismiss the preparation and experience of their contingent faculty colleagues. It is hard to say how widespread these sentiments might be, but it does suggest that continuing work on the advancement of contingent faculty might place an emphasis on engaging graduate students in these conversations.

Finally, SF State could advance the integration of its contingent faculty by placing a greater emphasis on including contingent faculty in significant university events. Only a small percentage of our contingent faculty participates in commencement or attends the annual faculty convocation. The university could do a great deal more to encourage attendance and participation in these activities by contingent faculty, and doing so would foster a greater sense of connection to the institution and to our students.

The evolution of the status of contingent faculty at SF State over the past 50 years has been dramatic, and those of us who hold those appointments today owe a huge debt to the work of those who came before us. Their work, beginning with the 1968 strike, transformed the culture of the institution and that transformation has been essential to advancing the cause of contingent faculty ever since. Maintaining these essential cultural commitments is a challenging task and will become even more so as resources become increasingly scarce. The legacy of success established by contingent faculty leaders at SF State was founded in their ability to demonstrate that the advancement of our institutional mission and the

| MOBILIZATION | IMPLEMENTATION | INSTITUTIONALIZATION |
|---|---|---|
| • Awareness through unions and rising numbers of contingent faculty<br>• 1968 strike<br>• First policy through union opened door for others | • Set of policies advanced over time through union<br>• Work with academic senate for more day-to-day policies and practices<br>• Create collegial relations and alliances with tenure and tenure-track faculty<br>• Increasing contingent faculty leadership | • Ranks not emphasized<br>• All faculty considered faculty |

**FIGURE 8.1** Overlay of three-stage model with San Francisco State University's progress toward change

quality of the educational experience for our students improved with the integration of our contingent faculty—themes that will continue to be critical elements to future success.

## Key Points:

1.   Having contingent faculty play a leadership role through governance can help alter culture and values and facilitate institutionalization. Rewards and pay should be allocated to support such efforts and make them sustainable.
2.   Campus values can be used to leverage change. At SF State they appealed to the strong social justice values of the regional area and campus.
3.   Unions provide powerful tools to enable the creation of change in terms of setting agendas, conducting surveys to identify key issues of concern, bargaining skills, models and benchmarks for comparison, and the like.
4.   Senate and unions can work together in a complementary way that fosters change at the broad policy level, but that also gets deeper into day-to-day practice.
5.   There is power in a broader collective like a statewide union. Participating in broader groups can help to advance change on campus.
6.   Small changes (getting the first policy in place) can lead to a cascading of other changes. Do not be frustrated if first changes take a long time.
7.   Flexibility and compromise without adherence to uncompromising principles can be important. Administrators may provide changes in some areas if there are concessions on the part of contingent faculty leaders and unions.
8.   It is important constantly to re-evaluate policies over time. New external conditions emerge (e.g., recession) and the contingent faculty profile might change (e.g., a rise in part-timers who need more attention). New areas may emerge as a concern—departments that suddenly become hostile. Surveying and meeting on an ongoing basis even after changes are made are essential.

## Key Questions:

1.   Do we provide avenues for leadership?
2.   What values might be appealed to for creating change on our campus?
3.   Is unionization an option on our campus? What would be the benefits? Should we join with the tenure-track faculty?
4.   What is the relationship between our senate and the union? How might they work together more productively? If you are not unionized, what role might the senate play in advancing change?
5.   Can our union work with others in the region and state? Is there any advantage in working at a more overarching level to leverage the power of several campuses?

6. Have we made any small advances that we might build on? Do we help people see the few key changes we have made to recruit more people to the effort?
7. What principles are we willing to compromise on? Are we willing to compromise? What issues need our attention and re-evaluation?

## Note

1  (CBA Article 12.13; see http://www.calstate.edu/laborrel/contracts_html/cfa_contract/ article12.shtml).

## References

Academic Senate. (1986a). Periodic evaluation of temporary faculty (S#86-189). [Unpublished manuscript.] San Francisco: San Francisco State University.
Academic Senate. (1986b). University policy on temporary faculty (S#89-160). [Unpublished manuscript.] San Francisco: San Francisco State University.
Matson, H. (2011). Personal communication, April 28.

# 9

# CREATING CHANGES FOR NON-TENURE TRACK FACULTY WITHIN A DECENTRALIZED UNIVERSITY ENVIRONMENT

*Ginger Clark and Jerry Swerling*

This chapter describes the emergence of non-tenure track faculty at the University of Southern California (USC) as part of a uniquely configured workforce that has altered the university from its traditional foundations, and has allowed it to become agile, responsive, and able to "turn on a dime" with the conditions of the times. As the university has begun to recognize the power and flexibility inherent in a non-tenure track faculty workforce, it has begun to think of itself as a continually shifting entity that can quickly adjust itself to meet the needs of the constituents it serves. The value of a contingent faculty work force however, has been a slow and strategic process. It has taken time for non-tenure track faculty to enter the consciousness of this historically "traditional" university in ways other than as full-time adjunct teachers, clinicians, or researchers. The timing of this emergence fortunately coincided with two university presidents' agendas for change that would transform the university into a progressive, dynamic, innovative institution of learning and knowledge. Without this timely movement away from traditional university models, it is unlikely that there would have been an opportunity for the university to recognize the untapped resources it had in its non-tenure track faculty.

The chapter will first focus on the environment of the university as a decentralized administrative culture, where each school is like a province in itself, run by the dean, but ultimately answerable to the provost and president. From this environment emerged a need for a centralized committee charged with monitoring the experience of, and conditions for, non-tenure track faculty. The chapter will explain how that committee was ultimately formed and emerged as a powerful voice within the university. We will describe strategies used by the committee, along with reactions within the university to various efforts made by the committee. Finally, we will share lessons learned: These address how

**TABLE 9.1** Institutional Snapshot of University of Southern California

| | |
|---|---|
| *Institutional type* | Private research university |
| *Student population* | Approximately 37,000 |
| *Unionized* | No |
| *State* | California |
| *% of non-tenure track* | About 50% |
| *Institutionalization phase* | Mobilization |
| *Main changes* | Adopted by some but not all departments: involvement in governance; mentoring; professional development; salary equity; promotion scheme; revised evaluation |

the committee will proceed in the future, now that there is a clearer picture of the overall environment and the various roadblocks that might be encountered as we move toward even more equitable integration into the university system.

## University of Southern California

The University of Southern California is a private research university with a very decentralized administrative culture, wherein the deans possess substantial decision-making and budgetary authority for their respective schools. Each school is responsible for its own revenue stream, budget, hiring structure, and governance policies. Certainly there are university-wide guidelines that are encouraged among all of the schools, and there are some policies that are uniform across the university. However, the rationale behind the decentralized model is that each school knows best what its needs are, and how it should be governed. In many ways this has contributed to USC's success as a top-tier research institution. Each school has been free to cultivate educational programs that serve their fields in ways that stay relevant and current. They are flexible and agile, and able to craft faculty and staff positions, raise funds, and cultivate partnerships that meet the needs of the school, the community, and the field in a changing global climate.

With regard to its faculty, though, there is operational variability, both within and between schools. The University of Southern California ascribes to the widely accepted norms around tenure-track faculty workload, benefits, and involvement in university governance that are common in most Tier One research institutions. So with some variability associated with field or leadership, the tenure-track faculty at USC work under a generally accepted set of broad conditions or guidelines that are uniform across the university, and set in place and carried out by the provost. The non-tenure track faculty, however, are affected differently because the final arbiter of their career trajectory within the university is their dean, and not the provost. This results in non-tenure track faculty experiencing vastly different environments within the same university, according to the structures and guidelines that each dean has created within her or his school.

On the one hand, some schools have been creative in developing non-traditional faculty positions that are exciting and challenging, allowing faculty to function in a variety of capacities outside of the typical workload of tenure-line faculty. On the other hand, the model still allows for inequities in schools where non-tenure track faculty policies have yet to be solidified. For example, some non-tenure track faculty have challenges with their contracts and benefits that are difficult to negotiate when they have no job security. When you have a year-to-year contract, saying no to a request to take on more responsibilities without benefit of release from other duties is a precarious decision. Negotiating salary when there are no clear guidelines around rank, promotion, or title puts the faculty member at a distinct disadvantage.

As non-tenure track issues began to emerge in the mid-1990s as an important topic within the university, and information was gathered about how non-tenure track policies were carried out across the different schools, the results varied widely, but overall indicated that change was needed. Within some schools, non-tenure track faculty were treated with respect, but were relatively limited in their role in the university as teachers, practitioners, or researchers. Changes were needed in titling, involvement in governance, promotion, and review policies, in addition to many other areas in order appropriately to recognize their expertise and to realize fully their value to the university. In the worst cases, non-tenure track faculty were not highly valued within schools, and in some schools were even excluded from all governance activities (e.g., meetings and governance committees). Certainly, no polices were yet in place that utilized the multifaceted intellectual capital offered by this large population of academic professionals. The perception appeared to be somewhat one-dimensional, where non-tenure track faculty served one purpose within the school. They were seen as either full-time adjunct professors whose only value was to teach courses or provide clinical care or training; or they were seen as self- sustaining, full-time researchers. There was no recognition of how these professionals could contribute to the school in a more meaningful way; they were primarily seen as ancillary faculty used to fill in the coverage gaps.

The widespread underemployment of these faculty was not serving their needs or allowing them to provide their full contribution to the university in a way that could foster significant growth in the system. The non-tenure track faculty were used to patch up the leaking areas. So, in many respects, the lack of general recognition of what non-tenure track faculty could offer the university as a whole led to policies that ranged from benign neglect to having to justify the reappointment of one's position every year. This issue of variable treatment across schools is one that many decentralized colleges and universities face. How can you create a far-reaching policy that attracts the best and brightest non-tenure track faculty when there is limited central oversight on the employment of these non-traditional faculty, and no overall institutional policies to guide action?

## Development of the Non-tenure Track Faculty Committee

It is within this context that the non-tenure track faculty at USC worked to develop a strategy and plan for improving their work environment. The non-tenure track faculty make up approximately 50 percent of the faculty at USC, not uncommon for an institution with many professional schools. With these large numbers emerges the ability to develop a persuasive voice. As a result, the non-tenure track faculty committee, an academic senate subcommittee, was established over 15 years ago to oversee issues related to the non-tenure track faculty experience. The academic senate is the elected and representative body of the entire faculty (tenure-track and non-tenure track alike). The non-tenure track faculty committee is comprised of primarily non-tenure track faculty, representing most of the academic units within the university. The prospective members of the non-tenure track faculty committee can either self-nominate or be nominated by others; then the executive committee of the academic senate appoints the membership from the pool of nominees. Thus—and this is a very important point—*the committee is neither elected nor technically representative.* Its primary purpose, then, is to serve in an advisory capacity to the senate's executive committee, rather than as a decision-making body.

Over the past 15 years, the non-tenure track faculty committee has made serious strides in bringing non-tenure track issues to the forefront of the university's consciousness; and more and more attention has been paid publicly, at the university level, to the work experience of non-tenure track faculty. The early history of the committee was not well documented; there was little activity and it had a relatively small membership. Merely forming the committee was, however, an important step in recognizing that non-tenure track faculty were on campus and should also be supported in their work. The committee was able to obtain some minor changes in the faculty handbook, through a collaboration with the vice provost for faculty affairs who had a concern that non-tenure track faculty were not receiving equitable treatment in some units. In the past five years there has been substantial, measurable change seen in the creation and publication of policies specific to non-tenure track faculty within the schools.

## Creating a New Charge and Delving into Policy

In the academic year 2007–2008, the membership concluded that the committee needed to become more involved in policies affecting non-tenure track faculty, both campus-wide and within the individual academic units. This was driven by very rich discussions that revealed the extent to which policies and processes affecting non-tenure track faculty varied widely among the academic units, including a few cases in which the policy of a unit actually violated the faculty handbook. Thus, as a first step, in 2008, the committee proposed a motion to the academic senate, which it adopted, that both changed the committee's name and refined its purpose. (It is important to note that the vice provost for faculty affairs, who had earlier worked to help initiate handbook changes, also supported these changes.)

Originally known as the non-tenure-track faculty committee, the committee's activities tended to focus on "soft" topics such as training and career development rather than "hard" policy matters like merit review, promotion, and contract terms. The new name was the academic senate committee on non-tenure-track faculty affairs (CNTTFA), which better reflected the committee's and the senate's view that it should be more actively engaged in providing policy-related advice to the senate's executive committee. But more important than a simple name change was the newly focused mission. The 2008 motion specified that the CNTTFA's responsibilities were to include the *monitoring* of "the working environment, conditions of employment, benefits eligibility, opportunities for participation in governance, opportunities for professional advancement, and participation in the academic life of the university provided for non-tenure-track faculty." The exact wording has changed somewhat since then, but the intent remains the same. This monitoring function is extremely important in a "federated" system like USC's, in which the academic units enjoy a great deal of freedom and independence of action relative to policy-making (within certain parameters established by the central administration). This autonomy results in a wide variance in non-tenure-track-related policies and practices found among the academic units.

Also in 2007–2008, and after a great deal of deliberation, the CNTTFA determined that its monitoring function could only be successfully undertaken if benchmarks were established for non-tenure track policies and procedures, and that the only way to establish such benchmarks was by conducting a comprehensive inventory of all 17 USC academic units, looking at the non-tenure track policies and practices that were then in place. In addition to helping fulfill the CNTTFA's monitoring assignment, a comprehensive inventory also gave the schools the tools they needed (i.e., the processes and procedures used by other units) better to support their own non-tenure track faculty. For example, the schools were beginning to recognize the value of their non-tenure track faculty in running their programs, teaching their students, and acquiring grant contracts. Some have stated that they want to support non-tenure track faculty career development and its contribution to the school, and have taken substantive action to demonstrate that support. However, when there is no centralized model or guideline to work from, each school must develop a model that respects the work and culture of that school, on its own. The decentralized culture also results in schools not knowing whether their practices are normative for the institution;

hence the need for a committee that created dialog among non-tenure track faculty across the various units. And as we will see in the next section, the use of data and sharing of promising practices can be useful in this decentralized model to help leaders become aware of policies that might work. The survey of practices across the schools that culminated in the first White Paper on exemplar non-tenure track faculty practices at USC showcased model policies so that all deans would have access to this information.

It is important to note that leadership of the committee consists mostly of full-time non-tenure track faculty, and that the data collection and the policies then reviewed have all been focused on full-time non-tenure track faculty. Discussions are now under way regarding how future work needs to include part-time faculty. This group has been harder to involve and organize because it is so large and is, by definition, also employed elsewhere, and is therefore not on the USC campus the majority of the time.

## Strategies for Change

### Creating an Inventory of Policies and Committee Growth and Visibility

While the challenges that came with undertaking such a never-before-attempted inventory were daunting (especially because the committee was a voluntary body), the potential benefits were clear and provided all the incentive that was needed. First, because the CNTTFA lacked hard data on current policies and practices, without an inventory, there was no sound basis on which it could provide the senate's executive committee with credible counsel and actionable recommendations. Second, the data would make it possible to compare objectively the practices and policies of the units within the university, thereby providing a clear frame of reference for all subsequent deliberations. Third, as described above, the results could be used by the academic units when assessing and improving their own policies. Fourth, any outliers, whose policies around non-tenure track faculty were underdeveloped or in violation of the university's guidelines, would be obvious by comparison with generally accepted norms, and, it is hoped, would be motivated to take corrective action.

Naturally, when undertaking an inventory, one must begin by identifying the items or concepts to be inventoried. Therefore, the CNTTFA conducted both a mini-survey and focus-group discussions within the committee itself. In the course of the committee's internal discussions, the astonishing extent to which non-tenure track policies and procedures varied among the units became clear. For example, here is just a sampling of the nomenclature used to categorize non-tenure track faculty:

- assistant clinical professor, associate clinical professor, full clinical professor;
- assistant research professor, associate research professor, full research professor;

- assistant professor of practice, associate professor of practice, full professor of practice;
- assistant lecturer, associate lecturer, and lecturer;
- visiting assistant professor, visiting associate professor, visiting full professor.

But perhaps more important than the maze of titles was the fact that, even in cases where similar titling was used in multiple units, the workload profiles and policies applied to those titles often varied widely. In addition, the very language used to describe non-tenure track faculty as a category was found to be problematic, because *non*-tenure track describes faculty as something that they *are not*, or that they *lack*, as opposed to something that affirmatively states what they *are*, and *possess*. Ultimately, though, through these very healthy discussions, the CNTTFA determined the eight core non-tenure track faculty issues:

1. titling language and categories;
2. workload profiles;
3. involvement in governance;
4. contract renewal and duration;
5. merit review policy;
6. promotion policy;
7. professional development;
8. availability of paid professional leave.

It is important to note that the issue that had the greatest overall importance was "job security." However, because job security is a broad concept with many contributing elements, the committee decided to address it by focusing on the policies and procedures that have a direct bearing on job security (i.e., merit review, contract renewal and duration, etc.). To optimize the extent to which policies could be compared on an apples-to-apples basis, a standardized questionnaire for the various academic units was developed that covered the entire eight core issues listed above.

As word of the committee's increasingly important activities spread, its membership had grown to more than 30 people, including non-tenure track faculty from all of the academic units. Thus, the work of gathering data from all of their units, most of which included multiple sub-units and departments, was distributed fairly equally among the committee members. In carrying out data collection, members met with the appropriate administrators in their respective units, reviewed numerous policy documents, and completed the standardized questionnaire. The results were then combined into a single, massive Excel spreadsheet that enabled unit-to-unit comparisons on any of the key issues. Much of the data collection took place in 2007–2008, but the scope of the project caused it to continue into 2008–2009.

## Creating a White Paper Showing Policies

Realizing that the data were not sufficiently accessible in the worksheet format, and that some degree of analysis and commentary was necessary to make the data actionable, in 2008–2009, the CNTTFA, with the support of the central administration and the senate's executive committee, decided to produce a "White Paper on Exemplary Practices and Policies Relating to Non-Tenure Track Policies and Procedures" (see Appendix A). As the title suggests, this paper went beyond simply listing the data gathered through the policy inventory, but presented a more thorough analysis of the data. The White Paper showcased policies not just from USC, but also compared policies at USC to those collected from peer institutions and an American Association of University Professors report (AAUP, 2006) on recommendations for non-tenure track faculty. Based on this additional data the committee developed a set of five criteria that could be utilized to distinguish "exemplary" practices, procedures, and policies from all others:

1.  substance (i.e., content that effectively addresses one of the eight core issues);
2.  clarity (i.e., adequate written detail and explanation);
3.  fairness and consistency (i.e., an indication that the policy can be applied fairly and consistently in multiple, similar situations);
4.  rationale (i.e., the reasoning behind the policy is logical and relevant);
5.  implementation (i.e., the extent to which the practice or policy is actually utilized in the unit).

Over several months a small subcommittee wrote, edited, and rewrote the White Paper, which was finally completed and submitted to the academic senate's executive committee in May of 2009—the very end of the 2008–2009 academic year. (Please see Appendix A for a copy of the White Paper.)

While the issue of titling language was addressed in the White Paper, a conscious decision was made not to take on the issue of what the term "non-tenure track" did or did not convey, because of its complex nature and the risk of it becoming a major distraction from other more pressing and actionable matters. Indeed, the committee developed many alternative terms, but all were found to be significantly flawed, usually because they did not adequately address the varying workloads and profiles to be found among the many units, which were a problem in themselves.

It was at this point that a very interesting phenomenon began to take place. While the White Paper was submitted too late in the academic year for it to have any immediate effect (which was not unexpected, given the scope of the project), and while it did not have any "official" status as a document formally adopted by the academic senate, it began to take on a life of its own. Because it had been, by its very nature, a high-visibility undertaking, committee members were often asked about the inventory and the resulting White Paper, and it was widely circulated among the academic units.

At least partially as a result of the White Paper, in the following 2009–2010 academic year there was much campus-wide discussion of non-tenure track faculty policies. A significant number of academic units undertook reviews of their own policies, and while the CNTTFA certainly cannot take credit for all the changes that have taken place (and continue to take place), it is worth noting that it is not unusual for those changes closely to resemble the exemplars described in the White Paper. And it is certainly true that colleagues in various units have told committee members that: "This change happened because of your committee's efforts."

More specifically, there have been many reports of schools making significant changes or creating entirely new policies or guidelines around their non-tenure track faculty employment practices based on the exemplars presented in the White Paper. One school reported that they had developed a promotion policy that allowed for advancement in rank, title, and salary, as well as multi-year contracts. Other schools reported that they had augmented their governance practices to include non-tenure track faculty in their leadership structure and decision-making processes. Still others were grappling with the workload issue, so that non-tenure track faculty are not unfairly burdened with teaching and administrative responsibilities in the school. These were all positive changes that did not result from a change in policy at the university level, but resulted from the sharing of best practices with both administrators and faculty so that each school was armed with information about what was working in other schools, leaving non-tenure track faculty in a more empowered position to advocate for themselves and the good of their school.

In 2010–2011, because it had been two years since the White Paper, and believing it was time to re-evaluate what was happening at USC university-wide, the CNTTFA gathered data for a follow-up inventory and also conducted qualitative focus groups with NTTF in each unit to understand policy implementation (see Appendix B). The results of the survey's focus groups will be showcased in an updated White Paper will be written in the 2011–2012 academic year. We have heard anecdotal evidence about powerful change, but would like to evaluate hard data about what is currently happening in the schools.

## *Use of Peer Comparisons*

In 2010, based on the White Paper and its end-of-the-year summary report, the CNTTFA was invited to develop a memorandum proposing some changes to non-tenure track faculty policy that the senate might consider and distribute to the deans. But in order to support such changes, the committee leadership realized that the legitimacy of the recommendations could be enhanced by providing peer benchmark data. The committee conducted a document analysis of the faculty handbooks of 11 peer institutions (Columbia University, Cornell University, Harvard University, New York University, Princeton University, Stanford University,

University of California, Berkeley, University of California, Los Angeles, University of Pennsylvania, University of Washington, and Yale University). A memorandum was sent to the executive committee of the academic senate with a summary of findings from these peer institutions about how non-tenure track faculty employment policies and benefits were addressed, and the changes that the CNTTFA would recommend based on the data collected.

This memorandum sparked an invitation to report these findings to the entire academic senate. An interesting note to this invitation was that the senate wanted original sources cited and *included* in the presentation during the meeting. It was clear they wanted more than a review of the original memorandum, in which the CNTTFA had simply summarized the findings of the peer review, but did not include raw data to support each recommendation. It was not clear whether the executive committee members were in support of the recommendations, or whether they were more curious about what the actual data reflected about non-tenure track policies. When the raw data was reported in the senate meeting, there appeared to be some surprise about the number of peer intuitions that were "non-tenure track friendly," and the extent to which they extended benefits to non-tenure track faculty. Whether the senate's point was to learn more about our recommendations or check on our data, the request to have the data presented clearly ultimately worked in the CNTTFA's favor. The data made it difficult to argue against better non-tenure track policies at USC, especially if our mission is to become a leading university with a critical mass of both tenure-track and non-tenure track faculty.

The key elements covered in the meeting were workload, profile, title, sabbaticals/professional leave, equity in work distribution, contracts, and governance. On the topics of workload, profile, and title, the committee was able to demonstrate to the academic senate that the handbooks for most of these institutions contained more clarity than our own, but still maintained enough flexibility for those institutions to allow their schools easily to fulfill their unique needs. While the senate may not decide to change the language in USC's handbook, its members were very open to working with the deans to clarify their own written guidelines and criteria within their schools around these and other issues, based on the comparative data our committee provided.

One of the other issues that came up for non-tenure track faculty was sabbaticals/professional leave. While the USC faculty handbook guarantees full-time non-tenure track faculty the same rights (excluding lifetime employment) as the tenure-track faculty, there is no support in place to fund non-tenure track sabbaticals at the provost (university) level. To do so would mean using the same funds for sabbaticals as already exist, while increasing the number of sabbaticals approved. The committee used the data collected from peer institutions to point out that seven out of the 11 handbooks provided for funded professional leaves for non-tenure track faculty (six at the provost level). While the administration is not yet ready to change the sabbatical funding structure, it is being more vocal about encouraging school-, rather than university-, funded sabbaticals or professional leaves (the latter term seems to engender less resistance) for non-tenure track faculty within the schools. As a result, one school reports that a new pilot program, considering applications from non-tenure track faculty for professional leaves, is being launched in the coming academic year.

The CNTTFA also advocated for more oversight on workload assignment equity within schools, by highlighting Princeton's practice of requiring the dean of faculty to regularly interview non-tenured faculty to incorporate their views into governance, and to monitor, on a consistent basis, their workload to ensure fair and equitable distribution of work. Many non-tenure track faculty at USC serve in leadership or service positions across the campus, and often these positions require far more investment of time than is allotted for typical service assignments. In addition, each school differs as to whether they provide release time from other duties, or if they do, how much time is provided to take on these responsibilities.

Another area presented was that all but one peer institution has multi-year contract options for their non-tenure track faculty. This point ignited a discussion which ended in an agreement that the university administration supports multi-year contracts, should the schools decide to implement them. This is important, since in the past, the school administrators were under the impression that the university would not allow anything but rolling contracts.

The topic of governance was another area that sparked great discussion. All but one of our peer institutions included non-tenure track faculty in its governance structure and in leadership positions within the schools and the university. Again, most were in favor of non-tenure track faculty serving at all levels of the university. In fact, the discussion of this topic at the senate meeting allowed the USC administration to voice its serious concerns over the fact that there are *any* schools in the university that do not include non-tenure track faculty in their governance structure. The University of Southern California stands out in this area, as many schools have non-tenure track representatives in the academic senate, chairing faculty councils, and in senior leadership positions. In fact, in a handful of schools, non-tenure track faculty serve on merit and promotion review committees for tenure-line faculty (although they cannot vote on the conferral of tenure). However, there are still a couple of schools adhering to the view that only tenured associate or full professors should have voting rights in the school and university because of the academic freedom that tenure provides. After much discussion, the university administration fervently argued that *all* faculty at USC enjoy academic freedom.

With data from our peer institutions, it will be interesting to compare current practices at USC to the practices of these other universities. Once the new White Paper has been written, we can include the information from peer institutions, and again present this information to the university community. The updated USC data, juxtaposed against the data collected from our peer institutions, may be a powerful incentive for USC to become a leader in non-tenure track policies and practices.

## Getting a Platform with the Senate

In addition to presenting data from the White Paper, the CNTTFA also used the opportunity to voice some of their other concerns. For example, since the senate asked for a set of recommendations to be presented (the above peer comparisons), the committee also used this as an opportunity to lobby the senate for other improvements in the experience of non-tenure track faculty. The following are some other suggestions that the committee presented to the senate:

- clearer guidelines and criteria for the merit pay and promotion process;
- regular and ongoing orientation at the unit, school, and university level for new faculty;
- consideration given to the time it takes to orient and prepare for new courses or apply for new grants, resulting in workload release in order to provide time to get new faculty up and running, similar to what is provided for new tenure-line faculty;
- formal mentoring for junior faculty, in order to enhance their likelihood of success within the university;
- university-sponsored/approved fellowships, training opportunities, leadership development, research and grant support, and professional travel funds that would contribute to a culture of creativity and growth across the university, since growth for all faculty members depends on the time, space, and opportunity afforded to them to learn and try new things.

Being a subcommittee of the academic senate keeps CNTTFA members connected to the policymakers and people with influence at this university. Having this platform creates a reciprocal relationship. The committee not only responds to the senate's requests with the data that is needed, but the senate also listens to the committee's concerns. Below we discuss the senate's response to our suggestions mentioned above and the White Paper research.

## The Senate's Reactions to the Committee's Work

The reaction to the presentation to the academic senate was positive. Comparing USC with the peer-institution data was by far the most compelling element of the presentation, according to the feedback we received. The senate is, after all, comprised of scholars who pursue knowledge and evaluate data. The data speak far more powerfully than a subgroup of faculty. The new president of the academic senate asked to meet with the CNTTFA co-chairs to help him craft a memorandum reflective of the plan that he and the other executive committee members are working on to address non-tenure track faculty issues across the campus; and the memorandum has happily included responses to all of the issues raised by the CNTTFA. The new president will be encouraging dialog and clarification of policy around all of the major points raised by the committee.

It is unlikely, based on the conversation after our presentation, that any sig-nificant changes will be made to the faculty handbook. However, the executive committee's memorandum will be sent to all of the deans, with the support of the provost's office, and will outline recommendations for non-tenure track faculty policy across the university. This memorandum is a good foundation for initiat-ing self-examination and conversations at the school level, and will further the work we have done in creating a forum of comparison and consultation that works well with USC's decentralized model. The CNTTFA has also pledged to present our peer-institution findings at faculty meetings in all of the schools across the university, so that all faculty are aware of what is happening nationwide. We foresee even more changes resulting from this information, and from the influ-ence of the academic senate, which will, it is hoped, continue to change the reality, attitudes, and culture of the university. Perhaps as everyone becomes more comfortable and familiar with these practices, there will be less resistance to putting these ideas in writing in the future, and this will eventually lead to permanent changes in the faculty handbook.

## Lessons Learned

### Working With the University Culture and Not Against It

Embracing and capitalizing on the culture of the university have been much more fruitful than working against it. The University of Southern California has a very independent, entrepreneurial spirit. This ideal is regularly communicated in the president's messages to the university, commonly reflected in the attitudes and productivity of the faculty and staff, and saturates the students throughout their USC training. The university wants to produce leaders among all of our constituents, and for the most part we are free to figure out for ourselves how best to lead. So to try to impose universal policy across all levels of a very complex and dynamic university landscape creates resistance. What the non-tenure track faculty have found is that it is more effective to work with the grain than against it. We trust that most of our administrators and colleagues want to be fair, and want all faculty to prosper. We often only need to point out what works well, and why current practices may not be effective any more.

For example, when the non-tenure track faculty asked the academic senate to clarify the language in the faculty handbook about workload, profile, and titles for non-tenure track faculty, there was much resistance about taking away the power and agility of the deans to create positions that filled a need in their own school, by replacing the general handbook language with limiting and specific language. This was a roadblock that we could not overcome, regardless of where the discussion took place. Still, the senate was not unconcerned with the problem; they simply did not want to replace it with another problem at the administrative level. They were willing to try to influence the issue at the school level, given adequate evidence to support the request.

## The Value of a Bottom-up Approach to Change

The bottom-up approach of gathering data about what is happening on the ground at USC, and at other Tier One institutions, and presenting these results to the academic senate, deans, and faculty, appears to work well with the decentralized model of the university. This data is presented not with the intent of shaming or uncovering unfair practices, but with the intent of highlighting best practices. In this approach, the schools maintain their individuality and autonomy, and have access to cutting-edge examples of how to cultivate creativity, productivity, and satisfaction among their faculty. So they take what makes sense from their perspective from that data, and reshape the model to fit their needs, without having a model that may or may not fit their current needs imposed on them from the top. The university itself is undergoing a transformative process where it is recruiting some of the top researchers, innovators, practitioners, and teachers in the world. The schools understand that recruiting and retaining this caliber of faculty will require that all of their faculty feel valued, respected, well-treated and well-compensated. So the bottom-up approach of helping the schools develop new or effective ideas on how to grow and enrich their faculty will ultimately help them to fulfill the university's charge to transform the face of USC.

## Data Creates Influence

While it can be painstaking to collect data—whether it be a distillation of policies on our campus or on others—it is critical for creating change. We were able to gain the attention of the senate leadership through the creation of the White Paper and even the policy repository itself. The benchmark peer data was even more influential in demonstrating that changes we were proposing were not outside the norm. Data may be particularly important within the university environment where faculty spend their careers invested in research.

## Creating Community

Another important lesson to note was the power in building a community of action. The very act of organizing the CNTTFA around the mission of collecting data from all the units was, in itself, a powerful tool for building morale and cohesion within the committee and throughout the non-tenure track faculty community. There was the obvious benefit of associating with others who share similar experiences, but the added component of being committed to action and change empowered the CNTTFA. As a result, this committee is held in high esteem within the non-tenure track community. The committee is seen as an advocate for non-tenure track faculty. It is a safe place to discuss concerns and celebrate progress. The findings from the committee's research were certainly essential to our purpose, but the process used to gather the data was, in itself, a galvanizing force. In a situation like this, it is often true that the distinction between *means* and *ends* is vague, at best.

## Increasing Visibility and Credibility

Finally, it is important to note that the CNTTFA has given a voice to a previously voiceless group. Because we are connected to the senate, we have been given the opportunity to represent the concerns of the non-tenure track faculty on a university-wide stage. In doing so, we have further demonstrated that the fear often associated with giving voice to under-represented groups is unfounded. Our concerns were not without merit, and our requests were not unreasonable. What the university is finding is that what is good for the part is good for the whole. In meeting the needs of the non-tenure track faculty more effectively, the university is also benefiting from their experience, knowledge, and social capital. In many schools, non-tenure track faculty are often considered the most valuable players in the school (e.g., the dentists, the film makers, the attorneys, the market makers). They bring to the university great visibility and real-world knowledge in fields that change so quickly, it is difficult for the elements of academia to keep up (e.g., algorithms, textbooks, technology). Better working conditions that connote respect and value for non-tenure track faculty now attract these key players, who have been leaders in the field, to come and work for the university. These people often make far more money outside the university and hold very high status in their own practices and fields. So when the university cultivates a culture of creativity and innovation, it provides powerful non-monetary incentives for these high-profile leaders to come to the university to provide the knowledge and insight they have about their changing fields. The university and non-tenure track faculty are now profiting from a more mutually beneficial relationship that taps into what each has to offer the other.

| MOBILIZATION | IMPLEMENTATION | INSTITUTIONALIZATION |
|---|---|---|
| • Development of the non-tenure track faculty committee<br>• Changed name and purpose of committee<br>• Conducted a comprehensive inventory of policies and practices<br>• Data collection from peer institutions<br>• Created a white paper | • Some academic units/departments/schools reviewed policies and made changes<br>• Conducting a follow-up inventory | |

FIGURE 9.1 Overlay of three-stage model with University of Southern California's progress toward change

## Key Points:

1. Work within the culture and institutional context in order to facilitate the change process.
2. A senate subcommittee can be a valuable starting place for change. It can have more impact if it has authority, or works closely with the overall senate which is charged with hard issues of policy. The subcommittee can also build a non-tenure track faculty community.
3. Data collection provides models, benchmarks, and information that can be influential.
4. Setting up monitoring systems (like the inventory of policies) or ongoing data collection of policies or climate can help ensure that change is continuous.
5. Having a vehicle for compiling data and making it more meaningful (such as the White Paper) provides a way to reach many audiences that can lobby for change.
6. Setting an agenda for change is critical. In this case, the CNTTFA established eight areas of focus that became the data-collection areas for the inventory and the committee's agenda for change.
7. Discussions in open and influential fora build support for changes and can create allies.

## Key Questions:

1. Have we examined our culture and identified the best way to work within it?
2. Can we form a task force, group, or subcommittee to focus on non-tenure track faculty issues? Does the group have the needed authority and avenues for accessing influence? Is the group primarily made up of non-tenure track faculty so that they can develop a community?
3. Have we identified the data, models, or benchmarks we need to collect?
4. Have we considered ongoing monitoring vehicles? Do we have a vehicle for compiling and making the data we have meaningful for different stakeholder groups on campus? It may be that more than one type of report or repository is needed and will differ according to its target group.
5. Have we created an agenda for change?
6. Are there key fora for communicating the findings of data collection that will provide visibility, opportunities for problem-solving, and a way to discuss the data that might question assumptions and generate key questions?

## References

American Association of University Professors. (2006). *AAUP contingent faculty index 2006.* Washington, DC: American Association of University Professors.

# 10

# BUILDING A MULTI-PRONG, CONTEXT-BASED STRATEGY FOR CHANGE AT A PRIVATE CATHOLIC COLLEGE

*Adrianna Kezar*

Like most chapters in this book, the story of change at Villanova University starts with non-tenure track faculty taking a leadership role to improve their working conditions. Villanova is a private Catholic teaching institution with a particular culture focused on community and social justice, and the non-tenure track faculty leaders realized that they needed to pay attention to their context and culture to make change effectively. Being aware of their particular context, non-tenure track faculty developed a multi-pronged strategy for change in which they engaged different stakeholders from tenure-track faculty to administrators, used political persuasion, utilized data and benchmarks, leveraged what peer institutions were doing, and capitalized on pressure from external groups such as the Middle States accreditation process. This chapter documents the changes that have happened at Villanova and highlights three elements: the changes they have accomplished to date; the process that occurred to create these changes; and the unique lessons they learned—some that are specific to their campus culture and institutional type, and other strategies that are more broadly applicable to most campuses trying to create change.

## Growth of Non-tenure Track Faculty and Understanding the Changes Needed

Similar to many campuses across the United States, Villanova has had the long-standing practice of hiring non-tenure track faculty to teach an occasional course in specific departments. However, in the last decade, the numbers of non-tenure track faculty have grown significantly and Villanova's use of non-tenure track

**TABLE 10.1** Institutional Snapshot of Villanova University

| | |
|---|---|
| *Institutional type* | Private liberal arts college |
| *Student population* | Approximately 9,500 |
| *Unionized* | No |
| *State* | Pennsylvania |
| *Institutionalization phase* | Mobilization |
| *Main Changes* | Multi-year contracts; governance; professional leaves |

faculty has increased. The non-tenure track faculty on campus were aware that their experience and working conditions were not the same as those of tenure-track faculty; and as they became a significant percentage of the faculty, it became apparent to them that changes needed to happen.

One of the main areas that needed change was the perceived lack of respect. Both full-time and part-time non-tenure track faculty experienced this lack of respect from colleagues, mostly through the lack of multi-year contracts, faculty governance and departmental voting rights, and paid leaves. The non-tenure track faculty knew that compared nationally to many of their non-tenure track colleagues—those with poor pay, no benefits, and high teaching loads— their conditions were quite good. However, a critical insight for them was not to compare themselves to non-tenure track faculty with the worst conditions, but to realize they deserved working conditions like the tenure-track faculty, at least as similar as makes sense. They also needed to realize that general plans or agendas for change would not work and that they must find out what their institution required, and what were the main concerns of non-tenure track faculty at Villanova.

This task is not always easy as non-tenure track faculty can be a very diverse group with different needs and experiences (see the Preface to this book for discussion of this heterogeneity). For example, like many part-time faculty, non-tenure track part-timers do not enjoy benefits, but the full-time non-tenure track faculty do enjoy these benefits. However, overall at Villanova there were more similarities than differences in the perspectives and experiences among the part-time and full-time non-tenure track faculty. This is not to say there are not different types of non-tenure track faculty who teach at the institution for varying reasons, and exist within unique departmental conditions—but there were some agreed-upon issues that needed to be addressed.

Non-tenure track faculty at Villanova decided their first task toward creating change would be to gather institutional data: both existing campus data, as well as a survey of the non-tenure track faculty. In general, becoming familiar with the public data that the university has submitted to federal agencies is an important tactic for non-tenure track faculty leaders. Universities have to submit accurate data on faculty for government reports, and this requirement provides non-tenure track faculty with valuable information to draw upon over time. For example, non-tenure track faculty leaders got their data from a contact in the institutional research (IR) office. It will benefit contingent faculty leaders to become familiar with IR offices on their campus. These offices produce federal reports and can provide data on a variety of topics, such as non-tenure track faculty numbers, course load, salary and benefits, and contact information for surveys. At public institutions, these data are available and must be provided if an information request is made; but at private institutions, data are not necessarily publicly available. Therefore, in the private institution context, it is important to develop relationships with the institutional researcher or IR office. On some smaller campuses, if there is not an IR office, a faculty member in the social sciences may be in charge of institutional research. A relationship can be developed with this faculty member in order to obtain help in the change process.

In addition to examining existing data, faculty leaders at Villanova knew it was important to collect specific data from non-tenure track faculty about their experience and concerns. They started by surveying the full-time non-tenure track faculty. Given that non-tenure track faculty often feel disconnected from the institution, they needed to identify people in various departments and encourage individuals to fill out the survey. While not everyone filled out the survey, they obtained a 40 percent response rate. They presented the three themes that emerged from the survey at a meeting open to all non-tenure track faculty, and to be sure they had obtained information that reflected the campus more broadly, they allowed faculty to discuss what emerged in the surveys and to provide feedback. They felt confident that the three key areas for change were:

1.   longer-term contracts—three or five years;
2.   clear governance representation throughout the university (both in the faculty congress and within departments);
3.   paid leave to conduct scholarship.

Before the changes occurred, faculty were on yearly contracts and felt a great deal of job vulnerability. Also, participation in governance was not systematic. For example, some departments invited non-tenure track faculty to meetings, but others did not. There were no non-tenure track faculty on the faculty congress, and there was no clear understanding of the full-time non-tenure track faculty voting rights within the university or the departments. Finally, there were no professional leaves for non-tenure track faculty, and they felt it was important that some process be available for people who wanted to engage in some form of scholarship to enhance their work.

## Accomplishments

In terms of progress to date, non-tenure track faculty leaders were able to obtain three-year contracts through appeals to the academic vice president. Villanova recently issued the first long-term contracts and tied them to successful evaluations within the department. The non-tenure track faculty also gained access to more representation in governance within the university. Prominently, there are now two representatives on the faculty congress who are non-tenure track, and one elected seat for full-time non-tenure track faculty on the faculty senate. While only two seats are being held by non-tenure track faculty, the congress is relatively small with only 20 individuals, and they feel that they now have a substantial voice within governance. They recognize, however, that they do not have proportional representation, and this is an issue that they may need to address, especially if future votes find non-tenure track faculty issues ignored. They have also gained greater representation within departments; instead of a few departments inviting non-tenure track faculty and others excluding them, they discovered that the faculty handbook granted all non-tenure track faculty rights to attend and to vote on most issues within departments (excluding hiring, rank and tenure, and the selection of the department chair). Although there are some exclusions, non-tenure track faculty have made substantial progress in obtaining governance participation.

Villanova has made little progress on the issue of paid leave at this point. The faculty have a proposal written up for an annual fellowship for one semester's leave with full pay for one full-time non-tenure track faculty member who demonstrates excellence in teaching and a commitment to service in the college. This individual would have at least seven years of continuous service within the institution and would have to return to teaching the next semester. They are hopeful that the proposal for a paid leave (fellowship) will be granted in the near future. Villanova non-tenure track faculty leaders also recognize that they will continue to need new data every couple of years to see if conditions for non-tenure track faculty need more alteration or work, and to consider new issues that emerge. It may come to their attention that a poor climate has emerged within a particular department, for example. They are also looking into benefits for part-time faculty and need to collect data about this issue. Villanova is moving toward being a model of support for non-tenure track faculty nationally, and the change process has included tenure-track faculty as well as the administration. Next, the process that brought about these important changes is described.

## Process for Creating Change

As described in the section above on needed changes, the process for creating changes began with a survey of non-tenure track faculty and data collection. Yet conducting the survey alone would not have guaranteed that these changes would be integrated into the institution. In order to open up discussions about NTTF policy, the faculty leaders inserted their conclusions into the handbook revision that had just begun work. Villanova had not revised the faculty handbook in over a decade, and there was campus-wide recognition that it should be examined and potentially updated. Updating the faculty handbook is an area in which all faculty engage, and it was a way to bring the non-tenure track faculty issues to the attention of the entire faculty. As the handbook committee (a subcommittee of the academic policy committee) began to look at changes to the handbook, it received information about the rise in non-tenure track faculty numbers and the ways that they were often not integrated into the language of the faculty handbook.

Just the process itself of reviewing the faculty handbook led to some campus-wide changes. For example, the tenured faculty realized that non-tenure track faculty had governance rights within the faculty handbook, but this policy had neither been instituted nor carried out by the departments. Many faculty throughout the institution were completely unaware that this was the policy. When tenure-track faculty attention was focused on the faculty handbook, they realized they were out of sync with current policies and needed to alert the departments that the non-tenure track faculty must be informed of their governance rights in terms of attendance privileges and voting privileges in meetings. A letter was sent to all department chairs from the senior administration along with the faculty congress, asking them to comply with the handbook policy on governance. Also, the full-time non-tenure track faculty representatives on faculty congress began to collect their own data to understand more fully how departments were treating non-tenure track faculty. By sharing the results of that data with the faculty congress, the full-time non-tenure track faculty representatives hoped that other non-tenure track faculty in departments might follow the lead of the more progressive departments, once they learned that several departments did include full-time non-tenure track faculty in all of their deliberations.

Through the handbook committee process, change leaders were able to engage tenure-track faculty in problem-solving activities around the practices involving non-tenure track faculty. Non-tenure track faculty leaders started by engaging tenure-track faculty in a discussion about the role of non-tenure track faculty and policies affecting them, but they quickly realized that they needed to work with the administration as well. The tenure-track faculty may develop proposals for change, but if the administration is not open to such changes, it may be resistant. Therefore, non-tenure track faculty leaders shared the data from the survey with the administration to demonstrate that the proposals being brought forward from the academic policy committee and faculty congress represented broader concerns across the institution, not just the voice of a few non-tenure track faculty. They established an information-sharing process with the administration to help sensitize them to changes in policies that would be coming forth from the handbook committee and the non-tenure track group.

Another successful strategy was the documentation of progressive policies within certain departments. In their efforts to update the handbook, the faculty congress and academic policy committee collected policies within various departments (see also Chapter 9). In reviewing data, certain policies emerged that served as models. However, without a comparison of data across campus documenting each department, the collection of disparate practices would not have been as compelling and convincing. The data provided evidence of differing practices as well as models. Making this information public and available was critical, particularly on a campus that prides itself on community. Faculty change leaders plan to continue to collect departmental data and distribute it from time to time, so that departments become aware of model practices and policies that evolve. An example is a department that highlights the accomplishments of non-tenure track faculty in its communications. By showcasing this practice and making other departments aware of this mechanism that honors and respects the work of non-tenure track faculty, faculty change leaders can improve departmental climates.

Faculty change leaders also realized the importance of drawing on Villanova's social- justice mission as they made their case for improving the poor working conditions. Villanova is built on an ethic that the campus should work to make the world a better place for historically and currently marginalized groups. This value permeates the teaching, research, and service of the institution. Yet equitable working conditions for non-tenure track faculty in terms of governance, professional development, or job security had not been identified as an issue of social justice; contingent faculty leaders helped bring that perspective to individuals who were making decisions about this issue. Non-tenure track faculty leaders knew that the social-justice mission had been the reason for more equitable pay and benefits for non-tenure track faculty at Villanova, so the mission was a potential lever for change. They recognized that it might not be as apparent to administrators and tenure-track faculty that the principles of social justice should also be drawn into areas such as governance or professional development. It was the contingent faculty leaders' role to make these connections.

In addition to social justice, community is a very important principle at Villanova, and most people at the institution know each other quite well. It is much harder in a smaller community for people to make decisions that are inequitable; drawing upon this principle of community is also a significant way to help create better working conditions for non-tenure track faculty that will enhance student learning. The administrators on campus were particularly drawn to principles about community and social justice, as they weighed decisions to make changes for non-tenure track faculty.

While change leaders worked from the inside drawing on principles of social justice and community, contingent faculty leaders also recognized the importance of external levers for change, such as accreditation and institutional peers. Higher-education institutions are always in some phase of the accreditation process and leaders can use this element to leverage change. Villanova was in the process of conducting its Middle States self-study and this was a vehicle that would allow the institution to examine and become aware of some of the needed changes related to non-tenure track faculty. As a part of the Middle States self-study, the Middle States Committee on Faculty conducted town-hall meetings with full-time non-tenure track faculty, and structured discussion groups. One of the recommendations in the current Middle States report is to create more predictability of employment for part-time faculty by better predicting of enrollments and teaching needs. While institutions have long found the prediction of scheduling classes a struggle, the self-study process asked the institution to take on this challenge of examining data for a better understanding of their enrollment patterns and teaching needs so that part-time faculty can be hired and have their classes scheduled ahead of time. This change would give faculty more time for preparation and improve the educational experience. The self-study report also noted that the pay level for non-tenure track faculty was below that of its peers, but not so much that it might affect recruitment of teacher–scholars who are non-tenure track. However, the documentation of lower levels of pay brings attention to an issue that the institution may need to address in the future in terms of keeping wages marketable.

The report also demonstrated that there was a retention problem with non-tenure track faculty because of campus climate issues. Non-tenure track faculty feel unsupported and have not enjoyed the same privileges as tenure-track faculty such as involvement in governance. The good news is that they are addressing this issue with the current changes, and over time, will be able to look back at data to see if the retention issue has been ameliorated. But the institution only became aware of the retention issue through the self-study process, and this helped make the case for the governance changes that non-tenure track leaders proposed. The accreditation self-study process served as an important opportunity for the campus to engage in learning and self-awareness around non-tenure track faculty issues. The contingent leaders appreciated how the administration and tenure-track faculty have been responsive to the issues identified in the self-study report.

Contingent faculty leaders realized that they also needed data about other peer institutions (see also Chapter 9) and their policies to help convince tenure-track faculty and administration further. The awareness they had developed among the tenure-track faculty and administration might not be enough. Therefore, they collected information about peer institutions to provide examples of how other campuses were developing policies. It was particularly helpful that one institution, for example, had some very progressive policies for non-tenure track faculty, including paid leaves. They collected data on aspirational peers in addition to their regional peers. They also capitalized on organizations such as the Association of Catholic Colleges and Universities, and publications that the association had written relating to campus policies for non-tenure track faculty.

Through these various external benchmarks, they helped provide the administration and tenure-track faculty with specific examples of policy language and a sense of promising practices used by their peers.

Change leaders at Villanova have continued to return to data collection throughout their process of change in order to navigate and develop direction. (One-time surveys are not enough and contingent faculty leaders should encourage regular data collection.) Not only do they collect new data, but they are drawing on past studies and examining how this data can inform the issue of non-tenure track faculty policies. Several years ago, the new president at Villanova had conducted a campus climate survey that hinted at some of the issues that contingent faculty leaders were addressing. In fact, the institution has used instruments that might be useful to other campuses attempting to understand faculty climate, such as the Higher Education Research Institute's faculty survey, available at http://www.heri.ucla.edu/facoverview.php. Many individual campuses have also developed surveys that one can model: for example, http://www.uwlax.edu/campusclimate/htm/survey.htm or http://www.sph.umn.edu/facstaff/sphfcc/climate/index.asp; a quick search of the internet provides dozens of examples. The *Diversity Digest* offers advice for conducting campus climate surveys at http://www.diversityweb.org/digest/sp.sm00/surveys.html. There is an ongoing commitment at Villanova to collect data every five years on faculty climate. This next climate survey will examine variations in the responses of full-time tenure-track, part-time non-tenure track, and full-time non-tenure track faculty.

## Lessons Learned

While the non-tenure track faculty leaders at Villanova have had much success in making changes, some strategies were more successful than others. When they veered from this multi-pronged process of working across the university and persuading different groups, or using multiple levers from inside and outside the institution, they did not always get the support to achieve the changes that they desired. For example, contingent leaders were working to have voting rights for non-tenure track faculty for the selection of department chairs, something which significantly influences the working lives of non-tenure track faculty. However, in the vote at the faculty congress on this issue, they overwhelmingly lost the vote with only one tenure-track faculty member voting with the two non-tenure track faculty. In reflecting about this process and the ways they could plan differently, they realized they had not done enough groundwork to build a case for this proposed change, establishing how it was important for creating an equitable environment.

Villanova faculty leaders experienced success when they obtained greater buy-in among all groups by engaging tenure-track faculty and administration as well as non-tenure track faculty members. This approach of working across campus and with various constituent groups on it is particularly important at an institution that has been espousing a live commitment to community. On some campuses, a more political approach of one group asserting its interests might work, but this strategy would not fit the culture of this institution or other collegial institutions. The non-tenure track faculty leaders also appealed to the Catholic values of the institution, and its underlying mission, to support the change process.

Another valuable lesson was the importance of balancing inside (appealing to values, collecting the practices of model departments) and outside processes (accreditation, benchmarking peer institutions). Institutional leaders may recognize the importance of change, but they may also be so locked into the way things have been done at the institution that they lack the imagination to create needed policies. External information and processes provide an outside lens, establishing a vision for the ways the institution may approach this task. This lens brings in ideas that would not have emerged if faculty and the administration had relied solely on internal ideas and information. For example, at one model peer institution, they did not call the paid professional leave "sabbaticals." The term conjures up the process used by tenure-track faculty, and a professional leave for non-tenure track faculty might entail different sorts of professional development; for example, one that focuses more on teaching. By changing the language of this professional development leave to a "fellowship," the institution overcomes the barrier of associating too closely the non-tenure track faculty leave with the traditional tenure-track sabbatical. By borrowing various external ideas, campuses create policies and practices that they may not have been able to imagine on their own. Furthermore, these external ideas provide pressure for campus change by demonstrating that the institution is not up to date with what is considered best or common practice. Faculty leaders at Villanova followed these best practices and used the term "fellowship" in their proposal for paid leave for non-tenure track faculty.

Non-tenure track faculty leaders at Villanova also learned an important lesson that making changes is a political process. When they relied solely on logic, empathy, morality, or rationale, their proposed changes were often met with resistance. The attempt to win the vote for full-time non-tenure track faculty participation in the department chair selection relied too heavily on logic rather than politics. One cannot underestimate the importance of maximizing existing relationships, advocating for the needed changes, and actually gathering votes. Pure logical or moral persuasion alone failed in various instances and they learned from those mistakes.

In the end, Villanova's story has its idiosyncrasies that relate to its history and culture in terms of appealing to the values of social justice and community or working with multiple constituents, but most of the tactics are transferable—use of data and benchmarks, importance of peer comparisons, accreditation as a potential site for learning and change, capitalizing on existing processes like

| MOBILIZATION | IMPLEMENTATION | INSTITUTIONALIZATION |
|---|---|---|
| • Initial meetings among departments with large numbers of non-tenure track faculty<br>• Survey<br>• Focus groups<br>• Three-part agenda<br>• Obtain allies in administration | • Revised hand book and realized rights to governance existed already<br>• Letter to deans<br>• Documenting policies that exist in different units<br>• Institute multi-year contracts<br>• Proposal for professional leave<br>• Benchmark peers<br>• Use external groups such as accreditors | |

**FIGURE 10.1** Overlay of three-stage model with Villanova's progress toward change

faculty handbook updates, informing and winning over the administration, showcasing model departments, and building support across the part-time and full-time non-tenure track faculty. The way, however, that they collect and use data or work with the administration may reflect their particular culture, and being aware of tweaking these tactics to fit the campus environment is important. They also developed changes that fit their context and met the problems they had identified as specific to their faculty concerns in terms of professional development, governance, and job security. Other campuses will find that they need to prioritize very different issues, but can use the processes for change and the lessons learned at Villanova to understand how to make the academy a better place for all faculty in order to create the best learning environment for students.

## Key Points:

1. Change can happen without unions through individual non-tenure track faculty leadership. Many of the same principles from union organizing can be used— consciousness raising, surveys, building an agenda, and creating allies.

2. When working outside a union, shared leadership with either the administration or tenure-track faculty is likely very important. Meeting with them and building those relationships is important. Find a collaborative process like revising the faculty handbook to bring people together for discussions.

3. Data should be collected—internally about problems and existing campus policies; and externally for models and benchmarks, which can be very compelling data to create change.

4. Reporting out data from data collection is important to obtain action. The creation of regular reports that compared different units' policies provided a helpful mechanism for individuals to digest information and act on it.
5. Campus values can be a critical lever for change.
6. External groups should be leveraged and used to exert pressure for change. This campus used the accreditation process. This is a lever available to almost every campus in the United States.
7. Ongoing data collection helps to identify emerging problems—at this campus, they were climate and part-time faculty issues.
8. Be careful to use several strategies for change and not rely too heavily on any one.
9. Change is a political process. While unions make this more obvious, those on non-union campuses must realize this as well, even if they are on what may feel like a very collegial campus.

## Key Questions:

1. What data do we collect related to non-tenure track faculty? What outside information would be helpful for comparing and understanding whether non-tenure track faculty are treated equitably on our campus?
2. Are we regularly communicating with stakeholders on campus about data we have collected and changes that are needed?
3. Are we becoming familiar with the institutional research (IR) office on our campus?
4. Are we working with the administration in addition to the tenure-track faculty?
5. What values on our campus can be leveraged for change? Can we use them toward the good of non-tenure track faculty?
6. What does our faculty handbook say about non-tenure track faculty?
7. What external groups can be leveraged for change? Accreditation bodies, disciplinary societies, local community, and/or alumni?
8. Are we collecting best practices from peer institutions?
9. After initial changes, do we continue to collect data that might help us identify problems?
10. What strategies are we using? Are we depending on several different types—data collection, external pressure, seeking allies, etc?
11. Have we acknowledged the political character of this change process? Do we regularly meet with people to see if we have their support?

# PART III

# Synthesis of Lessons Learned

# 11

# TAKING HEART, TAKING PART

## New Faculty Majority and the Praxis of Contingent Faculty Activism[1]

*Maria Maisto*

The research that provides the foundation for this book, and the case studies that are featured in it, are an important advance in the movement to confront problems associated with contingent employment practices in higher education. Although the anti-contingency movement has existed for nearly as long as contingent hiring practices have been in place, the movement's concerns—the need for equitable treatment and professional respect for all faculty—have been regarded, like the faculty who have led it, as essentially "adjunct" or "non-essential" to mainstream higher education concerns about such issues as curriculum, faculty professionalization, student success and access, diversity, campus–community relations and financial responsibility. Past and current crises have shown such neglect to be a serious mistake. While it may have been easy to dismiss the problem when the total number of contingent faculty was relatively small, the range of costs associated with the steady, well-documented growth of the contingent faculty population—in 2011, two-thirds to three-quarters of the total number of higher education faculty, depending on whether graduate students are included in the calculation—has made neglect of the issue both impossible and irresponsible.

The steep costs of contingency are now in full view. They include lost financial resources for professionals who made huge investments in their own education; lost talent, as colleges and universities have driven away faculty who could not abide the working conditions they were being asked to accept; and lost time, embodied in the administrative inefficiencies that are tied (for administrative staff) to processing huge numbers of temporary faculty, and (for contingent faculty) to learning to juggle multiple, often conflicting, procedures, platforms, and pedagogies. The educational ramifications of contingency include documented links to academic underachievement by students, as inconsistent and sub-standard working conditions, along with workload creep, often prevent both contingent and tenure-line faculty from devoting necessary time to their teaching (Jacoby, 2006; Umbach, 2007). There have also even been serious, sobering human costs as stories of stress-induced illness among contingent faculty members are increasingly common and seemingly in need of formal study.[2]

Thanks to the efforts of scholars and activists, including those featured in this book, however, the higher education community is finally realizing that the problems associated with contingent faculty hiring are not peripheral, but rather central to higher education's future. That scholarly research on contingency has increased at the same time that localized social and political activism has spread is a logical outcome of the rise in contingent faculty numbers and concern for its effects on the educational mission at the heart of higher education. New Faculty Majority: The National Coalition for Adjunct and Contingent Equity (NFM) and its affiliated educational and research arm, the New Faculty Majority Foundation (NFMF), were founded as a result of this increased research and activism—as contingent faculty activists and their allies, reflecting on both the history of their efforts and on research into the causes and effects of contingency, recognized that the time was finally right for an organization devoted exclusively to improving higher education by confronting the problem of contingency.

In this chapter, I reflect on the evidence presented by the research of Kezar and her contributors, as embodied in the case studies, as well as in her analysis of the change principles and strategies they illustrate (see Chapter 1 and Chapter 2 in this book) and in the conclusions she draws for the benefit of ongoing and future efforts (see Chapter 12 in this book). My perspective comes from my own background, which includes not only being intimately familiar with the founding and evolution of NFM, but also a brief stint as a faculty senator at the University of Akron and, prior to that, seven years working at two national higher education associations. Of course I also draw heavily on my own experience as a contingent faculty member, at both a research institution and a community college, in English composition, which is recognized as having one of the highest rates of contingent faculty among all academic departments.

In the first part of my reflection, I discuss what I believe to be the most instructive lessons and observations from the case studies and analysis, particularly in light of what NFM has also learned. Then I explain in more detail how NFM and the NFM Foundation see their roles in the contingent faculty movement, and offer some general thoughts on the relationship of this movement to social change efforts on a broader level. My hope is that my contribution, like those of my fellow faculty contributors to this book, will clarify the relevance of contingent faculty employment reform to the fundamental mission of higher education.

## Lessons

Two lessons drawn from the case studies and analysis presented in this book have particular relevance to what NFM and its Foundation have learned so far.

The first is the evidence that achieving some measure of stability for contingent faculty is a critical first step in the reform process. The second lesson, related to the first, is that certain long-standing assumptions about barriers to contingent faculty activism (especially fear, poor self-esteem, apathy, and heterogeneity) can be successfully challenged. These lessons lead to more general observations about the synergistic and dialectical relationship between the theory and practice, or praxis, of contingent faculty activism, the role of NFM (and indeed of projects like this book) in making such praxis possible, and the place of this activism in the broader context of social change movements.

## Lesson One: The Relationship of Stability to Strategy

It is notable that one of the most important messages that comes out of the case studies, and that has especially guided NFM's work in its formative years, is the basic, practical need to prioritize the *stabilizing* of contingent faculty work life as a critical first step in the change effort. Stabilization, in this framework, refers to the need to eliminate or at least reduce, the psychological and financial stress and uncertainty that obstruct faculty work and discourage activism. This stress, which can be good only because it often pushes faculty into activism and into seeking out the kind of support provided by NFM, also prevents contingent faculty from establishing institutional roots deep enough to build the kind of knowledge and relationships that facilitate both commitment and reform.

For many contingent faculty, as the case studies from SF State (Chapter 8), Cal Poly Pomona (Chapter 7), MATC (Chapter 4), and VCC (Chapter 3) show especially clearly, this kind of stability has been provided through formal union structures which are able to compel institutions to provide adequate working conditions. Having basic needs addressed then allows faculty to focus more effectively on issues like curriculum and governance. However, the very centrality of the union role in these exemplary case studies only highlights the fact that in a significant number of U.S. states, contingent faculty access to unions is blocked, either legally or culturally. In these places—my home state of Ohio among them—the enormous burden to students, faculty and the public of contingent faculty members' financial and psychological instability becomes painfully evident, as my colleague Matt Williams and I argued in an op-ed (opinion piece) for Cleveland newspaper *The Plain Dealer* in February 2011 during the height of the attack on public collective bargaining (Maisto & Williams, 2011). The proven importance of unions—and the inconsistency of contingent faculty experience with unions (having good ones, not having them at all, and having bad unions which do not adequately represent them)—seems to have vindicated NFM's practical objective of seeking stability as a prerequisite for more far-reaching reform efforts tackling critical issues like the quality of education and the integrity of the profession.

Another important component of stability is the length and depth of the relationship between contingent faculty members and the institutions and communities in which they work. The case studies in this book indicate that contingent faculty leaders who have been able to plant strong roots in their institutions and communities are usually the most successful change agents. Typically, contingent faculty, particularly those at institutions without union organization or in areas where "freeway flying" is common, already face the daunting challenge of trying to integrate into the broader campus and community culture. The importance of familiarity with campus and community culture, then, cannot be understated. For contingent faculty leaders, this includes connection with long-term colleagues: Long-time part-timers who may be unwilling to step forward in a more public way may still be invaluable resources because of their institutional memories and ability to identify the kind of opportunities that are illustrated by the faculty handbook revision episode highlighted in the Villanova case study (Chapter 10).

Recognizing these important dimensions of stability as a factor in effecting change, NFM in its first two years has focused on two basic goals. First, we are carefully building our national organization, in order to provide all contingent faculty, both within and outside of unions, with the reassurance of a formal, stable, independent organization that can serve as advocate, community, and information clearing house.[3] Second, we are working to provide contingent faculty with practical support to confront what they have identified as the biggest obstacles to their ability to work effectively and to engage in advocacy: lack of access to healthcare, unemployment insurance, and due process. As a result, we now offer health insurance to most NFM members and are working to provide even better coverage for all of our members. Similarly, our Unemployment Compensation Initiative (UCI) aims to secure unemployment insurance for all faculty who need it to survive the periods in between terms. (The UCI also promotes institutional accountability by seeking to end the "have your cake and eat it, too" institutional practice of preserving managerial flexibility while denying adjuncts the benefits that other seasonal workers receive.) Meanwhile, NFM's advocacy agenda has included public and private efforts (letter writing, petitions, connecting individuals to local resources both within and outside of unions) to support contingent faculty facing questionable or retaliatory behavior by institutions or even unions.

Significantly (since this sometimes puts NFM at odds with some faculty senates and unions), NFM's practical initiatives to provide contingent faculty with a measure of material and psychological security also include encouraging contingent faculty inclusion in governance, and discouraging tenure-line faculty course overloads (overtime) and caps on adjunct workloads. While some may find this position to contradict the finding in most of the case studies (notably Chapter 8 on SF State and Chapter 3 on VCC) of the importance of building faculty solidarity, NFM intends its position on overloads and caps to challenge a fundamentally class-based practice, and actually strengthen faculty alliances while also helping to change academic culture. And again, NFM has taken this position for the practical purpose of helping contingent faculty become more anchored to fewer campuses so that they can build relationships with colleagues, students, and community members that are more likely to lead to meaningful collaboration and change.

Stabilization is thus a precondition for the ability of contingent faculty to invest in campus life and culture in a deeply rooted way. As the case studies vividly demonstrate and the analysis of Kezar and Sam (see Chapter 2) makes clear, stability helps bring about the kind of culturally rooted collaboration that brings about positive, lasting change.

## Lesson Two: Conquering Stereotypes

In *The Practical Strategist: Movement Action Plan (MAP) Strategic Theories for Evaluating, Planning and Conducting Social Movements*, social change theorist Bill Moyer (1990: 2) observed that activists are regularly susceptible to the mistaken belief that they are failing, and instead need to learn to recognize when their efforts are "moving through the normal stages to success." For contingent faculty, who still often exist in a culture in which professional disrespect is rampant and in which, as Päivi Hoikkala points out (Chapter 7), their employment status is taken to be evidence of personal failure, published research like Kezar's (in this book; Kezar & Sam, 2010)—which not only recognizes their successful efforts, but also highlights the leadership roles that they themselves have undertaken in order to achieve success—is absolutely critical to empowerment, to movement building, and to the dismantling of powerful and pervasive stereotypes that have helped perpetuate the contingent hiring system.

Thus it cannot be emphasized enough that the efforts documented in these case studies were almost universally initiated and led by contingent faculty. Kezar is absolutely right when she says (in the Preface to this book) that this "is all the more remarkable since contingent faculty are often in marginal positions on campuses." The recognition that change is not only possible, but has in fact happened or is happening—and is being led by colleagues in similarly marginal positions—can propel contingent faculty into leadership roles.

As an example: Jack Longmate, one of the co-founders of NFM and co-author of Chapter 3 on VCC, often recounts how meeting his co-author Frank Cosco and hearing about the regularized system at VCC was a life-changing moment that re-energized his activism.[4] Encounters like this—what Chip and Dan Heath in their book *Switch: How to Change Things When Change is Hard* (2010) call the exposure to "bright spots" or exemplars of the change being sought—can come through networking and organizing, which NFM seeks to provide, as well as simply through a growing awareness of the successful history of activism, as Shawn Whalen experienced at SF State (see Chapter 8). Whalen's deep respect for fellow activists and what he calls the "enduring legacy of the campus's grassroots commitment to social justice and equity" has clearly been as influential to his leadership as has Longmate's friendship with Cosco.

Whalen also shows insight into the complexity of the psychological dimension of contingent faculty activism. While describing a faculty culture in which solidarity between contingent and tenure-stream faculty is common, Whalen's chapter demonstrates how the views of contingent faculty establish a psychological climate in which their activism takes place. At SF State, the long history of activism created a more hospitable climate for making changes. Like Hoikkala, whose case study on Cal Poly Pomona (Chapter 7) compares the experience of acknowledging one's contingent status to confessing to being a recovering alcoholic, Whalen is very much aware that the vast majority of contingent faculty must confront significant, long-standing psychological barriers to activism.

Discussions of barriers to faculty activism always highlight narratives of fear, self-hatred, and apathy. It has long been a truism among faculty activists that the biggest obstacle to reform is the fear that purportedly dominates contingent faculty life—fear is tied to the precariousness of their employment. No one involved in this activism would deny the extent of contingent faculty fear, particularly during the current economic recession. Periods of economic crisis, for example, can be the hardest times to recruit contingent faculty to activism, not just because they may be afraid of losing assignments, but indeed because they may be receiving welcome extra course assignments for which they are not usually eligible.[5]

Perhaps more pernicious than fear is the widespread observation (again vividly illustrated in Hoikkala's case study in Chapter 7) that contingent faculty often internalize attitudes of inferiority. In 2009, *The Chronicle of Higher Education* (Schmidt, 2009) reported on the presentation of the Kezar & Sam study at the annual conference of the Association for the Study of Higher Education (ASHE), noting the extent to which mobilization seemed to be "hindered by adjunct faculty members themselves, many of whom had absorbed the negative images that full-time faculty members had of them and did not think they deserved better working conditions" (Schmidt, 2009: paragraph 12). A more complicated version of this inferiority complex has been described as the dangerous tradition, within academia and in the so-called "feminized" professions in particular, of subjugating the perfectly rational—and honorable—right to fair compensation for one's labor to a false, martyr-like notion of service and vocation that is easily used to justify exploitation.[6] This tendency, sometimes called the fallacy of teaching for love, is particularly distressing given the statistics that show that the disciplines that are most likely to hire contingent faculty are also most likely to employ a majority or significant percentage of women.

Less widely discussed, but no less of an obstacle to contingent faculty-led reform initiatives is the problem of apparent apathy. This psychological barrier is linked to the more widely discussed characteristic of reported contingent faculty "satisfaction," which is in turn linked to public (mis)understanding of the nature of faculty work, and especially the nature of adjunct faculty work. Often perpetuated by institutional marketing campaigns (but certainly rooted in some reality), the narrative features the successful "practitioner" who is providing "real-world" expertise to students out of a sense of civic duty, professional pride, or a desire to "dabble" in teaching. A version of the adjunct who teaches for love, this type was once approvingly described to me by a foundation officer as someone who is so uninterested in financial remuneration for his teaching that "he just signs his check over to the foundation." Presumably, therefore, adjuncts who are apathetic about working conditions may simply have a high degree of personal satisfaction with their situation. The more important point, however, is that the satisfied/apathetic adjunct represents only one sector of a very diverse population, and that this heterogeneity is yet another barrier to faculty mobilization as the challenge facing reformers is how to find common core values that can unite and inspire all contingent faculty.

In response to the challenge posed by the psychological barriers of fear, apathy, and self-hatred, NFM's experience, along with the findings of this national study (this book; Kezar & Sam, 2010), unexpectedly and directly challenge these powerful stereotypes. On the issue of fear, contingent faculty have indicated that whether through active agency or the experience of forces beyond one's control, there is a point at which fearfulness is overcome. I include myself among the many who have discovered that events like the economic recession can simply be the final straw, providing a Janis Joplinesque sense of freedom.[7] I also discovered the strength that comes from community and solidarity, as the anxiety generated by my own family's temporary dependence on my part-time faculty salary of less than US$20,000 per year as our primary source of income was offset by the energy and friendship of my contingent colleagues, first at the University of Akron, then at the online community at the adj-l listserv, and finally with the cherished colleagues with whom I have been building NFM.

Unlike fear, apathy/satisfaction can present a stronger challenge. It can be difficult to critique this stance because it is an offshoot of the oft-cited heterogeneity of the adjunct faculty demographic profile, and falls under a rubric of respect for individual choice—not unlike the respect afforded to citizens who choose not to exercise their right to vote, as upsetting as that may be to those who cherish participatory democracy.

Yet the problem of apathy is also tied to the issues of professionalism and governance. Kezar refers (in Chapter 1, under "Governance") to a definition of professionalism that recognizes both a right and an obligation to attend to the conditions not just of one's own work, but also to the working conditions of one's colleagues. So the case studies and analysis suggest the importance of asking the question: To what degree do contingent faculty have an obligation to the profession and to society rather than just to themselves and their own students, and how do contingent faculty exercise such an obligation? Can the development of a more nuanced notion of faculty professionalism uncover the shared core values that will build faculty solidarity in spite of contingent faculty heterogeneity and across faculty ranks?

Developing that sense of outward-focused professionalism is a challenge faced by all faculty.[8] Promoting an understanding of contingent faculty professionalism that includes a place for activism, however, raises the particular challenge of overcoming fear and self-hatred. Like Ernesto Cortés, the social change theorist (cited by Hoikkala in Chapter 7) who points out these "corrupting" effects of powerlessness, Moyer (1990: 5) suggests that social activists have an obligation to attend to their own individual psychological and even spiritual health, by making "the emotional adjustments and changes required for them to redefine themselves as powerful and successful." Moyer's insight is that they "need to give up the psychological 'advantages' of inferiority and be willing to become successful citizen-activists in a movement that is creating real social change" (Moyer, 1990: 5). On the spiritual level, Moyer suggests that we must cultivate "awareness and active exploration of the deeper dimensions of being human [in order to] give us strength, appreciation of the potential that resides within all of us, and a greater understanding of the challenge that true change represents to the individual and society" (Moyer, 1990: 6).

The second lesson to be learned from this study, then, is that just as the stereotype of the fearful adjunct can be refuted by the evidence of contingent faculty engaging in and succeeding at self-advocacy both individually and collectively, so can the more complex tropes of the self-hating adjunct and the satisfied or apathetic adjunct be countered with the examples and testimony of contingent faculty who refuse to succumb to inferiority complexes and who see their professionalism as academic citizenship as much as, or more than, personal fulfillment. Part of NFM's mobilizing and culture-change function is to provide contingent faculty with information about these exemplary individuals in the form of interviews and profiles, as a sort of compendium of examples of "best practice" individual psychology.

New Faculty Majority has incorporated these insights about attention to individual well-being into its increasing use of a metaphor derived from the familiar experience of pre-flight emergency operation demonstrations on airplanes: Just as adults are instructed to put on their own masks before assisting others, so must contingent faculty engage in self-advocacy, not only so they can serve their students more effectively, but also so that they can model advocacy to others, making of their activism a lesson for students, many of whom will soon be facing the same challenges as the trend toward precarious, contingent employment continues to spread throughout the economy.

## Observations

### *Toward a Praxis of Contingent Faculty Activism*

The lessons that we at NFM have distilled from our own experience as well as from the case studies and analysis featured in this book lead to a question and observation that may be fruitful for all would-be reformers both within and outside of higher education. The question is whether the change principles that Kezar highlights (in Chapter 2) are being invoked *consciously* by the activists featured in the case studies. From NFM's perspective, it would be interesting to learn the degree to which these faculty leaders have used theoretically grounded action plans, particularly in the face of documented obstacles to successful activism, including active resistance from tenure-line faculty and/or administrators.

I raise the question because for many of the most active and experienced contingent faculty activists (including many who were critical to NFM's founding), the organizing principles of the American labor movement, as embodied by the Coalition on Contingent Academic Labor (COCAL) and Joe Berry's groundbreaking book *Reclaiming the Ivory Tower* (2005), have been guiding lights. Berry's work, in particular, is a study in the evolving praxis of contingent faculty activism, as it situates this activism in the context of both the labor movement and academic culture. Indeed, NFM has manifestly adopted the "inside/outside" strategy endorsed by Berry: inside as working within academic culture and outside as invoking unionization. This strategy is evident, for example, in NFM's explicit stance supporting the existence and efforts of faculty unions, while at the same time declining to endorse unionization as the *only* path to reform (particularly since there are so many places in which unionization is either illegal, legal but difficult/impossible to support culturally, or characterized by the same injustices and power imbalances that plague the faculty workforce within higher education institutions). The idea is that NFM needs to be an organization that works within institutional structures, be they unions or colleges and universities, to effect change from within, while also exerting pressure from outside when necessary.

At the same time, NFM has also operated and evolved—much like many contingent faculty activist groups—without any particular additional formal grounding in social movement/social change theory. This is probably because the history of the rise of contingency has been, paradoxically, both systematic and haphazard, and the resistance to it has been largely reactive and localized. Although NFM was always intended to be a national organization with a singular focus, its emergence and evolution, particularly during its initial launch into mostly uncharted waters, were the result, in part, of sheer collective determination and more than a little luck.

However, as we evolve, we appreciate more deeply the insights and advantages that social change theory provides. The case studies and analysis in this volume provide an extremely coherent illustration of the strategic principles that Kezar and Sam highlight in Chapter 2 as critical to the change process: the elements of the institutionalization continuum (mobilization, implementation, and institutionalization) and (in Chapter 1) the change-culture framework (focus on policies, practices, and values). Significantly, each of these principles guides NFM's work, though until this point we have not studied or invoked them formally. Insofar as doing so will strengthen our efforts to support reform, we are prepared to adopt them more intentionally, especially since we would like to continue constructing an authentic praxis of contingency-focused higher education reform: one that encourages reformers to reflect on experience and create change principles that are grounded in that interaction between experience and reflection, as well as the interaction between the individual and the group, that are so fundamental to both education and democracy. Our mission, after all, includes the idea embedded in the well-known maxim about teaching a person to fish rather than just giving him a fish—we aim not just to engage in advocacy on behalf of contingent faculty and their students, but indeed to provide activists and their allies with the resources (both research-based as well as experience-based) they need to engage in effective self-advocacy.

## Refocusing the Conversation

Another observation is a reflection on the assumptions and goals that are at work in local and national reform efforts related to contingent academic employment. It seems critical to seek answers to the following questions: Is the operative assumption of such efforts that contingency is simply here to stay and that we all have to learn to live with it? Is the goal of reform simply to make contingency more palatable?

New Faculty Majority's perspective is that higher education has an obligation to identify the faculty hiring practices and principles that *best* serve the missions of individual institutions and of higher education more generally. Our hypothesis, which we believe is supportable with even more comprehensive and more focused research data, is that well-supported, well-respected faculty are absolutely critical to the integrity and efficacy of higher education, and that regularization, and not contingency, is the path to achieving that objective.

Put another way, NFM wants the higher education community, which includes the community at large, to explore more critically reforms focused on "productivity," "completion," and even "innovation", terms that are currently ubiquitous in the national conversation about higher education. We believe that it is important to note that these kinds of terms have been co-opted in some contexts as code for eliminating faculty altogether, or for downgrading them from professionals to "content delivery specialists" overseeing standardized, computerized modules. These terms should not be tied to those definitions.

In other words, it is important for change agents to understand the essential nature of the change being sought. Given the often adversarial relationship between the goals of the contingent faculty movement (improved working conditions and equal pay for equal work) and those of tenure-line faculty (protecting tenure, reversing part-time to full-time ratios) and administrators (managerial flexibility and control), is it possible to come to consensus about ultimate goals, to forge common ground, and to be attentive to whether the goals sought are really innovative or simply the preservation of the status quo, whether that status quo is (pick your phrase) the expense of/investment in tenure or the flexibility/precariousness of contingency?

On this question, a lesson that NFM has learned in its first two years may be instructive. Consistent with the framework of the change theory that Kezar outlines in Chapter 1 of this book, NFM has always recognized the fundamental importance of changing culture, but has also had to learn to understand the complex reality that "[c]ulture incorporates both the policies and practices of an institution, but also moves to more abstract values, ideas, and principles" and that it is important to find "ways to link change to values and specific contexts [that] can be beneficial for the change" (Kezar & Sam, Chapter 2 in this book). The values and specific contexts that obtain equally at local and national levels are those that include one of the most essential features of the institutions' educational missions and the faculty's academic values: the learning experience of students.

On one level, this is hardly revelatory, particularly for a movement whose most powerful and longest-lived slogan is "faculty working conditions are student learning conditions." Yet like many principles, the meaning of this one had become obscured in spite of its ubiquity. For NFM, the evolution of this realization was prompted by our interaction with a surprising entity: the Internal Revenue Service (IRS).

In early 2010, after a year-long process of launching the organization, including crafting a mission statement, creating by-laws, and working through our own internal "intercultural communication" issues, NFM was finally ready to submit its application for 501c3 nonprofit (tax-exempt, charitable) status. We considered acquiring such status essential to the "implementation" phase of our work, as we need resources in order to build the infrastructures that will allow us to fulfill our organizational goals more effectively. We contracted with an experienced consultant, also an adjunct faculty member, who had helped establish a number of 501c3 nonprofit organizations.

The nonprofit application process involves convincing the IRS that the mission and activities of the prospective nonprofit organization are truly charitable, educational, and ultimately "in the public interest." To us, this requirement seemed the easiest to meet, as our operative assumption, not just as an organization, but certainly as individual faculty members, was that these qualities defined our work as educators. Furthermore, we were certain that the social justice component of our mission—to end exploitative employment practices—would solidify our application, and since we were not interested in operating as a union, we would not have to worry about being placed into that category. We were surprised then, when the IRS informed us that based on our application, we did not meet the definition of an organization whose activities are primarily charitable, educational, and in the public interest. Instead, we were given 501c6 status, which is for a "business league that works to improve the working conditions of its members."

We realized that a 501c6 designation did in fact describe many of our activities, particularly since we fully intended to engage in direct advocacy and lobbying where necessary, and since we hoped to provide services that could directly benefit our adjunct and contingent members (as part of our overall strategy to stabilize working conditions in order to support faculty work and encourage faculty self-advocacy). However, we continue to believe that our mission is in fact ultimately in the public interest, and we are now much more solidly on the way to acquiring 501c3 status for our affiliated foundation by separating out the research, education, and outreach activities that fall more properly into the purview of a 501c3 organization, while still advancing our overall mission. The process of doing so has led to the insight that our operative principle that "faculty working conditions are student learning conditions" is a message that has to be defined, explained, and practiced in a way that makes the latter half of the equation much more prominent and understandable.

In other words, we realized that like the IRS, the general public, whose support is essential to the achievement of our goals, would likely *not* see the connection between faculty working conditions and student learning conditions that is so obvious to us, and that we would have to rethink our communication strategy in order to introduce and explain and illustrate it.

## Conclusion: Learning from Experience

The insight that faculty dedication to the mission of higher education has somehow been lost in debates over education reform is certainly not unique to NFM: Both the American Federation of Teachers (AFT) and the National Education Association (NEA), for example, have recently issued publications or statements clarifying the importance of student learning to their missions.[9] Other groups and efforts that NFM has joined, like the Coalition on the Academic Workforce (see its brief titled "One Faculty Serving All Students")[10] and the Campaign for the Future of Higher Education (see its core principles)[11] have similarly emphasized the need to put learning back at the center of higher education reform efforts.

For NFM, the seemingly peripheral administrative challenge with which the IRS literally blindsided us, which, as Kezar and Sam point out (Chapter 2 under "Utilizing Allies"), often happens in the implementation phase of a change movement, has also had the effect of strengthening and focusing our efforts so that we can work more effectively toward institutionalization. Thus NFM has revised its mission statement to emphasize the goal of improving education, and as I write this (in May 2011), it is even entertaining the possibility of revising its name in order to emphasize further the education-centered principle that drives our work. As NFM works to identify data, concrete processes, and benchmarks to serve as practical tools and guides for reform efforts that can be implemented in context-specific ways and shared with a wide variety of higher education stakeholders, we have learned that we must continue to emphasize the fundamental importance of the educational process and the connection of faculty working conditions to student learning conditions.

Separating NFM's operations into the work of direct organizing and advocacy for improved faculty working conditions on the one hand, and education and research to demonstrate the centrality of those working conditions to higher education's fundamental mission of promoting learning, on the other hand, has been critical to the praxis of our activism. It has allowed us to understand and explain the "faculty working conditions are student learning conditions" principle more clearly. Similarly, the experience of reflecting on the case studies and analysis provided in this book has allowed us to understand better the dialectic between individual and collective experience, which slowly builds in intensity and confidence and leads to coalition building as the best way to effect culture change more generally.

NFM sees its function as constantly encouraging and supporting advocacy as well as engaging in it directly. This advocacy must occur at individual and collective levels, often simultaneously. For example, through our UCI, a contingent faculty member can practice self-advocacy by trying to secure unemployment compensation based on her individual professional context, but also contribute information from her experience (through our interactive website) to the group, which includes colleagues at individual institutions throughout the state and across the United States. The data collected will then be used to help other individuals and other groups of contingent faculty members.

The success of the efforts highlighted in the case studies can be explained in terms of this dynamic of interaction between individual and group advocacy, and can also be explained by the concept of synergy. It is easy to see how the case studies embody the most basic definition of synergy, which according to *Webster's Dictionary* is "combined action or cooperation" (Webster's, 1913). Each of the case studies showcases the ways in which important changes in policy and practice were carried out through "combined action" and "cooperation." As anyone who works in higher education knows, it is no small feat to effect institutional change in this way.

Yet a fuller definition of the term provides a second, more nuanced sense of synergy: "an effect of the *interaction* of the actions of two agents such that the result of the combined action is *greater than expected* as a simple additive combination of the two agents acting separately" [emphasis added] (Webster-Merriam, 2011). The combined action suggested by the word synergy is constitutionally different from the combined action that consists in two or more agents simply working simultaneously to achieve one goal.

Instead, the case studies and efforts like NFM's UCI initiative suggest that it is the *interactive* nature of the collaboration—for example, in the engagement by faculty at Virginia Tech (Chapter 6) and Villanova (Chapter 10) and SF State (Chapter 8) with institutions that take their mission and cultural values seriously—that seems to be critical to overcoming fear, building solidarity, and effecting change.

The interactivity suggested by the concept of synergy is also significant because it acknowledges the independence and "separateness" of the agents who are working in tandem. This provides a theoretical framework that could be useful in addressing the challenge (mentioned above) of the heterogeneity of the contingent faculty population, as well as the challenge of collaborating with both allies and erstwhile adversaries. For NFM, which aims specifically to be a "coalition," communication and interaction across cultural divides both within and outside of academia are critical.

My final point is that it is notable that the major, but subtle, shift in our understanding of the central guiding principle of our work, that faculty working conditions are student learning conditions, has been the result of a dialectical, synergistic process in which a reflective and interactive combination of efforts is carried out by agents who are not even necessarily linked in purpose and function. Clearly the unions and higher education coalitions which have come to the same conclusion are linked in purpose and function, but who would ever imagine the IRS to be an agent of higher education reform? The result so far has been "greater than expected": a "reclaiming," in the words of Joe Berry's title (2005), of faculty commitment to its professional status, which is not merely self-interested, but indeed outwardly and comprehensively focused on education as an essential public good, in the public interest, and critical to the future of our students and our democracy.

## Notes

1   Thanks to Anne Wiegard for suggesting this title.
2   See, for example, http://www.cpfa.org/journal/11spring/cpfa-spring11.pdf.
3   While many of NFM's founding members were actively involved in the Coalition for Contingent Academic Labor (COCAL), NFM has actively sought formal structure while COCAL has always rejected it, conceiving of itself as "a loose network of activists involved in contingent faculty issues." See http://www.aaup.org/AAUP/issues/contingent/cocal. htm. NFM believes that both approaches are necessary to effective reform.
4   Jack has made this point in many personal conversations with me as well as in public fora like the adj-l listserv.
5   Thanks to Steve Street for this important observation.
6   NFM board member Alan Trevithick has been a vocal critic of the embedding of the ideology of "teaching for love" into contingency, as have Marc Bousquet, Michelle Masse, and Eileen Schell.
7   Thanks to Steve Street and Gary Rhoades for making this insightful and whimsical connection.
8   See, for example, Hamilton & Gaff's (2009) White Paper on the future of the professoriate.
9   See AFT Higher Education's *Student Success in Higher Education*, available at http://www.aft. org/pdfs/highered/studentsuccess0311.pdf; and the South Carolina Education Association (SCEA) press release on the National Education Association (NEA) July 2011 statement from the Representative Assembly, available at http://www.thescea.org/assets/document/ Press_release_from_2011_RA_re_Obama.pdf.

10  See http://www.aft.org/pdfs/highered/presentations/ib_coalitionaw0210.pdf.
11  See http://futureofhighered.org/Principles.html.

## References

American Federation of Teachers Higher Education. (2011). *Student success in higher education*. Washington, DC: American Federation of Teachers.

Berry, J. (2005). *Reclaiming the ivory tower: Organizing adjuncts to change higher education*. New York, NY: Monthly Review Press.

Hamilton, N., & Gaff, J. (Eds.). (2009). *The future of the professoriate: Academic freedom, peer review, and shared governance.* [White Paper.] Washington, DC: Association of American Colleges and Universities.

Heath, C., & Heath, D. (2010). *Switch: How to change things when change is hard*. New York, NY: Broadway Books.

Jacoby, D. (2006). Effects of part-time faculty employment on community college graduation rates. *The Journal of Higher Education, 77*(6), 1081–1102.

Kezar, A., & Sam, C. (2010). *Understanding the new majority: Contingent faculty in higher education.* ASHE Higher Education Report Series, 36(4). San Francisco: Jossey-Bass.

Maisto, M., & Williams, M. (2011, February 27). Go to college to learn what Senate Bill 5 will do. *The* Plain Dealer [op-ed]. Retrieved from http://www.cleveland.com/opinion/index. ssf/2011/02/go_to_college_to_learn_what_se. html.

Merriam-Webster. (2011). Synergy. In *Merriam-Webster* Dictionary online. Retrieved from http://www.merriam-webster.com/dictionary/synergy.

Moyer, B. (1990). *The practical strategist: Movement action plan (MAP) strategic theories for evaluating, planning, and conducting social movements.* San Francisco: Social Movement Empowerment Project. Abstract available at http://www.thechangeagency.org/_dbase_upl/practical_strategist.pdf.

Schmidt, P. (2009, November 1). When adjuncts push for better status, better pay follows, study suggests. *The Chronicle of Higher Education.* Retrieved from http://chronicle.com/article/When-Adjuncts- Push-for-Better/48988/.

The South Carolina Education Association. (2011). NEA delegates vote to support President Obama for second term, and on policy on teacher evaluation and accountability [Press Release]. Retrieved from http://www.thescea.org/assets/document/Press_release_from_2011_RA_re_Obama.pdf.

Umbach, P. D. (2007). How effective are they? Exploring the impact of contingent faculty on undergraduate education. *The Review of Higher Education, 30*(2), 91–123.

Webster's. (1913). Synergy. In *Webster's 1913 Dictionary* online. Retrieved from http://www.webster-dictionary.org/definition/Synergy.

# 12

## WE KNOW THE CHANGES NEEDED AND THE WAY TO DO IT

### Now We Need the Motivation and Commitment

*Adrianna Kezar*

This chapter captures themes that emerged within the case studies and which were not summarized earlier in Chapters 1 and Chapter 2. Furthermore, I explore some larger overarching questions that are raised by the case studies, building on Maria Maisto's contribution (Chapter 11). As a reminder, Chapter 1 speaks to: creating a vision for change that acknowledges the diversity of non-tenure track faculty with different contracts, motivations, and interests; addressing policies, practices, and principles that make up the overall campus culture; and developing context-based changes that reflect the institutional culture and needs. Chapter 2 describes strategies used to create better policies and practices and which unfold during the different phases of institutionalization. These different phases were also touched upon at the end of each case study, giving the reader more insight into the institution's progress on change. In addition, the reader was given *key points* and *key questions* to help understand the change process. These areas will not be reviewed in this chapter, and I ask readers to seek these points within the earlier chapters. I begin and end this chapter by focusing on motivation for change, as I believe this is a primary challenge that remains.

### Creating Motivation through Principles

Motivators for change reflected in the case studies include rationales such as improving student learning, respect for colleagues, and inequities that violate campus missions and goals. The case studies clearly demonstrate that respect is a driver for change and that leading with principles is important. Vancouver Community College (VCC) (Chapter 3) suggests that their model is built on acknowledging that non-tenure track faculty deserve to be treated equitably.

San Francisco State University (Chapter 8) also was able to make progress because of a sense of respect between faculty. Other campuses [Madison Area Technical College (Chapter 4), University of Southern California (Chapter 9), Virginia Tech (Chapter 6)] used fora such as strategic planning, accreditation, or senate floor meetings to build respect. Principles also provided a rationale for why changes were needed that motivated people to create change. Campuses across the country need to be aware of (and model) this attention to values and principles and see how these can be strong levers for change.

## Accountability: Needed Mechanisms to Monitor Policies

Principles then led to policies, but most campuses have no way to follow up on policies and practices. Departments and divisions often do not reflect campus-wide policies. Departments routinely violate policies, but there are limited ways to ensure that policies are actually implemented. The University of Southern California (Chapter 9) developed a monitoring system, but few campuses have a robust system for ensuring that policies are translated into practice at the local level of the department. The result is that policies do not always ensure change. Also, many campuses are not addressing negative practices like last-minute scheduling of classes, informal hiring, and climates of incivility. So, we need not only to think about the connection between policies and how to enforce them, but how to undo negative practices and norms that develop within units. We also need to move our focus from the institution to the department. Many of the problematic practices that arose in the course of our research were departmentally driven. Until non-tenure track leaders dig deeper into the institution, these violations of policy and poor practices will likely remain. Building a council of non-tenure track faculty across campuses to unearth violations of campus policy as exercised at Cal Poly Pomona (Chapter 7) is one excellent way to monitor policies and to have a reach into departments. While it is often difficult to focus on accountability when leaders are just trying to get changes off the ground, ignoring accountability can mean that changes are never implemented, as people see there will be no follow-up on the policies.

## Key Strategies: Data Collection and Relationship Building

Data collection and relationship building were used at each campus and were believed to be extremely important to advance change. Data collection fed into other strategies—providing trends and patterns for discussion in strategic planning, providing accreditators a baseline understanding in order to develop recommendations, and highlighting areas for task forces to work on. Many contingent faculty leaders initially look at data collection as a passive strategy, delaying needed change. But the time used up front to collect data turned out to be pivotal to long-term change. When conditions have been bad for so long, it is easy to see why contingent faculty leaders would want to use strategies that would garner immediate change in the short run. But the case studies speak to the value of data for creating strategic and thoughtful changes that are sustained. Sustainability is another theme woven throughout the chapters. Monitoring, a compelling rationale or set of principles, relationships, and data are strategies that lead to institutionalization.

Relationship building is also deeply important within all these case studies and also often does not result in immediate change. Relationship building needs to happen at multiple levels—between different non-tenure track faculty on campus, between non-tenure track and tenure-track faculty, between non-tenure track faculty and students or the outside community, between faculty across different units and divisions, between faculty and administrators, and between non-tenure track leaders across the United States. These relationships all add to a larger web of social contacts that the non-tenure track leader can draw upon for reform ideas, strategies, empathy, problem solving, and resiliency. Successful non-tenure track faculty leaders realize that change is a long-term proposition, and different contacts will be needed at different times in the change process. Chapter 7 on Cal Poly Pomona epitomized the way that relationship building fosters change and the non-tenure track faculty leader explores how each level of relationship moved their change agenda forward.

## Context and Culture Matter for Change Strategies

Chapter 1 introduced the notion of change agendas and strategies varying by institutional type. The case studies provided ample evidence of this theme. The University of Southern California (Chapter 9) emphasized the decentralized and entrepreneurial spirit of the campus and the research university as shaping their approach of collecting policies and making them available for comparison among deans. Villanova (Chapter 10) spoke to the importance of harkening to the sense of community and its mission of social justice as pivotal for change. At Virginia Tech (Chapter 6), the shared leadership, multi-campus system, and research mission affected their agenda and approach to change. San Francisco State University (Chapter 8) drew on its history of activism and had to adjust to the resource constraints. Each institution was able to shape and hone its approach to draw on strategies that would have the most success within its particular setting.

## Understanding Obstacles is Just as Important as Understanding Tactics

For each campus (and non-tenure track leader) there are different obstacles—faculty apathy, resistance from tenure-track faculty or administrators, internalized inferiority, leadership turnover, difficulty with data collection, money concerns, the challenges of getting changes made in writing, bringing policy into departments, etc. Obstacles will abound and they can become overwhelming if non-tenure track leaders and their allies do not anticipate some of these barriers and create more seamless solutions for overcoming obstacles. Many campuses have stories about failed efforts at change: what made these case-study campuses differ is their ability to respond to obstacles in productive ways. And as various case studies demonstrated, non-tenure track leaders cannot rest after a few victories, they need to be diligent in continuing to scan the landscape for resistance and obstacles and be ready with tactics to address the obstacle. Villanova (Chapter 10) provides an example of this when the contingents' proposal for involvement in selecting department chairs was denied. They had stopped communicating about why their involvement was critical and, in consequence, resistance emerged that could have been addressed. The model we presented in Chapter 2 provides an outline of common challenges and ways in which campuses overcame these challenges. These lessons can then be used by other campuses to overcome challenges more smoothly and keep moving forward in stride.

## Union Versus Non-union Campuses: Are They So Different?

While unions provide a unique change mechanism through collective bargaining agreements and the ability to strike, many union strategies can be used outside the union setting and represent key strategies for any campus or leader. While union and labor literature often speaks to strategies as bundled, and clearly there is strength in being able to use them together (bargaining is more powerful when you can strike), the strategies used individually can also lead to change (AFT, 2010). Take the various case-study examples. Surveying non-tenure track faculty for their concerns and issues is a standard union tactic and was also used by several non-union campuses (see Villanova in Chapter 10 and USC in Chapter 9). In addition, data collection related to benchmarks and models is another union tactic used by non-union campuses. Working collectively through subcommittees, task forces, and informal groups is similar to the union in that a large group creates a coalition. These groups need to push for some authority or work closely with decision-makers. As the USC case (Chapter 9) illustrated, a campus subcommittee can fail to make changes for years and be largely symbolic if it has no authority. Unions have authority, so that makes a difference in what they can accomplish, and if collective groups like campus subcommittees cannot garner some authority, they will be significantly weakened. Negotiation and formal policymaking differ, as non-union groups must operate more through persuasion, until they get more standing in formal governance within institutions. So there are some ways that union strategies can be used outside a union setting.

It is noteworthy that campuses that made major progress tended to be unionized—Vancouver Community College (Chapter 3), Mountain College

(Chapter 5), and Madison Area Technical College (Chapter 4); the formal authority and power that unions have appears to be significant for making changes. It is also important to note that non-unionized campus changes—unless captured in faculty handbooks—are fragile and subject to modification, and are hard to enforce; the changes have no legal standing. Many campuses within our larger study had implemented a set of changes that were altered when new leadership came in. Without formal policy development, change can be fleeting and dependent on leaders' whims. Unions also help make advances on salary, benefits, and job security that may be ignored through a senate-driven process.

## Reflecting the Framework for Effective Faculty

Like the recommended changes in the literature (see Chapter 1 and Chapter 2), these case studies suggest that certain changes receive more focus—employment equity, for example—while others continue to get short shrift and are not part of the change agendas that campuses put forward. None of the campuses were addressing issues of flexibility (even the most institutionalized ones). None of the campuses were looking at childcare, or involvement in the curriculum. San Francisco State University (Chapter 8) suggests the dilemma that arises when non-tenure track faculty leadership is ignored and not rewarded; the campus potential to continue to move forward is now hampered. Therefore, while these case studies show campuses making progress on equity, they are not necessarily addressing all the areas needed for an effective professoriate. The case studies also reflect the fact that campuses began with the most critical changes as identified by their own contingent faculty, through surveys of their concerns. This is extremely important, as then the changes addressed will reflect the actual struggles and needs of the particular campus. It is important to note that campuses should try to align changes with principles. If campuses declare that changes are necessary to improve student learning, focusing on salary and benefits alone and ignoring professional development and orientation might seem mismatched.

## Basic Principles and Local Flexibility

Maisto's chapter (11) questions whether contingency is a viable model and argues for stabilization (not tenure, but stabilization). Will changes in policies and practices, argued for in this book, be enough if stabilization of faculty is not accomplished? Campuses may put in place professional development, but if faculty have no job security, will this work to professionalize the non-tenure track be enough? There is a concern that by speaking about altering policies and practices and leaving a future model of faculty role open to campus leaders and their various cultures and contexts (which is needed), we may not address an underlying problem with contingency—that without some level of stabilization, the new professoriate is doomed to be an unproductive model. Maisto makes the argument that while flexibility in policies and practices is important to a national strategy, some basic principles about the new professoriate need to be agreed upon in order for it to be a viable alternative to past versions of the professoriate. We need discussion on basic principles about what is needed for an effective faculty. We do need to decide on some basic principles of the new professoriate along the lines of historic documents created by the American Association of University Professors (AAUP) (e.g., 2006) in the past. Stabilization seems to be one principle on such a list, and we need more discussion about other items to be included on it.

## Intentionality in Creating Changes

In Chapter 11, Maria Maisto brought up an important question: Were non-tenure track leaders consciously drawing on theories of change or labor studies in order to create these successful examples? Were non-tenure track leaders intuitively drawing on ideas of change or driven by any systematic ideas? What difference would conscious strategizing about change make? As Maisto notes, union tactics emerge from well-known organizing strategies that have been studied over time. Maisto also points to New Faculty Majority (NFM) encouraging contingent activists to use research-based strategies and not to depend only on experience in order to create change. She notes the influence of Joe Berry's work (2005) on NFM's own strategizing and planning.

One of the perennial problems in higher education is the lack of a conscious adoption of change strategies when trying to create reforms. Business and corporations have become much more systematic in adopting theories of change as they innovate to respond to challenges. External pressures and crises drove businesses to look to theory for answers (Kezar, 2001). Higher education leaders, by contrast, tend to be intuitive in their approach to change (Kezar, 2001). While intuition can certainly work as theory is often built upon good practice, it often takes a tremendous amount of experience to amass enough examples to operate successfully on the basis of intuition. As Plato once quipped (Plato, 1966), it is a wise person who knows what they do not know. If higher education leaders could see the benefit in drawing from theory and research rather than relying so exclusively on intuition, there would be a benefit in terms of more successful change efforts. My own research has shown a bias for leaders to focus on the reform and to ignore the change process; both need equal weight if we are to have more success with change (Kezar, 2011). This is not to say that intentionality in understanding change processes is a panacea for success, as powerful interests working against the change, politics, and leadership turnover can arise to defeat the best-laid plans. But the chances of success are much greater if non-tenure track leaders have an arsenal of known strategies and can create synergy to make them work in combination.

## Making People Care about Change

One of the most fundamental problems that exist related to non-tenure track faculty is motivation to create changes. While campus policies, practices, and principles have been in need of change for decades, there has been little or no motivation to do so. In Chapter 11, Maisto notes that focusing on the ways that student learning and experience are impacted by this shift in faculty is the most important way to make people care. This is why I opened the book by describing research that points to the detrimental outcomes as campuses have moved to contingent labor, but have not changed campus policies and practices to make new faculty successful. It is also intriguing that somehow stakeholders do not see faculty as important to student learning and success, and that even making that argument connecting faculty working conditions with student learning has not been compelling enough. In a conversation with an executive at the U.S. Department of Education, I was recently told: "I am not aware of any relationship between faculty and student learning. I do not understand why this is an issue—contingent faculty." What is so odd is that this is the same department that thinks there is a strong link between K–12 students' learning and teachers. The U.S. Department of Education is demanding evaluation of school teachers' effectiveness, holding them directly accountable for student learning, in fact. But somehow when students are between 17 and 18 years old, teachers stop mattering? In a review of all the national documents proposing change in higher education by the Bill & Melinda Gates Foundation (2009), the Spellings Commission (U.S. Department of Education, 2006), the National Commission on Accountability in Higher Education (2005), the Council for Higher Education Accreditation (2008), the Lumina Foundation (2009), and the College Board (2008), none refer to faculty as a partner in improving the access and success of students. In fact, none of the reports refer to faculty at all. Yet, there is a plethora of research that suggests that faculty–student relationships are among the most important for student retention and success in college. In fact, the major and most recent definitive meta-analysis of higher education research by Pascarella and Terenzini (2005) identified that faculty–student interactions have a substantial impact on student persistence, success, and completion, *more* than any other known intervention program or policy—*faculty matter*. Pascarella and Terenzini (2005) did acknowledge that the link between faculty–student interactions and outcomes related to persistence, success, and completion may not be causal, as high-achieving students may be the ones seeking additional contact with faculty; however, the authors note that the weight of the evidence suggests a strong beneficial effect on student outcomes from having more frequent interactions with faculty as well as other measures of faculty contact and engagement. This research strongly supports the view that faculty need to be a part of the conversations on student access and success. Why is it that the public is not aware of such evidence, or does not find it compelling? Are we not communicating the right message? Is there a deeply embedded stereotype that faculty are not important to college learning and is there a need to address this topic more directly? Both Maisto's and my own experiences with policymakers nationally, as well as the policy documents created in the last decade, suggest that stakeholders do not see a connection between faculty and student learning. This broader narrative is a significant barrier to change and provides no motivation to tackle the changing professoriate. So while I have focused on understanding how change can happen and helping make that a more seamless process, we also need greater motivation for change so that the change process is not so difficult. I am heartened that the New Faculty Majority will be working on creating motivation among policymakers and higher education stakeholders. We know some of the changes that need to be made, we know how to put them in place, and through this book and other writings, we hope there are more allies. Now we need some basic principles to help us move forward with the new professoriate (such as stabilization) and we need political will among higher education stakeholders, which may be harnessed by seeing the harm to student learning that results from our broken academic model.

## References

American Association of University Professors. (2006). *AAUP contingent faculty index 2006*. Washington, DC: American Association of University Professors.

American Federation of Teachers Higher Education. (2010). *American academic: A national survey of part-time/adjunct faculty*. Washington, DC: American Federation of Teachers.

Association of American Colleges and Universities. (2002). *Greater expectations: A new vision for learning as a nation goes to college*. Washington, DC: Association of American Colleges and Universities.

Association of American Colleges and Universities and Council for Higher Education Accreditation. (2008). *New leadership for student learning and accountability: A statement of principles, commitments to action*. Washington, DC: Association of American Colleges and Universities.

Berry, J. (2005). *Reclaiming the ivory tower: Organizing adjuncts to change higher education*. New York, NY: Monthly Review Press.

Bill & Melinda Gates Foundation. (2009). *Postsecondary success*. Seattle, WA: Bill & Melinda Gates Foundation.

Kezar, A. (2001). *Understanding and facilitating organizational change in the 21st century: Recent research and conceptualizations*. ASHE-ERIC Higher Education Reports 28(9). Washington, DC: Jossey-Bass.

Kezar, A. (2011). Scaling up innovation in higher education. *Innovative Higher Education, 36*(4), 235–247.

Lumina Foundation for Education. (2009). *A stronger nation through higher education*. Indianapolis, IN: Lumina Foundation for Education.

National Commission on Accountability in Higher Education. (2005). *Accountability for better results: A national imperative for higher education*. Denver, CO: State Higher Education Executive Officers.

Pascarella, E., & Terenzini, P. (2005). *How college affects students*. San Francisco: Jossey-Bass.

Plato. (1966). Apology. In *Plato in twelve volumes*, Vol. 1 (H. N. Fowler, Trans.) (section 23b). Cambridge, MA: Harvard University Press.

The College Board. (2008). *Winning the skills race and strengthening America's middle class: An action agenda for community colleges*. New York, NY: The College Board.

U.S. Department of Education. (2006). *A test of leadership: Charting the course of U.S. higher education*. Washington, DC: U.S. Department of Education.

# APPENDIX A

# WHITE PAPER ON EXEMPLARY PRACTICES AND POLICIES

## Relating to Non-Tenure-Track Faculty*
## Submitted to the Academic Senate Executive Board
## by the
## Senate Committee on Non-Tenure-Track Faculty Affairs

## May 15, 2009

*This report identifies practices and guidelines at some USC schools or other universities that are not current USC general practice or policy but that, in the view of the Committee, should be drawn to the attention of other USC schools, the University administration, and the Academic Senate.

## I. INTRODUCTION

### A. Background

As defined in a motion unanimously approved by the USC Academic Senate in the 2007/2008 academic year, the mission of the Committee on Non-Tenure-Track Faculty Affairs (CNTTFA) is

> To monitor, evaluate, advocate, and make recommendations to the Executive Board of the Academic Senate regarding: the working environment; conditions of employment; long term security; compensation; benefits eligibility; opportunities for participation in governance; opportunities for professional advancement; titling nomenclature; status; participation in the academic life of the university, and other matters of concern to the non-tenure-track faculty.

In the 2008–2009 academic year the principal task of the Committee on Non-Tenure-Track Faculty Affairs was to develop an inventory of exemplary practices and policies relating to Non-Tenure-Track (NTT) faculty. The inventory, on which this White Paper is based, is intended to serve as a resource for faculty and administrators involved in the review and formulation of NTTF-related policies, guidelines and procedures in the University and in their respective units, in keeping with the requirement stipulated in the USC Faculty Handbook that schools formulate such policies and submit them for review by the Academic Senate Executive Board and approval by the Provost. Having a common reference point will enable different units on campus to compare the practices of their own schools with those of others, identify proven options, and make more informed decisions.

This report identifies practices and guidelines at some USC schools or other universities that are not current USC general practice or policy but that, in the view of the Committee, should be drawn to the attention of other USC schools, the University administration, and the Academic Senate. At USC, practices vary widely among schools, while policy requires the approval of the President or Provost. The sharing of information is encouraged and it is hoped that the NTTF Policy Inventory and this White Paper, both of which will be updated as appropriate, will become valuable resources.

## B. Research

A combination of primary and secondary research served as a basis for the development of the criteria to be utilized in distinguishing "exemplary" practices from others, and in selecting those policies:

1.  Primary:
    a.  Development of an inventory of the NTTF faculty-related policies of all USC academic units compiled by means of interviews with, and or completion of questionnaires by, appropriate administrative staff.
    b.  In-depth discussions among the committee membership, which consists of NTT faculty from all USC academic units.

2.  Secondary research sources included:
    a.  The practices of other major universities (Stanford, Cornell, Carnegie Mellon, and the University of Texas at Austin);
    b.  The American Association of University Professors (AAUP) 2006 Contingent Faculty Index (which reviews and assesses national trends in hiring of full-time faculty off the tenure track);
    c.  A 2001 report on contingent faculty compiled by the American Association of Universities (AAU);
    d.  A 2002 Academic Senate "White Paper on Non-Tenure-Track Faculty."

## C. Core Issues

The research revealed that the most important issues pertaining to NTT fall into five interrelated categories:

1. Workload profile
2. Annual merit review
3. Periodic evaluation, promotion, non-reappointment, and contract
4. Professional development
5. Participation in governance

## D Criteria

The research also indicated that criteria to be utilized in distinguishing "exemplary" practices, procedures and policies from others should include:

1. Substance, i.e. content that effectively addresses one of the five issues listed above.
2. Clarity, i.e. adequate written detail and explanation.
3. Fairness and consistency, i.e. an indication that the policy can be applied fairly and consistently in multiple, similar situations.
4. Rationale, i.e. the reasoning behind the policy is logical and relevant.
5. Implementation, i.e. the extent to which the practice or policy is actually utilized in the unit.

## II. EXEMPLARY

### Overarching Qualities

The CNTTFA identified two factors that can be seen as ideally applying across the board to NTT Exemplary Practices and Policies:

1. Recognition of the administrative flexibility required by the varying needs of the many schools and departments in the University.

2. Recognition of the interconnected and interdependent nature of the five Core Issues listed above, so that they are seen collectively as an interdependent whole (or system) that, in its entirety, governs the relationship between the NTT faculty, the academic units, and the University.

### Workload Profiles

#### 1. USC Inventory

    a. The Schools of Law, Business, and Social Work have clear definitions of service that include four levels: (1) school; (2) university; (3) professional; and (4) public, community and society.

b. The School of Social Work has clear definitions of both teaching and research. Regarding teaching, Social Work describes the role of faculty in student advisement, field placements, and other out-of-classroom teaching obligations.

c. The School of Cinematic Arts utilizes a three-component profile: Teaching, Professional Development/Creative Work, and Service. These components, with varying percentages, apply to TT and NTT faculty.

d. The Schools of Business and Education apply flexibility when developing the Workload Profiles of NTTF. Varying levels of Service and Scholarship (i.e. scholarship of discovery, application, teaching, and/or integration) can be negotiated and substituted for each other.2

e. The Schools of Journalism, Social Work and Education provide teaching release for faculty involved in significant, teaching-related, out-of-classroom activities.

## Secondary Source Input

a. A memo from the Provost dated July 24, 2006, on Part-time Non-tenure Track Instructional Faculty, based on a report of the Senate NTT committee, said "We have extended NTT faculty eligibility for university prizes, the Zumberge Research Innovation Fund, and appointment as Center for Excellence in Teaching faculty fellows."

b. An invitation to apply for research fellowships, distributed to all faculty by Vice Provost for Faculty Affairs Martin Levine on January 23, 2009, included the following statement: "USC faculty members from all ranks, both tenure-track and non-tenure-track, are eligible to apply. Successful proposals are those that describe a concrete, well-defined set of activities that promote research development at USC."

c. The 2001 AAU report on contingent faculty recommends that Workload Profiles should be made public and serve as the bases for annual and merit reviews, renewal, promotion, development, etc.

d. The same AAU report recommends the adoption of clear, consistent, definitions of "standard courses."

## 2. Workload Profile: Exemplary Practices and Policies

a. Schools and units are encouraged to comply with the Provost's memo of July 24, 2006, on Part-time Non-tenure Track Instructional Faculty, and the Vice Provost for Faculty Affairs' message distributed on January 23, 2009.

b.  Preference for full-time (versus part time or adjunct) appointment, in accordance with University policy and the past recommendations of the Senate Committee on Non Tenure Track Faculty Affairs.

c.  Clear, concise definitions for teaching, scholarship (as previously defined), professional development, and service, as appropriate for each unit and positions within the unit. While definitions may vary, specific descriptions of each component of the profile can be established with NTTF participation, published, and implemented.

d.  Individual Workload Profiles, using the established definitions, developed by the unit after consultation with the affected faculty member or members.

e.  Use of individual Workload Profiles, and the definitions on which they are based, as points of reference for annual and merit reviews, contract terms, contract renewal, promotion, development, etc.

f.  Establishment and maintenance, to the extent reasonable, of parity and transparency vis-à-vis the Workload Profiles of faculty within specific ranks in each unit.

g.  Application of flexibility, wherever appropriate and possible, in assigning percentages to the components of Workload Profiles, recognizing that there will be variances in the scholarship, teaching, service, and professional development loads of faculty within similar ranks. (In adherence to the general guidelines outlining professional responsibilities of faculty members in the University Handbook Section 3-B (2).)

h.  With regard to the teaching element of Workload Profiles, clear definition of a "standard course," based on units, enrollment, and/or contact hours, along with a maximum teaching load (for purposes of fairness and consistency in Workload Profiles).

For example, in an academic unit where the definition of a "standard course" includes three units and four contact hours per course, Workload Profiles for NTT faculty operating under nine-month contracts might include a maximum of three courses per term (for a total of six courses within nine months); Workload Profiles for those operating under twelve-month contracts might include a maximum of eight courses. (It must be noted that these examples refer to maximum course loads only. The teaching expectation is defined by the school and some units may require different, i.e. smaller, workloads.)

---

1  Throughout this document the term "Scholarship" refers to scholarship of discovery, application, teaching, and/or integration, as defined in Boyer, E. L. Scholarship Reconsidered: Priorities of the Professoriate; San Francisco: Jossey-Bass, 1990. (E. L. Boyer was president of The Carnegie Foundation for the Advancement of Teaching.)

Voluntary teaching "Overloads" agreed to by the instructor and academic unit would not be affected by such a policy. Such arrangements are also subject to special approvals by school deans and the Provost, as noted in the University Handbook Section 3-D (2).

i.   With regard to the teaching element of Workload Profiles, recognition of situations and/or responsibilities that may fall outside the common classroom teaching scenario, i.e. very large class size, online courses with significant numbers of students, the variations in workload associated with four-unit versus two-unit courses, etc. For example, two large online courses may equate to three regular courses taught in person.

j.   With regard to the teaching element of Workload Profiles, recognition of out-of-classroom activities and/or situations such as advising large numbers of students, supervising large numbers of students in internships and/or field assignments, mentoring students and/or faculty, etc., whether that recognition takes the form of compensation or the provision of course release.

k.   With regard to scholarship (as previously defined), professional, and/or creative activities commonly conducted by NTTF and designated by the unit as part of the responsibilities of NTTF, recognition in Workload Profiles of the actual scope and substance of such activities as a separate and distinct category, apart from Teaching, Service, etc.

## Annual Merit Review

### 1. USC Inventory

a.   The Schools of Business and Social Work utilize a systematic, comprehensive and regular process of review of non-tenure-track faculty. Each year non-tenure-track faculty complete a detailed annual review form that assesses their performance relative to clear criteria that were developed by faculty, with the full and equal participation of NTT faculty. These criteria are shared with faculty well before the review process, simultaneous with the explanation of their Workload Profile. These schools employ a peer review process through which one or more non-tenure-track faculty members review each file to ensure that the process includes input from people with comparable experience.

b.   The Schools of Business and Social Work utilize several methods to evaluate teaching, including peer observation, classroom assessment, review of class materials, and professional development, as well as teaching evaluations. (Concern has been raised by non-tenure-track faculty that they are often measured on very limited criteria such as student evaluations only, when other valid measures are available.).

c.   The Schools of Business and Social Work provide specific feedback to NTT faculty each year as part of its merit review process, including guidance regarding progress toward promotion. (The School of Social Work also has a Professional Development Committee that provides feedback and guidance to each non-tenure-track faculty member.)

## 2. Annual Merit Review: Exemplary Practices and Policies

a.   A consistent, comprehensive, and systematic evaluation process for NTT faculty, based on written criteria; process and criteria developed with the full participation of NTT and TT faculty.

b.   Review criteria that assess the individual's performance relative to the specifics of his/her Workload Profile.

c.   Allocation of merit pay increases based on instructors' performance relative to annual merit review criteria.

d.   Comprehensive, consistent, yet individually relevant measures applied to the evaluation of teaching, scholarship, professional development and service.

e.   Use of the annual review process as a mentoring opportunity, including discussion and guidance regarding future prospects, i.e. retention, promotion, and/or non-renewal.

f.   With regard to scholarly (as previously defined), professional, and/or creative activities commonly conducted by NTTF and designated by the unit as part of the responsibilities of NTTF, distinct recognition of such activities as a separate category in Annual and Merit Reviews, rather than potentially diminishing these contributions by categorizing them as either Teaching or Service.

g.   Inclusion in the annual merit review process of peer review by NTTF colleagues.

## Periodic evaluation, promotion, non-reappointment, and Contract

### 1. USC Inventory

a.   The School of Education utilizes clear promotion standards that have been thoroughly communicated to faculty, as well as a three-level structure through which non-tenure-track faculty are actively progressing. Social Work also has exemplary criteria for promotion of non-tenure-track faculty.

b.   The School of Cinematic Arts requires two years of experience with the school for appointment as a Lecturer; three years as a Lecturer to be eligible for promotion to Senior Lecturer; and six total years as Lecturer/Senior Lecturer to be eligible for promotion to Master Lecturer.

c.   The School of Journalism requires non-tenure-track candidates for promotion to compile a comprehensive dossier demonstrating their accomplishments in their current positions and potential for success in the next level position. NTTF promotions are voted upon by the entire faculty, with the Director of the unit, and the Dean of the school, determining their ultimate disposition.

d.   The School of Business employs a very clear promotion track with varying criteria for advancing levels.

e.   With regard to non-renewal, the School of Business has a detailed policy that includes review by a Committee on Clinical Faculty.

## Secondary Source Input

a.   The Provost's Non-Tenure-Track Faculty Initiative of February 3, 2006, "asked schools that do not have promotion tracks for NTT faculty to establish them and to evaluate NTT faculty for such promotions on a schedule they establish."

b.   The aforementioned 2001 AAU report on non-tenure-track faculty recommends, and such peer institutions as Stanford, Cornell, and University of Texas offer additional compensation and longer-term contracts to non-tenure-track faculty who are promoted.

## 2. Periodic Evaluation, Promotion, Non-Reappointment, and Contract: Exemplary Practices and Policies

a.   Schools and units are encouraged to comply with the Provost's Non-Tenure-Track Faculty Initiative of February 3, 2006.

b.   A clear, systematic, written, and published process for periodic evaluation, promotion, contract renewal, or non-reappointment, with written criteria directly reflecting the Workload Profile and annual review process. Factors to be addressed in the process include:

- The scheduling of merit reviews, i.e. exactly when and how often they will take place. (At a minimum such reviews should take place prior to the renewal of a multi-year contract.)
- The criteria by which each element of an instructor's Workload Profile will be evaluated.
- The metrics to be applied to those criteria.
- Possible outcomes of the review (reappointment, non-reappointment, promotion, postponement of consideration for promotion, multi-year contract, etc.).
- The methodology and/or metrics applied to (i.e. select) each outcome.

c.  A three-level system for rank and title designations (i.e. Assistant, Associate, Full) that embodies sufficient flexibility to make it adaptable to the variety of rank and/or title designations currently given to NTT.

d.  A clear timeframe and three-level promotion progression that specifies the required minimum length of time in the school and in each level. For movement from Level I to Level II a 3 year to 6 year window may be appropriate. For movement from Level II to Level III an additional 3 year to 6 year window may be appropriate.

e.  Recognition that merit, rather than time in rank, should be the determining factor in the promotion process.

f.  Explanation in criteria for promotion of the role to played in the promotion decision-making process by prior academic and/or professional experience.

g.  Granting of an increase in pay in recognition of promotion from one rank to the next (while allowing flexibility necessitated by the school's budgetary situation).

h.  A clearly defined, rigorous promotion review process that includes preparation of a comprehensive dossier demonstrating the candidate's accomplishments based on the Workload Profiles of both the current and next position; dossier reviewed by all departmental faculty at or above the rank being sought by the candidate for promotion, as well as cross-departmental subcommittees, as may be appropriate; a vote by all faculty at or above the rank being sought determines a recommendation on whether or not to advance the promotion decision to the Dean or Director of the academic unit for final disposition.

i.  Recognition of promotion from one rank to the next by the granting of a multi-year contract (as distinct from a series of individual, rolling, one year contracts); recognition in such contracts of the academic unit's need to maintain staffing flexibility in times of financial difficulty. For promotion from Level I to Level II a three year contract may be appropriate. For promotion from Level II to Level III a five year contract may be appropriate.

j.  With regard to scholarly (as previously defined), professional, and/or creative activities commonly conducted by NTTF, distinct recognition of such activities in the promotion and contract renewal process, in direct reflection of Workload Profiles, rather than potentially diminishing these contributions by categorizing them as either Teaching or Service.

k.  Within the context of the need to maintain the privacy of any affected party, as well as the contract employee nature of non-tenure-track appointments, clear, written, published policies and procedures for the performance-related non-reappointment of NTT faculty, including (but not limited to): the criteria by which the individual's performance relative to each element of his/her Workload Profile will be evaluated, the metrics to be applied to those criteria, prior merit reviews, etc; and review of the matter by a faculty committee that includes in its membership a representative number of non-tenure-track faculty.

## Professional Development

### 1. USC Inventory

a.    The School of Social Work has a professional development committee that works to assist non-tenure-track faculty in becoming oriented to the university, the annual review process, and the promotion process.

b.    The School of Education provides the same level of support for non-tenure-track and tenure track faculty in terms of professional development funds.

c.    The Schools of Business, Law and Pharmacy have all awarded paid, 6-month sabbaticals to non-tenure-track faculty members active in scholarship and/or teaching-related work.

### Secondary Source Input

a.    The University Handbook guarantees that non-tenure-track faculty are entitled to share equally in professional development benefits and makes no distinction between tenured and non-tenure-track faculty in matters such as applying for sabbatical leaves. See Sections 4-C(2) and 3-E(2) of the Handbook.

b.    Various peer institutions, such as Stanford, UCLA, and Cornell, offer professional development leaves for non-tenure-track faculty after they have been with the institution for approximately 6 years. During leaves faculty can work on projects related to the scholarship of teaching, create new programs, re-immerse themselves in professional practice, or conduct other scholarly activity depending on their field.

c.    While leaves times vary by institution, they are typically a quarter/semester in duration. Some schools also offer unpaid leaves of up to a year with guaranteed employment upon return, for faculty who want to renew themselves professionally.

### 2 Professional Development: Exemplary Practices and Policies

a.    Schools and units are encouraged to comply with the Faculty Handbook as it applies to NTTF professional development and other NTTF-related matters.

b.   Comprehensive, written processes designed to meet the need for non-tenure-track faculty to continually enhance their expertise relating to teaching, service, and scholarship (as previously defined).

c.   Mentoring and other faculty development activities for non-tenure-track faculty at the department, school and university level.

d.   Availability of professional development funds for non-tenure-track faculty to attend conferences and be involved in professional activities.

e.   Consideration of professional development leaves, for scholarly (as previously defined), creative, and/or professional development activities, the duration of which might be a minimum of one month up to a maximum of one semester. Such leaves could be available every five years to non-tenure-track faculty who have reached the associate level.

Traditionally, such leaves (also known as sabbaticals) involve freedom from teaching duties to concentrate on scholarship duties, and so generally have been available for those who have both teaching and scholarship assignments. Given that many NTTF are involved in both teaching and substantial scholarship (as previously defined), it is possible that scholarship related to pedagogy, curriculum development, etc., may qualify. Under current budgetary practices, leaves for non-tenure-track faculty are school-paid. Funding for such leaves by the Provost, as is done for tenured and tenure track faculty, is a topic worthy of consideration.

## Participation in Governance

### 1  USC Inventory

a.   A number of USC academic units, including Architecture, Social Work, Cinema, Education, and Computer Science have recently undergone changes in their governance and now fully include non-tenure-track faculty.

b.   The School of Education specifies that NTT faculty participate in its Faculty Council, and rotates the chair of the Faculty Council among non-tenure-track and tenure track faculty on an equal basis. Non-tenure-track faculty participate in all decisions (other than those relating to the granting of tenure), and provide input on the merit reviews of NTT and tenure track faculty alike.

c.   The School of Business, the Dean of which was until recently a member of the NTT faculty, sends both NTT and tenured faculty representatives to the Academic Senate, and includes NTT faculty on its Faculty Council.

d.   The Law School and Medical School have long had NTTF on their elected faculty bodies.

e.   NTTF have been nominated and run for the position of Academic Senate President, and have been elected and served as Senate officer and Executive Board member, as well as chair of school elected faculty council.

## Secondary Source Input

a.   The University Handbook explicitly calls for/refers to such participation in Sections 2(B)(1) and 4(C)(2), among others.

b.   The Provost's Non-Tenure-Track Faculty Initiative of February 3, 2006, said, "We have already increased NTT faculty participation in a wide range of University committees. I join in the Academic Senate's call to increase the participation of NTT colleagues in faculty councils and other school and departmental bodies."

## 2 Participation in Governance: Exemplary Practices and Policies

a.   Schools and units are encouraged to comply with the Faculty Handbook as it applies to NTTF participation in governance and all other NTTF-related matters, as well as the Provost's Non-Tenure-Track Faculty Initiative of February 3, 2006.

b.   Full participation by NTT faculty in governance and administrative processes, with the sole exception of tenure decisions.

c.   Encouragement of NTT faculty to run for positions representing their units in the Academic Senate and in their units' Faculty Councils, and eligibility for appointment to all administrative task forces and committees. In principal the NTT/Tenure Track make-up of a unit's Faculty Council should reflect the NTT/Tenure Track makeup of its full time faculty.

# APPENDIX B

# USC COMMITTEE ON NON-TENURE-TRACK FACULTY AFFAIRS (CNTTFA)

# INVENTORY OF FULL-TIME NTT FACULTY-RELATED GUIDELINES AND CRITERIA

## 2011 UPDATE
## INTERVIEW QUESTIONNAIRE: QUALITATIVE

Committee Member: _____

School: _____

Academic Unit (if more than one is being assessed within a school):

_____

## Workload Profile

1. What are the strengths and weaknesses related to Workload Profile in your unit (e.g., clear, written guidelines; publicly available; guidelines consistently used in Workload assignments)?

## Merit Review

Merit Review of Clinical Faculty (Skip this question if there are no Clinical faculty in the school/unit.)

2. What are the strengths and weaknesses related to Merit Review in your unit (e.g., clear, written guidelines; publicly available; guidelines consistently adhered to in Merit Review; known schedule for Merit Review)?

## Promotion

Promotion of Clinical Faculty (Skip this question if there are no Clinical faculty in the school/unit.)

3.   What are the strengths and weaknesses related to Promotion in your unit (e.g., clear, written guidelines; publicly available; guidelines consistently adhered to in Promotion Process; known schedule for Promotion)?

## Contracts

Contracts for Clinical Faculty (Skip this question if there are no Clinical faculty in the school/unit.)

4.   What are the strengths and weaknesses related to Contracts in your unit (e.g., clear, written criteria; publicly available information; criteria consistently adhered to in awarding Contracts; length of contracts; multiyear contracts; rolling contracts, etc.)?

## Sabbaticals

5.   What are the strengths and weaknesses related to Paid Professional Leave or Sabbaticals for NTT faculty in your unit (e.g., no sabbaticals for NTT; clear guidelines; fair process; awareness of opportunity; not granted in recent years; funding sources, etc.)?

## Governance

6.   What are the strengths and weaknesses related to Governance that includes NTT faculty in your unit (e.g., participation in faculty council; participation in senior committees; leadership roles; participation in academic senate; awareness of opportunity to participate in governance, etc.)?

## Orientation

7.   What are the strengths and weaknesses of the orientation process for new NTT faculty in your unit (e.g., orientation to handbook, workload, merit review process, promotion process, organization, leadership, governance participation, access to resources, etc.)?

## *Other Issues*

8.   What are the other strengths and weaknesses related to NTT faculty within your unit?

# CONTRIBUTORS

## Adrianna Kezar

Associate Professor for Higher Education, University of Southern California

Adrianna Kezar's research focuses on leadership, change, and equity in higher education. She has published 14 books, 75 articles, and over 100 book chapters and reports. Her most recent book is *Enhancing Campus Capacity for Leadership* (2011). She has worked to improve the working conditions of non-tenure track faculty as part of her service and leadership at the three institutions where she has been employed.

## Cecile Sam

Research Associate, Rossier School for Education, University of Southern California

Cecile Sam is a research associate for the University of Southern California's Center for Higher Education Policy Analysis and a doctoral candidate in higher education policy. Her qualitative research interests include organization theory as applied to faculty work in higher education, with a special interest in online/offline communities and ethics. She has a BA in English Literature and Philosophy, an MA in Education, and an MA in Philosophy, all from Loyola Marymount University, Los Angeles.

## Frank Cosco

President, Vancouver Community College Faculty Association

On the Vancouver Community College Faculty Association (VCCFA) executive since the late 1980s, Frank Cosco has taken on a number of roles for his union including vice-president, bargaining chair, and president. He is currently also a member of the executive of the Federation of Post-Secondary Educators of

BC (FPSE). He has worked at VCC for over 30 years as an English as a Second Language (ESOL) faculty member.

## Jack Longmate
English Instructor, Olympic College

An adjunct English instructor at Olympic College since 1992, Jack Longmate has served as vice- president and secretary of the NEA-affiliated union. He is a board member of the New Faculty Majority (NFM), past chair of the Employment Issues Committee of Teachers of English to Speakers of Other Languages (TESOL), active with the Washington Part-time Faculty Association, and participates in conferences such as those of the Coalition of Contingent Academic Labor (COCAL), where in 2010, he and Frank Cosco co-presented the Program for Change: Real Transformation over Two Decades. He is also employed as a technical writer for BAE Systems.

## Nancy McMahon
English Faculty, Madison Area Technical College

Nancy McMahon has decades of part-time teaching experience at a two-year technical/community college, which has provided her with first-hand experience of changes in higher education at Madison Area Technical College (MATC). She was one of the founders of the MATC Part-Time Teachers' Union in 1996, where she held various offices. She has been a delegate to American Federation of Teachers (AFT) local, state, regional, and national meetings; she co-presented sessions at the 2006 National Council of Teachers of English conference on College Composition and Communication in Chicago and at the 2010 American Association of University Professors (AAUP) conference in Washington, DC. She was the 2005–2010 adjunct representative to the Two-Year College Association (English) Midwest Board.,

## Patricia Hyer
Associate Provost Emerita, Virginia Tech

Patricia Hyer served the office of the provost at Virginia Tech for 23 years prior to her recent retirement. She oversaw faculty personnel issues and was deeply engaged in policy development and implementation, university governance, and diversity efforts throughout her career. She was named fellow of the Association for Women in Science (AWIS) and received the WEPAN University Change Agent Award for her work on behalf of women faculty in the fields of science, technology, engineering, and mathematics (STEM).

## Päivi Hoikkala
Lecturer, Department of History, California State Polytechnic University, Pomona

Päivi Hoikkala received her doctorate from Arizona State University. Since 1997 she has been teaching in the Department of History at California State Polytechnic University, Pomona. She is the elected lecturer representative to the Pomona chapter of the California Faculty Association (CFA) and also serves on the campus faculty rights committee. To decompress, she spends time hiking and camping with her husband and two dogs.

## Shawn Whalen

Lecturer and Director of Forensics, San Francisco State University

Shawn Whalen has served at San Francisco State University since 1997. He earned his BA and MA degrees in Speech Communication from San Diego State University and did doctoral work at the University of Utah in the areas of argumentation, rhetorical theory, and rhetorical criticism. He has just completed three terms as the chair of the San Francisco State University academic senate. He has been a significant contributor to the recent overhaul of the institution's general education and baccalaureate degree requirements, its ongoing accreditation review, and to strategic planning efforts that have streamlined the institution's college structures.

## Ginger Clark

Associate Professor of Clinical Education, University of Southern California

Ginger Clark is the curriculum coordinator of the marriage and family therapy program in the Rossier School of Education. She has served on the academic senate committee for non-tenure track faculty affairs (CNTTFA) for three years; she co-chaired the committee with Jerry Swerling in 2010–2011, and will be co-chairing with Rebecca Lonergan in 2011–2012. Ginger has been employed at USC as a non-tenure track faculty member for six years.

## Jerry Swerling

Professor of Professional Practice and Director of Public Relations Studies, Annenberg School for Communication and Journalism, University of Southern California

Jerry is also responsible for the management of the undergraduate and graduate programs in public relations. He also serves as director of the USC Annenberg Strategic Communication and Public Relations Center, the mission of which is to "advance the study, practice and value of public relations by means of practical, applied research."

## Maria Maisto

President, New Faculty Majority: The National Coalition for Adjunct and Contingent Equity and Executive Director, The New Faculty Majority Foundation

Maria Maisto is a co-founder of New Faculty Majority (NFM), founded, together with the NFM Foundation, in 2009. These national non-profit organizations focus exclusively on improving higher education by improving the working conditions of the majority of its faculty. She has been an adjunct faculty member in English for five years at two institutions in Ohio in addition to having worked at two national higher education associations in Washington, DC. She has a BS in Foreign Service and an MA in English from Georgetown University and is ABD (partial doctoral work) in Comparative Literature from the University of Maryland at College Park.

# INDEX